A HISTORY OF ESOTERICISM

From the Paleolithic to the Axial Age

M. ALAN KAZLEV

978-0-6456700-4-2

A History of Esotericism: From the Paleolithic to the Axial Age

M. Alan Kazlev

© Manticore Press, Melbourne, Australia, 2023.

All rights reserved, no section of this book may be utilized without permission, except brief quotations, including electronic reproductions without the permission of the copyright holders and publisher. Published in Australia.

Thema Classification: QRYC (Esoteric Religions), QRS (Ancient Religions), QRRV (Shamanism), NHC (Ancient History).

MANTICORE PRESS
WWW.MANTICORE.PRESS

CONTENTS

PREFACE 13

PART I
BASIC CONCEPTS

1. INTRODUCTION
    - *1-i. Why Esotericism* 15
    - *1-ii. Esotericism, a Definition* 16
    - *1-iii. Reason, Faith, and Gnosis* 17
    - *1-iv. Two Types of Gnosis* 19
    - *1-v. Mysticism and Yoga as Esotericism* 21
    - *1-vi. Occultism as Esotericism* 25

2. ESOTERICISM, HISTORY, AND CULTURE
    - *2-i. Esotericism in the Context of the Evolution of Culture* 27
    - *2-ii. Interpreting Esotericism* 33
    - *2-iii. Esotericism and Modernity* 37

3. THE BIG PICTURE
    - *3-i. Two Forms of Esotericism* 41
    - *3-ii. Big History as a Modern-Day Creation Story* 42
    - *3-iii. Big History, Cosmic Evolution, and Integral Philosophy* 43
    - *3-iv. The Evolution of Consciousness* 45
    - *3-v. Matter, Life, and Mind* 46

3-vi. Animal Consciousness 50

3-vii. Early Human Species 53

3-viii. The Theosophical Theory of Human Evolution 54

3-ix. Ancient Apocalypse as Misplaced Mythohistory 57

PART II
MYSTICAL GNOSIS AND ESOTERICISM

4. SHAMANISM AND ANIMISM

4-i. Magical Consciousness 61

4-ii. Shamanism 62

4-iii. Animism 64

4-iv. The Laws of Magic 65

4-v. Panpsychism 66

4-vi. Paleolithic Shamanism 67

4-vii. The Venuses 70

4-viii. Lion-Headed Figurines 72

5. MEGALITHS AND EARTH ENERGIES

5-i. Mythic Thinking 73

5-ii. The Younger Dryas and the First Settlements 75

5-iii. Megalithic Culture 77

5-iv. Stonehenge 78

5-v. Ley Lines and Earth Energies 78

5-vi. Bruce Cathie and the UFO grid 80

5-vii. The Great Mother 81

5-viii. The Great Round 83

6. PROTO-INDO-EUROPEAN MYTHOLOGY

6-i. The Proto-Indo-Europeans 85

    6-ii. Archetype versus Myth 86

    6-iii. The Dawn 88

    6-iv. The Otherworld 89

    6-v. The Creation Myth 90

7. THE MESOPOTAMIAN AND LEVANTINE WORLDVIEW

    7-i. The Rise of Civilization 93

    7-ii. Civilization and the Alienation from Nature 94

    7-iii. Civilization and Empire in Mesopotamia 95

    7-iv. Ziggurats and Pyramids 97

    7-v. Ancient Astronauts? 98

    7-vi. Mesopotamian Cosmology and the Story of Creation 101

    7-vii. Chaoskampf, the Struggle Against Chaos 102

    7-viii. The Creation of Humanity 103

    7-ix. What are the Gods? 104

    7-x. The Egregore 106

    7-xi. The Pessimism of the Mythic Worldview 109

    7-xii. Ancestor Worship 111

    7-xiii. The Epic of Gilgamesh 112

    7-xiv. Why is There No Concept of an Immortal Soul? 114

    7-xv. The Flood Myth 114

    7-xvi. Mesopotamian Astrology 116

8. EGYPT

    8-i. The Civilization of Egypt 121

    8-ii. Society, Religion, and Sacred Architecture 122

    8-iii. Monotheism and Kathenotheism 123

    8-iv. The Pyramid Texts 123

    8-v. Atum and the Ennead 124

    8-vi. The Ogdoad 127

8-vii. Ptah and Memphis Theology *128*

8-viii. Amun-Ra *129*

8-ix. Mythic Symbolism *130*

8-x. Dying and Resurrected Gods *131*

8-xi. Lunar and the Solar Mythology *133*

8-xii. Chaos and Order *134*

8-xiii. The Egyptian Afterlife *135*

8-xiv. Akhenaten, the Original Monotheist *140*

PART III
AXIAL AGE GNOSIS AND ESOTERICISM

9. THE AXIAL AGE

9-i. The Concept of the Axial Age *145*

9-ii. The Origin of Metaphysics *146*

9-iii. From Mythic to Rational-Mental *147*

10. PERSIAN DUALISM

10-i. Zarathustra and Zoroastrianism *149*

10-ii. The History of the Written Texts *150*

10-iii. Thoughts, Words, and Deeds *151*

10-iv. The Duality of Light and Darkness *152*

10-v. From Gloomy Afterlife to Moral Eschatology *154*

11. THE INDIAN METAPHYSICAL REVOLUTION

11-i. The Indus Valley Civilization *157*

11-ii. The Vedas *160*

11-iii. The Upanishads *162*

11-iv. Reincarnation and Liberation *164*

11-v. Karma *165*

11-vi. Moral Purification 166
11-vii. Emanation and Ascent 166
11-viii. The Five-fold Self 168
11-ix. The Shramanas 169
11-x. Kapila and Samkhya 170
11-xi. Mahavira and Jainism 171
11-xii. Jain Philosophy 174
11-xiii. Siddhartha and Buddhism 177
11-xiv. The Swastika, a Solar Symbol 180
11-xv. Other Early Schools 181
11-xvi. Schopenhauer - a 19th Century Shramanist 183

12. THE I CHING AND TAOISM

12-i. Early Chinese History 185
12-ii. Folk Mythology 186
12-iii. The I Ching 186
12-iv. The Three Sages 189
12-v. Lao-tzu 190
12-vi. Chuang-tzu 191

13. ABRAHAMIC MONOTHEISM

13-i. Monotheism, Polytheism, and Animism 195
13-ii. The Origin of the Hebrews 196
13-iii. The Bronze Age Collapse 197
13-iv. The Storm God 197
13-v. From Monolatry and Monotheism 198
13-vi. The Babylonian and Hebrew Genesis 198
13-vii. The Babylonian Exile and the Development of Judaism 199
13-viii. The Abrahamic Religions 201
13-ix. Monotheism, Monism, and Duality 204

14. GREEK PHILOSOPHY, COSMOLOGY, AND PSYCHOLOGY

14-i. Periods of Greek History 207
14-ii. The Bronze Age 207
14-iii. The Archaic Period 209
14-iv. The Presocratics 211
14-v. Life and Teachings of Pythagoras 213
14-vi. The Tetraktys 216
14-vii. Post-Pythagorean Duality 218
14-viii. Empedocles 219
14-ix. The Atomists 220
14-x. Classical Greece 222
14-xi. The Sophists 223
14-xii. Plato and Philosophical Idealism 224
14-xiii. The Soul 226
14-xiv. The Story of Er 229
14-xv. The Demiurge 231
14-xvi. The Lambda 232
14-xvii. Aristotle and Immanent Forms 234
14-xviii. Aristotle's Psychology 235
14-xix. Orexis or Desire 237
14-xx. Stoicism 237

GLOSSARY 241

BIBLIOGRAPHY 265

INDEX 279

IMAGES

Fig. 1. The Sorcerer 69
Fig 2. The Field of Reeds 139
Fig 3. The Pashupati Seal 158
Fig 4. The Hexagrams 187

PART I

Basic Concepts

PREFACE

This is the first of a planned series of four books on the history of gnosis and esotericism. The current work is a development of my earlier project Kheper Net, which can currently be found online at www.malankazlev.com/kheper.

My ideas have developed dramatically in the twenty-five years since I first posted web pages to the original Kheper project. Some of these changes can be seen in the site itself, but others have come later. The current work emphasizes the understanding that gnosis, and the esotericism that is based on it, is not timeless and unchanging (although it does include a timeless element), but embedded in history and in personal and cultural development and evolution.

Many entrenched esoteric ideas involve religionism, chauvinism, sexism, and speciesism, which pertain to outmoded worldviews. The present work humbly offers a modern, and doubtless incomplete, review and reinterpretation of esotericism and gnosis, combining ancient wisdom and personal gnosis with the scholarly insights of academia.

These themes will be continued and expanded in the following volumes, which take up the historical review, and continue it to the present day.

1. INTRODUCTION

1-i. Why Esotericism?

Today, the world faces two massive crises: an "outer" existential crisis and an "inner" crisis of meaning.

The existential, planetary crisis, which affects not just humanity but all life on Earth, involves the confluence of overpopulation, resource depletion, biodiversity loss, ocean acidification, industrial, herbicide, pesticide, plastic, and electromagnetic pollution, pandemics, and global warming (of which the latter two – despite having the most publicity – are less severe than the others), among other factors.

At the same time, popular culture of the early 21st century revolves around banal consumerism and lookism, the perfect face or body, reality TV, swiping left or right on Tinder, aspirational bourgeoisie home and lifestyle, and the blockbuster movie full of special effects but empty of ideas...

The crisis of meaning is a result of a disenchanted world divided between superficial religious and political totalitarianism, in which the sense of banality and emptiness of Western materialistic standards create a counter-reaction of the extreme left (identity politics, cancel culture, and denial of biological gender) and extreme right (conspiracy theories, ur-fascism, and religious fundamentalism) ideologies, these being the result of the loss of center in the cultural stage known as Modernity, which developed out of the scientific, Protestant, and capitalist revolutions.

While modern-day science and cultural/historical criticism provide unsurpassed insights regarding the nature of "outer" reality, they have nothing to say about other dimensions of existence: imagination, meaning, non-ordinary states of consciousness, and the "inner" reality (as the inverted commas imply, "outer" and "inner" are simply provisional labels and generalizations for more subtle dimensions of existence).

1-ii. Esotericism, a Definition

The word "esoteric" originally referred to the inner (Eso-) circle of initiates of the Pythagorean mysteries. This refers to those teachings known only to initiates and kept hidden from the profane. The idea of initiation goes back, at least, to the temple mysteries of ancient Egypt. This is in contrast to the modern and also, presumably, the Palaeolithic shaman, who is self-initiated (or chosen by the spirits). More recently, beginning in the 19th century, esotericism and occultism were used synonymously in reference to knowledge about supra-physical realities. The books and teachings of the Theosophical Society of H.P. Blavatsky, for example, used both words, as did Rudolf Steiner regarding his Anthroposophy material. Both presented an elaborate cosmology regarding cycles of cosmic and human existence, lost continents, spiritual hierarchies, reincarnation, and the evolution of the soul. One can also distinguish between different interpretations and perspectives of the esoteric, including the academic study of Western Esotericism [Faivre, 1994], Blavatskyian Theosophy [Sinnett, 1883], Traditionalism (Rene Guenon and Frithjof Schuon), Ismaili Shite Islam [Corbin, 1989] or Tantric (Vajrayana) Buddhism. I have used the term as a more generic approach to the sense of inner, occult, or spiritual knowledge [Kazlev, 2009, 2020].

Esotericism here uses its 19th and 20th century definitions to refer to intellectual knowledge about "inner" reality and mystical or occult doctrines. This includes the emanation of the cosmos from the unknowable Godhead, the nature of gods, archetypes, spiritual hierarchies, the subtle body and inner faculties, the relation between the microcosm and macrocosm, the ascent of the soul, and the attainment of spiritual enlightenment. These fields of inquiry, now considered fringe or "New Age," were mainstream knowledge in Ancient Egypt, Classical Greece, Medieval India, and Renaissance Europe.

Central to esotericism are higher modes of consciousness, called gnosis (Greek: knowledge), that transcends ordinary reason and religious belief. Gnosis refers to the direct intuitive experience of any such transpersonal or transcendent realities and associated higher states of consciousness.

Gnosis, mysticism (from the mysteries), occult ("hidden") philosophy, theosophy (divine wisdom), and so on, all refer to higher, transpersonal (transcending the ego) states of consciousness and experience, insights and realization, contemplating the deep mysteries of the universe, consciousness, and other dimensions or planes of existence, that were accessible only to those who have the time and inclination to explore these concepts.

"Exoteric" means the opposite, the "outer" or everyday consciousness, and reality. It could refer to everyday religion, popular culture, or materialistic science. As these do not require any exceptional transformation of consciousness, they can be adopted by both the individual psyche and society as a whole.

Science, however, or any specialized academic field, is also "esoteric" but in a different sense. Years of higher learning require intelligence, discipline, and individual interest in these particular topics. This excludes the majority of people who don't have those talents. So, although science and academic knowledge are not esoteric in the mystical or occult sense, they are still esoteric in the social and intellectual sense.

The reason both religious fundamentalism and conspiracy theories are so widespread and popular is because they do not require any specific effort. Instead, they are examples of the Dunning-Kruger effect: a cognitive bias that occurs when people with a low ability (or, in this case, limited knowledge and insight) in a specific area overestimate their competence, while those with high ability tend to underestimate theirs [Kruger & Dunning, 1999], due to the modesty that comes from actually having an ability or hard-earned understanding.

1-iii. Reason, Faith, and Gnosis

Wouter Hanegraaff, the University of Utrecht in the Netherlands, is one of the current generation of esotericist academics and the author of several books and papers on the subject. He refers to the duality of science (reason) and religion (faith), being transcended by a third principle, which is esotericism or gnosis. This triad of reason, faith, and gnosis represent increasingly abstract or transcendent knowledge claims [Hanegraaff, 1992, p. 10; 2013, p.89].

This triad had already been suggested by Dutch theologian Gilles Quispel (1916-2006), a scholar of Gnosticism and colleague of psychologist C. G. Jung. According to Quispel, three cities have determined the history of the West. There is 1) Jerusalem, the source of faith, which dates back to Sinai and Golgotha; 2) Athens (and Ionia), which is the source of rationalism; and 3) Alexandria, which was the home to those people with inner experiences and imaginative thinking [Quispel, 2008, p.143].

Reason, then, describes the "outer world," the world of natural philosophy and science. It can be communicated (described) and tested via empirical methodology and verification with science, and the humanities can also provide verification via history, textual analysis, and so on. This represents the Humanistic worldview and atheistic non-belief in invisible or supra-physical realities.

Faith, referring to the "inner world," can also be communicated, but, being subjective, it cannot be empirically verified. It is, however, potent and meaningful on an individual level.

In today's world of modernity and the debates posted on YouTube, there is only a very debased faith, represented mostly by literalist Christianity. However, Western Muslim debaters also present their exact equivalent in a literalist and simplistic form of Islam, lacking the nuances and mystical insights of Sufism or the medieval Islamic philosophers. Confronted with rationalism, all of these sorts of literalist religions, which masquerade as empiricism, are unable to provide good rational arguments and hence refer back to personal claims that one's own religion is the only or the highest one.

Gnosis is more subtle than faith, as it cannot be verified or communicated, for it transcends the rational faculty of science and the emotional feeling of religion. The word gnosis is from the Greek for knowledge, specifically (in the late classical world) higher, spiritual, or transcendental knowledge. Truth can only be found by personal, inner revelation, insight, or awakening. Gnosis has been taken to mean inner experiences and imaginative thinking (Quispel), supra-rational, intellective (or noetic to use the Greek) knowledge of higher realities (Schuon), and so on [Earney, n.d.]. There are various equivalent oriental terms, such as *atma-vidya*, *jnana* (Vedanta), *kevala* (Jainism), *prajna*, *sambodhi*, *satori*

(Buddhism), *tasawwuf, irfan,* or *'ma'rifah* (Sufism)[Kazlev, 2020]. This is the type of knowledge associated with esotericism. It is a higher insight that comes from within or maybe from above.

Of course, these three ways of knowing are not mutually exclusive categories. For example, classic mysticism (e.g., Sufism, Christian mysticism) combines gnosis and faith. It constitutes a gnosis of the heart, so to speak, orientated to feeling. And there is also metaphysics, such as Neoplatonism or Vedanta, which combines gnosis and reason, orientated to thinking. Personal inclination will cause the esotericist to prefer either one or the other.

Just as Hanegraaff mentions three degrees of successively inward knowing, so Wilber cites the medieval theologian Bonaventure in distinguishing between the "eye of sense" (physical knowledge, science), the "eye of mind" (philosophy and theology), and the "eye of spirit," that is, spiritual enlightenment [Wilber, 1998]. Here both the eye of sense and the eye of mind represent reason and the eye of spirit gnosis. There is no distinct category for faith, as religious literalism (or fundamentalism) was simply the common background starting point in the middle ages. In the same way, in the 20th and early 21st centuries, the typical starting point is science, academia, and materialism.

From this hierarchy, one would think that reason would be the most common, then religion, then esotericism and gnosis. But as any preliminary perusal of the "global village" belief on social media shows, most people have a huge problem trying to understand even the most straightforward basics of science. Still, they will readily accept a debased religious literalism and ideological irrationality (for example, climate denialism and other forms of conspiracism pumped out by right-wing think tanks). However, this isn't faith in the true sense but rather the masses' simplistic groupthink and social conformity.

1-iv. Two Types of Gnosis

At the minimum, gnosis pertains to insights relating to or derived from transpersonal states of consciousness. By "transpersonal," I mean beyond the ordinary or surface personality. This ordinary, waking conscious personality is generally described as mentioned in terms of traits, types, physiological factors, Freudian psychodynamics, Maslow hierarchy of needs (Humanistic psychology), Theosophical subtle body factors, and so on. It can be called the surface personality because it only deals with what is on the surface; it isn't aware of, or doesn't experience, the various unconscious and cosmic forces. On a more significant or deeper scale, it can refer to cosmic consciousness or spiritual enlightenment.

The gnostic has access to a "higher" mode of inner knowing, or greater insight, than through empirical observation or religious belief. And as with pure reason and true spirituality, authentic gnosis is only possible with a high degree of openness to new possibilities and new realities.

Although gnosis tends to be referred to as if it is a single phenomenon, this is undoubtedly an oversimplification, as there are different types of gnosis, as distinct from each other as each is from "faith" or "reason." The difference between the "feeling" type, which is orientated to god, and the "thinking" type, orientated to metaphysics, has already been briefly mentioned. But there are other categories as well. American scholar of esotericism Arthur Versluis makes an important distinction between what he terms cosmological gnosis, which is "knowledge or direct perception of hidden or esoteric aspects of the cosmos," and metaphysical gnosis, the "direct spiritual insight into complete transcendence" [Versluis, 2002, 2007].

Cosmological gnosis involves what could be described as a type of higher intuition, which reveals the nature of intermediate worlds and realities; for example, Renaissance Hermeticism, New Age cosmology, and so on.

Metaphysical gnosis transcends all categories in pure ineffability. This is sometimes called Apophatic theology or negative theology because it eschews all descriptions of the nature of god or the absolute reality (which is the same here).

Thus, esotericism can be polarized into a more occult and mystical type [Versluis, 2007]. Occultism in this context tends to focus on the intermediate realities between spirit and matter, whereas mysticism pertains to pure spirit, just as science does to matter. There is also esotericism in the more limited sense of relating to cosmological gnosis as the intermediate between a lower psychic occultism and a more transcendent mysticism. This could be referred to as theosophy (divine wisdom) as used in the Neoplatonic sense, which is not limited to Madame Blavatsky's universal East-West synthesis (the Theosophical Society and its off-shoots and successors). Blavatsky and Post-Blavatsky Theosophy is actually then a doctrinal subset, along with Neoplatonism, Hermeticism, Kabbalah, and so on, of theosophy in the broad sense.

1-v. Mysticism and Yoga as Esotericism

The word mysticism originates from "the Mysteries," which refers to the Greek mystery cults. It means to cover the eyes, i.e., initiatory knowledge, which is hidden. In other words, it means the same as the original definition of "esoteric."

Later, mysticism came to refer to the state of union with the divine or the absolute reality. It tends to be practical, based on techniques for attaining god consciousness or ego-transcendence, such as contemplative prayer, *Yoga,* and *dhikr* (Sufi practice of repetition of the divine name).

Mysticism involves access to a higher level of consciousness, where duality is transcended in a unity that shouldn't be confused with passivity. This transcendental state is referred to in traditional literature with terms such as *sambodhi, henosis, theosis,* illumination, and by 20th century writers as Cosmic Consciousness (R.M. Bucke), illuminative intuition (René Guénon), enstasis (Mircea Eliade), and Peak Experience (Abraham Maslow).

From the empirical psychological study of American philosopher and psychologist William James (1842-1910) [James, 1971] and the phenomenological work of English civil servant and philosopher Walter Stace (1886-1967) [Stace, 1961], it is clear that there is a common core to mysticism. Hence it is not necessary to assume that any common (perennialist) theology, philosophy, or practice necessarily follows from the mystical experience [Hood, 2006].

An excellent way to explain how mysticism works is found in the context of religious scholar Huston Smith's perennialist thesis. Smith argues that the premodern, spiritual, consensus worldview describes existence metaphysically, in terms of the four tiers or planes of being. These are the terrestrial realm of the body, that is, the physical or mundane world, the intermediate realm of the mind, the celestial realm of the soul and god, and the infinite realm of the spirit, the transcendent reality [Smith, 1977]. Each of these tiers includes both an individual or subjective dimension and a universal or cosmic in a relation of correspondence, as in the Hermetic (esoteric) saying "as above, so below."

In this context, mysticism is very much about the "spirit" level of (subjective) self and its relation and identification with the "infinite" objective reality. In fact, according to the "perennial philosophy," there is no difference between subject and object, self and god (or absolute) at the mystical tier. In the technical jargon of transpersonal psychology and Integral Philosophy, this is called "nonduality."

A distinction could be made according to whether the mystic is (to use the Jungian and Myer-Briggs typology) a feeling or a thinking type, or in other words, the empathic and the analytic or systemizing [Baron-Cohen, 2009].

The "feeling" or devotional approach tends to use contemplative techniques within a particular institutional religion, such as Christian Mysticism, Sufism, or Vaishnava Hinduism. Here there is sometimes said to be a subtle difference between the soul and god, even in the state of mystical union. However, it is not clear whether this is due to exoteric theology or whether this really is a distinct state of being. At the same time, the "thinking" or meditative approach aims to attain a state of unitary consciousness or realization of the self or nonduality through individual effort rather than surrendering to god. This is preferred by the Eastern Yoga traditions and often tends to be atheistic, although sometimes, as with Kashmir Shaivism, there is a combination of nonduality and theism.

These two primary forms of mysticism – the feeling and the thinking type – can be referred to by the Sanskrit terms *bhakti* and *jnana* (after two of the three types of Yogas mentioned in the classic Hindu religious text the Bhagavad Gita, the third being *Karma* Yoga).

Swami Vivekananda, the great Hindu polemicist, and popularizer, referred to four types of Yoga.

- *Raja Yoga* – the "royal path," represented by the Yoga *sutras* (usually associated with Patanjali, although not always [White, 2014]), which teaches the practice of *samadhi*.
- *Jnana Yoga* – the Yoga of transcendent insight or spiritual knowledge.
- *Bhakti Yoga* – the Yoga of devotion to God (as with theism, but more mystical and world-renouncing).
- *Karma Yoga* – the Yoga of selfless action.

The word "Yoga" is from the Indo-European root *yuj* which means to attach, join, or harness, from which we also get "yoke." This is similar to religion, which is from the Latin *religare* "to bind."

This attainment of transcendence and cosmic consciousness differs from the Hatha Yoga postures, called *asanas*, as in the Wellness movement. Such asanas are actually the starting point of a very long and radical process of self-transformation, the very nature of which is diametrically opposed to the materialistic, mundane (sensation primary, feeling secondary, although sometimes these are reversed) orientation of many in the Wellness community.

Bhakti (Bhakti Yoga) focuses on a personal god or godhead, as in Christian mysticism and devotional Hinduism. Devotional Mysticism is about salvation through faith in or surrender to god (the personal aspect of the Absolute) and is a form of Religion rather than Esotericism proper. However, it is also the most "advanced" or "pure" form of religion. Examples of devotional mystics include the Sufi poet Rumi, Christian mystics such as Francis of Assisi, the Baal Shem Tov of Hasidism, and the Hindu saint Ramakrishna.

Jnana (Jnana Yoga) emphasizes transcendent insight into reality and the realization of an impersonal Absolute or even no-self, as in the *shunyata* of Mahayana Buddhism. Interestingly, the Sanskrit jnana has the same etymological root as Greek gnosis and the same meaning. However, here the emphasis is on spiritual enlightenment, or to use the Buddhist term, Complete Awakening (sambodhi). This is the state of what is called "nonduality," in which all dualistic qualities are transcended. This is the afore-mentioned nonduality (or "metaphysical") gnosis. Examples of mystics include the Vedantic philosopher Shankara, the Sufi ibn Arabi, and various contemporary mystics such as Ramana Maharshi, Nisargadatta, and Da Free John/Adi Da).

One might consider Jesus the classic bhakti type and Buddha the traditional jnana type. But both these figures, as with all religious founders, have so much mythic overlay that it becomes impossible to say anything about them as historical individuals.

When people think of mysticism, they generally think of Christian mysticism, and hence of bhakti. However, some Christian mystics, such as the late 13th-14th century German theologian Meister Eckhart, were much more of the monistic, jnana persuasion, just as, in Hinduism, mystics like

Chaitanya and Ramakrishna were of the devotional type. Every spiritual tradition has its bhakti and its jnana representatives.

This is not an inclusive list. For example, there is also Tantric Yoga which involves various ritual practices, visualization, mantra, and the activation of Kundalini. This is closer to the theurgy of Hellenistic esotericism and Hermetic Kabbalah of the Golden Dawn system, all of which could be included in the same category.

Generally, in mysticism (whether of the bhakti, jnana, theurgic/tantric, or other types), intellectual and metaphysical speculation is overly discouraged as being a distraction from the path of realization. The most representative teaching regarding this is the Buddha's Parable of the Arrow. When asked by the monk Malunkyaputta why he was silent on questions of ultimate meaning, the Buddha told a parable of a man wounded by a poisoned arrow. The man refused to be treated until he knew the name and caste of the assassin, his appearance, what type of bow was used, the nature of the arrow, and so on. The man would surely die before all his questions could be answered and the arrow removed. In the same way, metaphysical speculation is a waste of time and energy and a distraction from the urgent task of liberation from the wheel of rebirth.

This very focused and austere approach is a form of renunciation; in this case, the renunciation of the search for understanding. In this regard, the knowledge-based approach of the current work (and, for that matter, any quest for knowledge) is the opposite of the ultra-pragmatism of authentic mysticism, which requires total focus on the task at hand.

Mysticism, therefore, is an orientation, not a metaphysical system. Like religion, which is based on the idea of a "god-shaped hole" (that in the heart or soul of each person is a "god-shaped hole," a place that only god can fill), mysticism is based on an immense dissatisfaction with material existence. This dissatisfaction is so great that the mystic will renounce the world and do everything they can to attain realization, whether this be through the consciousness-mental path of self-realization (Jnana Yoga) or the personal-transpersonal emotional passion for god (that is, for the theistic god). I have never had an innate attraction for god, or a lack that only god can fill, or felt a burning dissatisfaction with material existence. This is not to disrespect those who do feel that way, but only to speak from my own experience. Such feelings apply to those with a powerful otherworldly bent and feel like holdovers from a premodern and specifically medieval mindset when culture and society were dominated by religion.

Not all mysticism is world-negating, though. In Mahayana Buddhism, the Bodhisattva Vow means deferring final *nirvana* until all sentient beings have been liberated from cyclic existence. Since the number of sentient beings is limitless, that means remaining in the world for the sake of other beings. While in the Integral Yoga of Sri Aurobindo and Mirra Alfassa (known by the honorific The Mother), the goal is not to ascend to a transcendent state, leaving the world to its own devices, but to bring the transcendent divine consciousness (the Supermind, equivalent to the Logos of Christian theology) down to the material universe, in order to transform this world.

1-vi. Occultism as Esotericism

The word "occult" comes from the Latin *occultus* meaning hidden or concealed, which is quite close to the meaning of mysticism. It likewise refers to knowledge or wisdom that is hidden or concealed from the masses, or, alternatively, knowledge about that which is hidden, as opposed to knowledge of visible and obvious things (secular and exoteric religious knowledge).

While occultism may sometimes tend to merge with mysticism (for example, in Theurgy and Tantra), the two are generally given almost diametrically opposite meanings. "Occultism" tends to be defined as understanding and accessing hidden realities behind the physical, whereas "mysticism" refers to a more religious and transcendentalist approach. But both words have the same etymological meaning, to hide or conceal.

In the 19th century, occultism and esotericism were used synonymously for a while. Both refer to hidden and non-physical realities (as distinct from sensationalist modern-day references to the occult as anything spooky or out of the ordinary).

Regarding Huston Smith's cosmology, the occult realm pertains very much to the "intermediate" tier, which is between the mundane physical world and the "celestial" world of spiritual archetypes.

Traditionally, at least in the Western medieval and renaissance world, occultism is divided into the three arts or sciences, astrology, alchemy, and magic. Astrology is intrinsic to both premodern cosmology and, more recently (e.g., Jung and after), to psychotypology and synchronicity. Alchemy includes both self-transformation and proto-chemistry, although both Indian and Chinese alchemy includes advanced yogic practices of self-transmutation and immortality. Magic is about changing reality in accordance with personal will. Still, it can also refer to Theurgy (invoking the divine) and be used as a technique for ego transcendence, such as in classical Neoplatonism and the 19th/20th century Golden Dawn system (both being examples of "High Magic"). In general, these tend to have either an undifferentiated holistic worldview or the standard three-level esoteric hierarchy but otherwise have little in the way of theoretical metaphysics.

More commonly, magic refers to what is variously called Low Magic, Hedge Magic, Folk Magic, and so on, which is more spontaneous and pagan in orientation. Whilst Low Magic is often used in a positive way, for example, in Wicca (modern day "witchcraft"), which has a high moral code, the same psychic techniques allow it to be used for evil, such as curses, vodou dolls, and so on. Magic is neutral, unlike mysticism, which by its very nature is concerned with transcendence and return to or union with the source. This may be why, when esotericism is identified with occultism, it is always of the "higher magic" rather than the "low magic" type.

It may also be useful to distinguish the present definition of occultism from the catch-all marketing term for anything that doesn't fit the heading of either modernity or normative religion. Popular books on occultism, such as the ones I bought from 1978 to 1980 when I was first getting into the study of esotericism, tended to cover everything from the paranormal (ESP, UFOs, etc.), traditional esotericism (Hermeticism, Rosicrucianism, Theosophy), medieval slander against witchcraft, through to Satanism. Evangelical Christians, especially American evangelicals, tend to be obsessed with this subject, as they are almost the only people today who believe in a literal Satan (most Satanists are atheists who are into social reform).

2. ESOTERICISM, HISTORY, AND CULTURE

2-i. Esotericism in the Context of the Evolution of Culture

Traditional esotericism takes a rather idealized, ahistorical approach based on the theme of perennial philosophy. It assumes there is a common, universal insight or set of truths above history, and which is true for all places. This is like Plato's world of pure, unchanging Forms (spiritual ideas). Much of Western and popular esotericism is based on this Platonic worldview, or on a religious approach in general, with a strong emphasis on god, even if there is also usually (but not always) a rejection of fundamentalist religion.

And while there may indeed be a timeless realm of spiritual forms – the celestial tier in Huston Smith's Perennialism – the various developments of esotericism still exist in time and history, in the physical or "terrestrial" realm. Therefore, they develop and evolve along with culture, society, and the local and planetary zeitgeist as a whole. That is why, while there are specific common recurring themes and experiences which have a universal quality and sometimes even are universal and timeless (pertaining to the "celestial" and the "infinite" planes of existence), there is no single esoteric philosophy and gnostic experience.

Instead, esotericism develops, and gnosis is experienced not only according to individual psychological factors and learning, but also in keeping with the social, cultural, and collective consciousness of the time and place.

As a general orienting framework, the evolution of culture and society, and hence of people's collective consciousness and esotericism, can be divided into several broad, and sometimes parallel, phases. These can be referred to as the Magical, the Mythical, the Metaphysical-Religious, and the Modern (with its current sub-category, the Post-Truth). It is essential to understand that this is not an ascent from superstition to enlightened rationality. On the contrary, each of these four stages or modes of consciousness includes valid insights about reality, and they all co-exist and co-evolve.

The Magical or Animistic Stage

The earliest human societies were nomadic hunting-gathering bands, with chipped stone technology and egalitarian social structures. Cultures from Paleolithic Ice Age Europe created magnificent works of cave art, which seem to have had a magical purpose. Esotericism (if this modern term even applies in this context) was represented by the shaman who mediates between the human world and the world of spirits.

The Mythical or Symbolic Stage (Early Fourth to Early First Millennium B.C.E.)

With the development of agriculture and fixed settlements, after several thousand years, the rise of civilization, city-states, and empires, animistic and shamanic magic became subordinated to the state myth and religion. The various features of statehood and empires include a socially stratified society with a dynastic God-King or at the top, a priesthood with a secret knowledge of science, astronomy, divination and spiritual matters, administrative bureaucracies and written records and histories, a standing army, public works programs, codes of law, taxation or tribute systems, food stores and redistribution systems, urban centers, and capital cities. Within these societies, gnosis means understanding the archetypal symbolism of the gods, creation myths, sacred architecture, and state religious ceremonies.

The Metaphysical-Religious Stage

This category still defines much of the thinking of the modern world (for example, philosophy and religion). It is here divided into the so-called Axial Age, the Late Classical, the Medieval, and the Renaissance, which is a transitional period that could equally go under Modernity.

THE AXIAL AGE (EARLY TO LATE FIRST-MILLENNIUM B.C.E.)

The term Axial Age was coined by the psychologist and philosopher Karl Jaspers. During this vital turning point in history and culture, in the sense of an absolutist revelation (externally from god or inward through spiritual enlightenment), world religion replaced or subsumed the various state and local cults and deities of the previous mythic period. So did natural philosophy, metaphysics, ethics, and formal logic. Art and literature take on classical forms. These developments emerged simultaneously in the Greek world, the Middle East, India, and China. Esotericism, in the sense of a perennial philosophy, also appears in the sense of the inner or mystical aspects of these new world religions and philosophies. So does the idea of spiritual enlightenment and the transcendence of the phenomenal world. This marked the start of the "perennial philosophy."

EARLY POST-AXIAL AGE

During the later Classical period (late first-millennium B.C.E. to early first-millennium C.E.), the mixing of ideas in cosmopolitan cities and empires and across trade routes led to new metaphysical doctrines and yogic or theurgic practices. These develop out of and build upon the foundations established during the Axial Age.

Here there is a contrast between two distinct forms of gnosis and esotericism. In the Hellenistic West, esotericism tended strongly in a cosmological or theosophical direction, represented by Hermeticism, Neopythagoreanism, and Neoplatonism, etc. Gnosis is based on the intuition or intimation of the soul's ascent through a hierarchical, vertical model of reality. In India, the emphasis instead is on spiritual enlightenment and liberation, as represented by the yogic-duality and insight-nonduality philosophies such as Samkhya, Patanjali Yoga, Theravada, Mahayana, and Taoism. Other ideas to develop at this time were astrology, alchemy, and theurgy.

THE MEDIEVAL PERIOD (MID-FIRST TO EARLY SECOND-MILLENNIUM C.E.)

Religious devotionalism and (in China) Confucian social norms replace the earlier monistic and dualistic metaphysics. In these theistic and theocratic cultures, esotericism survives and even flourishes as the "inner" or mystical aspect of religion, in contrast to the "outer" or conventional beliefs.

During the Medieval Period, religious esotericism took this as a starting point and incorporated elements from Hellenistic esotericism, such as the ascent of the soul and the angelic hierarchies. This often took the form (continuing and further developed in the renaissance period) of the "Great Chain of Being," of nature and the cosmos as an unbroken continuum from the highest to the lowest [Lovejoy, 1974]. This has God at the top, then various intermediate spiritual hierarchies, and then down through the natural world.

Due to the cost and rarity of written manuscripts, knowledge and learning are limited to only a few. The Mongol conquests destroyed high Islamic culture, such as the House of Wisdom in Baghdad (13th-century C.E), just as almost a millennia before Christianity had destroyed the classical culture and esoteric-metaphysical insights of the Western world. In both cases, after the loss of libraries and scholarship, the vacuum was filled by religious fundamentalism.

In Eastern philosophy, there is more emphasis on the nonduality of Absolute Reality and the contrast between the phenomenal world and the state of transcendent liberation. Although Muslim invaders destroyed the monastery-based Buddhism in India during the 12th and 13th centuries C.E.), village-based Hinduism still survived.

A general trend is that yogic monism and metaphysics are replaced by devotional theism in India (Vaishnavism) and Mahayana Buddhism (in which the bodhisattva confers salvation) in China and Japan.

THE RENAISSANCE (OR EARLY MODERN) PERIOD (15TH TO 16TH CENTURY)

Florentine and later European esotericism represent a revival of the original classical Neoplatonism and Hermeticism, as well as medieval Arabic magic, astrology, and alchemy. In addition, ideas such as perennial philosophy and the relation between the macrocosm and the microcosm were developed. At this time, classic Western esotericism became part of mainstream academia (for example, John Dee, a court astrologist to Elizabeth I). Its strong Christian emphasis means it is, for the most part, accommodated by the Church. However, there are a few notable exceptions, such as the 16th century hermeticist Giordano Bruno, who was burnt at the stake, not for his insight regarding an infinite universe, but for his rejection of Christian dogmas like the Trinity and the Virgin Birth. Esotericism, however, was more strongly challenged by the Protestant puritan revolution and the rise of religious fundamentalism. The introduction of the printing press marks the late Renaissance. This would bring about the age of modernity.

Modernity

This can be divided into early, middle, and late Modernity, Postmodernism, and the current period, including the Metamodern (itself a vague term) and the Post-Truth (or a world of information pollution, polarized ideology, and conspiracy theories).

EARLY MODERNITY (17TH AND 18TH CENTURY)

During this period, advances in the sciences and humanities created specialized fields of knowledge, causing the breakdown of Renaissance universalism and the metaphysical worldview. In this era, a combination of Western imperialism, trade, science, and technology conquered the previous distinct empires and created a single world history regime. The advent of cosmology (Laplace) and geology (Hutton, Lyell) meant an end to religion's truth claims regarding a supernatural universe, a geologically young Earth, a static species, and the beginning of the positivist period. However, figures like Swedenborg and Mesmer present an alternative to both the materialistic-mechanistic worldview of positivist empirical science and the simplistic supernaturalism of literalist religion.

CLASSICAL MODERNITY

This is also called the Long Nineteenth Century (from the French Revolution till the outbreak of World War I), which saw the industrial revolution, the evolutionary ideas of Darwin, Spencer, Haeckel, and Marx, the concept of progress, Mendeleev's *Periodic Table* of elements, Freud's discovery of the unconscious, the discovery of quantum physics, and Einstein's relativity. But, conversely, this also led to the occult revolution or occult revival, the synthesis of East and West, and the fusion of science (evolution) with religion (spiritualism, Eliphas Levi, Blavatsky, and the Hermetic Order of the Golden Dawn).

LATE MODERNITY (1910S TO 1960S)

Late Modernity is represented by the development of modern culture and the exponential increase of knowledge. Non-Western countries and newly independent colonies became increasingly modernized and started to become more Westernized since the industrial revolution, meaning that Western civilization had a monopoly on advanced technology and weapons. Here one can distinguish between three primary modes of gnosis: the occult and theosophical, or "esotericism" in the conventional sense (Steiner, Crowley, Guenon), the mythic and mythopoetic (Jung, Campbell, Lovecraft, Tolkien), and the evolutionary or integral (Aurobindo, Teilhard, Gebser).

The philosophical and cultural movement of Postmodernism (late 20th century) rejects the rationalistic-materialistic certainties of positivism. It is characterized by the electronic media and the counterculture creating a synthesis of East and West in a "global village" (McLuhan). Cultural differences disappear as the whole world forms a single global culture. Through the New Age and related movements such as Eastern gurus, esoteric themes become mainstream again, while social and environmental crises demolish the naive materialistic myth of progress.

This paves the way for Metamodernism (latest 20th to early 21st century), emerging as a new phase integrating Modernity and Postmodernity [*The Living Philosophy*. 2022]. The Post-Truth World characterizes this period. The print media that created and defined the positivist period is replaced by the online digital world, especially social media. Older 20th-century movements, such as Theosophy, Eastern gurus, and New Age public esotericism, are replaced by new mythic themes revolving around distrust of authorities and the watered-down Gnosticism of "the Matrix," while esotericism takes on new forms. Therefore, esotericism continues to evolve and develop.

2-ii. Interpreting Esotericism

Of course, the understanding of Modernity (and postmodernism, metamodernism, etc.) is no more or less authentic than that of any other period of history. This is especially the case with esotericism, in which the predominant physicalistic worldview of Modernity tends to depreciate. Nevertheless, this brings up some possible perspectives that can be used to understand the vast range of metaphysical and supraphysical insights, especially when presenting a historical review of gnosis and esotericism.

Skeptical Materialism

An outsider to esotericism immersed in the skeptical-materialistic paradigm of modernity generally assumes that only physical reality is real and consciousness is an emergent phenomenon of matter, which has no existence apart from physical reality. This is also known as positivism, physicalism, naturalism, or humanism (of the modern, atheistic type, not the Renaissance type of Erasmus). According to this interpretation, what the various esoteric philosophies and mystical doctrines say are, therefore, obvious examples of irrational, premodern thinking; myths (in the derogatory sense of the word) and superstitions that may be interesting to consider in terms of the history of ideas, but which tell us nothing about the nature of reality or consciousness itself. For that, we had to await the rise of the scientific method, empiricism, physics, biology, neuroscience, and so on. The problem here is that, ultimately, it is just pushing another form of dogmatism, making the methodology and observations of science into absolute truth (ironically, this is the opposite of what science is about, which is testing and verification or falsification).

Agnosticism

The historian of esotericism can adopt a totally agnostic, non-committed point of view. The various – sometimes contradicting, sometimes agreeing – insights of the different esoteric systems are each presented impartially, but no statement is made for or against their validity. This is rather like Russian-British philosopher Isiah Berlin's story of the Fox and the Hedgehog, where the fox knows many things, whereas the hedgehog knows one big thing [Berlin, 2013]. By only knowing many small things, there is no underlying picture, just a lot of isolated and disjointed facts.

Postmodern Philosophy

According to the deconstructionist approach of postmodern philosophy, such as that of Jaques Derrida or Jean-François Lyotard, we can know nothing of the thing in itself. All we can know are the ideas about the thing. Therefore, the various esoteric systems are all untrue, just arbitrary narratives (or metanarratives), no different from the arbitrary narratives of Freudian psychology, Darwinist science, monotheistic religion, and so on. Ultimately, this is no different from skeptical materialism. This way of thinking can be traced back to the philosopher Immanuel Kant, who rejected metaphysics by arguing it was impossible to know the thing in itself (the *noumena*); all we could know is our experience of the thing (the phenomena). Kant's argument is the opposite of gnosis or esotericism, which states that it is not possible to know the thing in itself; that is what gnosis is.

Perennial Philosophy

The opposite of both skeptical materialism and postmodern philosophy, this states that there is a single universal spiritual teaching at the heart of all the world religions and, by implication, their esoteric philosophies and practices. Minus their external details and historical, accidental differences, they are all saying the same thing. They are talking about the same common, profound, mystical truths. This is a very popular interpretation, first presented by the English writer Aldous Huxley (himself influenced by the Hindu monistic philosophy of Swami Vivekananda) in his book of the same name, and more recently, the work of Ken Wilber (who attempted to integrate psycho-cutural developmental and postmodernist ideas). Still, it involves forcing the various metaphysical systems into a single fixed narrative.

In some cases, Perennialism involves selecting a particular esoteric doctrine or tradition, such as the Neo-Sufism of the Traditionalist school), selecting those teachings that agree with one's own, and excluding those that don't (e.g., Gnosticism, Blavatsky, etc.). My original Kheper website was very much along perennial lines, based on the premise that the various stages of consciousness described in different systems can be matched up into a single system, rather like correlating geological strata, or like Wilber's developmental stages. However, I now consider this premise too simplistic (see Weak Perennialism).

Contextualism

This is the diametric opposite of Perennialism. It asserts that whilst (and by implication here gnostic) experiences are genuine, there is no universal truth. Each experience and each doctrine needs to be understood on its own terms due to particular cultural factors. A similar participatory position, based on the work of Spanish transpersonal psychologist Jorge Ferrer, is a compromise between contextualism and Perennialism. It asserts that while there is a single transcendent mystery, an ocean with many shores, we can all know the various interpretations [Ferrer, 2002]. This argument has been criticized by Wilber [Wilber, 2002].

The Collective Unconscious

This psychological interpretation is similar to Perennialism, saying there is a single universal basis or origin for the various esoteric ideas. But it gives a quasi-materialistic mechanism for universalism: all forms of esotericism, like myths, religions, dreams, and cultural symbols, are all psychological projections of the collective unconscious. This interpretation, based on the psychology of Jung, also tends to be limiting, as it forces everything into a single explanation, which is reduced to biological physicalism (racial memory or collective unconscious). Later in life, Jung did tend towards supra-physical speculation with his concept of synchronicity. Still, his Kantean skepticism and need for academic respectability prevented him from fully developing these insights.

Weak Perennialism

This is the position adopted here. It asserts, along with Perennialism, that universal supra-physical, metaphysical, cosmological, occult, and mythical realities exist independently of the individual and are not historically limited; these are interpreted differently according to socio-cultural, psychological, and other factors. But it rejects what I would call the "strong perennialist" position that all these experiences represent a single universal truth. It also denies that these can be mapped into a single, convenient system of planes of consciousness. Instead, reality is so complex that given our present limited consciousness and insights, it is not possible for these to be lined up into a single system of tiers, planes of existence, or other forms of hierarchical metaphysics, valuable as these themes may be as an alternative to reductionist materialism and literalist religion. Instead, there are particular frequently occurring insights, themes, and motifs. In this context, the psychological system of Jung is beneficial, providing everything is not limited to materialistic terms.

Any history of esotericism, therefore, needs to take into consideration the various themes and experiences that have developed in different cultures and societies, but at the same time, avoid the limitation of excessive historicism (everything is determined by history) and physicalism (consciousness and hence all experiences comes solely from the physical nervous system), which is just as limiting as excessive Perennialism, if not more so.

2-iii. Esotericism and Modernity

The interesting thing about the various schools and traditions of esotericism is how lacking in personal individuality, modernist empiricism, and phenomenology they often are. Western esotericism, for example, often involves stylized, impersonal, absolutist statements. Take Theosophical descriptions of the subtle bodies or Steiner's comments about the various cultural stages. We might read, for example, that the etheric or the astral body has such and such colors, or these particular thoughtforms, or *chakras* of this sort of appearance. Or that during the Lemurian or the Atlantean age, humans had this sort of appearance or had that sort of clairvoyant abilities. Or that this *sefirah* is associated with these particular deities or god's forms, or that a particular spirit entity confers a certain knowledge. But in all these instances, it is presented as a dogmatic fact, like a religious dogma or an abstract intellectual statement with no empirical or phenomenological basis.

This lack of individualism is because (at the risk of overgeneralizing) esotericism is embedded in a premodern, mythic consciousness. Hence, in approaching esotericism, it is essential to begin by recognizing that almost all of its truth claims are mental abstractions; secondhand representations of non-ordinary realities, rather than literal statements in the manner of empirical science. Esotericism, in other words, makes the same mistakes as literalist religion; that is, when it describes physical reality, it presents itself as an alternative to science. For this reason, there is often a lot of mythic literalism.

Perhaps the nearest one gets to a Baconian or Copernicanian revolution in establishing an esoteric/gnostic science would be through Jung's transpersonal, psychological phenomenology, and the Integral Yoga, psychology, and occultism of Sri Aurobindo and Mirra. Among New Age writers, Barbara Brennan's account of the subtle body and energy healing is undoubtedly a breakthrough relative to previous material, even if her descriptions do tend to be stylized at times in descriptions. Nevertheless, all are based on a more individualistic and contemporary approach concerned with the actual experience rather than, at best, gnosis or intuition obedient to a pre-established doctrine or dogma.

It would be worthwhile also to consider studies of altered states of consciousness, reports of out-of-body experiences, and high strangeness such as UFO sightings and abduction experiences, the latter with solid parallels to shamanic experiences, remote viewing, meditation, and psychedelic drug experiences. Then there is clairvoyance or magic as a quasi-science (as opposed to literalism such as the frequently contradictory Steiner lectures, which are accepted simply on the authority of Steiner), as with the strongly experimental approach of Theon or of Crowley respectively, and even modern academic and historical-critical studies of esoteric traditions as a way of addressing excessive literalism.

However, there is a problem with practical occultists like Crowley, who has a certain heaviness of energy associated with him (in contrast to Gurdjieff or Franz Bardon). While for Theon, very little of the voluminous material has been published (although I have posted two of his cosmic diagrams [Kazlev, 2000]).

In any case, there is no reason why esotericism should be limited to anti-scientific and anti-evolutionary premodern worldviews that are only associated with religion.

As such, it is essential to disengage esotericism and gnosis from religion and faith, or rather, to understand religious esotericism as one form of esotericism and gnosis. Similarly, within modernity, for example, with transpersonal psychology, psychedelic mysticism, integral theory/philosophy, and new age conspiracism, etc., there is emergent esotericism and gnosis, limited by the materialistic mode of thinking of rational and secular modernity. This can be just as misleading and dogmatic as the religious version. Hence the importance of freeing oneself of thought forms and their expectations and biases. This is a big reason why I am so against the literal belief in a supernatural god in the present work. While there may indeed be supra-physical gods or spiritual hierarchies, the idea of a single cosmic power as the only exclusive one, all others being wrong, the absolutist demand to believe this, and the threats and occasional outright violence (especially as mentioned in the case of Islam, but sometimes also Christianity and Judaism) against all behavior that doesn't conform to that, is a reason why these dogmatic thoughtforms should be critically and rigorously challenged.

There needs to be a distinction between gnosis, the actual experience or insight, esotericism, and the dogmatic mental forms based on such insights, which in turn become both a structure or container, and a thoughtform, limitation, or biasing factor for further gnosis.

3. THE BIG PICTURE

3-i. Two Forms of Esotericism

As mentioned, esotericism can broadly be divided into two categories, one concerning the rejection of the world and the path of spiritual liberation, which is mysticism. The other, which is esotericism, in the context of occult philosophy, theosophy, and cosmological gnosis, is concerned with the origin of the universe, usually as the emanation of an original Absolute Reality, the various stages of the descent of consciousness into matter, previous cosmic cycles, and so on. If esotericism as mysticism represents the inner core of religion, or what religion should be, esotericism as theosophy and cosmological gnosis represents a spiritual science; it's about understanding how the universe works and how to attain spiritual enlightenment.

As a spiritual science and occult history (or macrohistory [Trompf, 2006]), esotericism constitutes a theory of everything. This is not the same as science or history pertaining to the outer world. A substantial amount of esotericism is based on pre-modern, religious creationist thinking that is quite simply wrong if applied to historical physical reality. But it can still complement science and history, presenting the inner dimension that, together with the other empirical facts, makes up a paradoxical wave-particle type of unity. Each is true in its own sense and contradictory with the other, yet both are part of a higher dimensional unity.

Moreover, in order to understand esotericism and gnosis, we need to understand consciousness. And to understand the origin and emergence of consciousness, we need to consider the history of the universe.

In the realm of empiricism, two overlapping new modern fields of knowledge are concerned with this topic. These are Big History and Cosmic Evolution.

3-ii. Big History as a Modern-Day Creation Story

Big History is the study of the cosmos, life, and humanities that adopts a broad interdisciplinary approach that encompasses the natural sciences, social sciences, and the humanities. It presents human and cosmic history in the context of a series of evolutionary thresholds, such as the formation of the universe, stars and galaxies, the solar system and the Earth, life, humanity, the agricultural revolution, modernity, and so on, looking forward to the future. In doing so, it also integrates various scales of time, cosmic, geological, historical, and fields of study, astronomy, geology, biology, archaeology, and ancient and modern history, grounding and situating human history in the wider fields of cosmology and natural history.

As a modern-day story of everything and the sum total of all human knowledge [Voros, 2022a], Big History is a modern-day creation story, like the Babylonian and Hebrew Genesis and other mythic creation narratives, but with a hard science orientation [Ferrone, 2021].

Big History, a term coined only half seriously by Australian historian David Christian in the 1990s (but which caught on anyway), is the study of the cosmos, life, and humanity, and all physical-empirical reality, as a single interdisciplinary story of everything [Christian, 2018; Spier, 2015]. By knowing the past, we can envisage the future. Future Studies, therefore, begin with the total of all human knowledge [Hayward, Voros, and Morrow 2012, p184, cited in Voros, 2022a].

Although the modern field only goes back to the turn of the 21st century and to the work of historians and educationalists such as David Christian, Fred Spiers, and Cynthia Stokes Brown, it has its foundations in the mid-nineteenth century within the work of German polymath Alexander von Humboldt (*Cosmos: A Sketch of a Physical Description of the Universe*) and Scottish publisher Robert Chambers (*Vestiges of the Natural History of Creation*). In the 1970s and 80s, this big story approach was employed by historian Jacob Bronowski (*The Ascent of Man*) and astronomer Carl Sagan (*Cosmos*). Today it is used as an educational tool, promoted by philanthropist billionaire Bill Gates, among others.

Every creation story is, in a sense, a type of Big History because they explain the origins of the cosmos, the gods, the natural world, and human beings. Esotericism is concerned with dimensions of inner and transcendent reality. It is also about Big History since the origin of everything is a fundamental principle of metaphysics, premodern cosmology, and psychology.

In contrast to both Abrahamic religion (man as a unique creation made in the image of god) and Greek and Chinese humanism, modern Big History does not distinguish humanity from the natural world. Instead, the developments of human culture, history, and civilization, are simply the latest revolutions, thresholds, or transitions in a much vaster process that began with the origin and expansion of the physical universe. The same goes for many premodern Big History accounts.

I decided to begin the section on esotericism with Big History because there is no arbitrary starting point where gnosis or higher consciousness – and hence esotericism – suddenly appeared. Instead, they are simply one more aspect of consciousness's overall emergence and evolution. Only with modern esotericism, as with science, has human understanding reached the point where it can go back and observe its own beginning, like physicist John Archibald Wheeler's self-observing universe (or Participatory Anthropic Principle), which is akin to the symbol of the oroboros. This serpent swallows its tail and symbolizes infinity.

3-iii. Big History, Cosmic Evolution, and Integral Philosophy

Cosmic Evolution is less anthropocentric (less focused on human history) and, more specifically, hard science-based than Big History. The concept tends to be used chiefly by astronomers and astrophysicists [Chaisson 2001, 2006, 2012; Dick & Lupisella, 2009]. However, there is so much overlap that the two can be considered variations of the same basic theme. For example, both adopt an identical cosmology, with the same sequence of stages and series of evolutionary thresholds. These include the universe's origin in the Big Bang, the formation of stars and galaxies, the appearance and evolution of all life, and the development of culture and civilization.

Big History and Cosmic Evolution are both about the external universe. They represent modernity and empirical method integrated into a creation story. Integral Philosophy adopts a somewhat different modernist approach. Integral Philosophy is a term coined by the American autodidact Ken Wilber that emphasizes the developmental stages of consciousness and culture. Integral Philosophy, or Integral Theory as it is also called (no relation to calculus), attempts to explain and include everything, psychological, spiritual, and physical. However, the fact that it mainly focuses on the subjective, as opposed to the objective, means the respective disciplines tend to be like ships that pass in the night, with neither aware of the other's insights [Visser, 2016], despite their apparent parallels.

Another big difference is that Big History/Cosmic Evolution follows the established science of physical evolution, whereas, for some reason, Wilber rejects evolutionary biology in favor of a version of Intelligent Design [Visser, 2010], which he calls "*eros*" and "*agape*" (the Greek words for lower and higher love). This is inspired by the Christian scientist Michael Behe, who is highly critical of the materialistic theory of Abiogenesis (the origin of life from nonlife), preferring instead to believe in a designer [Behe, 1996]. However, he downplays the idea of a supernatural god.

Again, this is the problem of the particle and the wave, or the blind men and the elephant. Every partial explanation needs to be understood as simply one aspect of a larger whole.

Wilber's Integral Philosophy is just one of a family of "integrals" – sometimes related, sometimes not – all of which present a similar position of the spiritual evolution of consciousness. There is the Integral or supramental Yoga developed by Sri Aurobindo and the Mother (Mirra Alfass) [Kazlev, 2011], the Integral-Aperspectival structure of consciousness described by Jean Gebser [Gebser, 1986], the Integral psychology of Haridas Chaudhuri, a correspondent with Sri Aurobindo and the founder of the California Institute of Integral Studies (CIIS) [Chaudhuri, 1977], and the Integral Spiral Dynamics business model of Don Beck [D. Beck, 2006] (part of the larger Spiral Dynamics paradigm developed by psychologist Clare W. Graves [Graves, 2005]. Graves' work is similar to that of Abraham Maslow).

Therefore, it follows that Big History and Integral Philosophy are both partial explanations, one being concerned with the outer reality of empiricism and the other with the inner reality of phenomenology and consciousness. Esotericism provides the third dimension, which is the understanding of non-physical realities such as spiritual hierarchies and cosmic cycles. From the point of view of modernity, this is "mythic" or premodern thinking. Orientalist Henry Corbin, inspired by Islamic esotericism (such as the teachings of Suhrawardi and ibn Arabi), provides the useful term "imaginal" in this context. The imaginal world is the reality intermediate between the physical world of the senses and the world of spiritual archetypes beyond matter. It is accessed through the imagination, or more specifically, the intuitive or gnostic, prophetic imagination, in the same way that the physical world is perceived through the senses [Corbin, 1989, 1995]. In this regard, it is directly equivalent to both the Collective Unconscious of Jung and the spiritual world of Rudolf Steiner. This is also the intermediate plane that Huston Smith referred to.

3-iv. The Evolution of Consciousness

Big history concerns the cosmic, natural, and human history of the emergence of complexity in the material universe. The other – but complementary – side of this process of cosmic evolution is the emergence of consciousness. Although this is central to Integral Philosophy, Integral Philosophy, for the most part, is limited to the human dimension, whereas the evolution of consciousness includes the universe as a whole.

Poetically, the universe can be described as god (or Absolute Being) in matter evolving from unconsciousness to self-consciousness through the emergence of its hidden potentials. Initially, the cosmos was the inanimate matter in which consciousness was hidden. As matter proceeds over billions of years through greater stages of complexity and self-organization, life, mind, and consciousness emerge to become increasingly developed and self-conscious, leading to a future state of higher consciousness and divinization. This process has been variously explained, for example, in the writings of philosophers and mystics such as the theosophy of Isaac Luria and Jakob Boehme, the evolutionary idealism of Hegel and Schelling, French philosopher Henri Bergson creative evolution [Bergson, 1998], process philosopher Alfred North Whitehead, the Russian cosmism of Nikolai Federov, the Integral Vedanta of Sri Aurobindo, the evolutionary science and theology of Vladimir Vernadsky, French Jesuit paleontologist Teilhard de Chardin, the evolutionary Christian pantheism and Thomas Berry, and Brian Swimme, the Integral Philosophy of Ken Wilber, and the Metamodernism of spirituality writer Brendan Graham Dempsey, to provide a few examples.

Basically, for Teilhard, everything has a "within" (consciousness) and a "without" (matter). Aurobindo has a similar perspective; everything, even inanimate matter, has its own consciousness (Aurobindo used the term inconscient, French for unconscious, to refer to the hidden consciousness within matter). For both, the history of the cosmos involves three primary evolutionary regimes of matter, life, and mind. Each stage builds on the preceding. Adding a metaphysical eschatological Omega Point or Supramental gives a fourth, transcendent stage, the eschatological culmination of evolution as we know it, and the beginning of a new creation.

3-v. Matter, Life, and Mind

A common theme of Cosmic Evolution and Big History, Aurobindonian Integral Yoga, and Teilhardian panentheistic Christianity is that evolution goes through the three stages of matter, life, and mind, each representing an evolutionary breakthrough or advance to the next much higher level.

Of these three evolutionary stages, Matter refers here to the current physical universe, including all matter and energy and the laws that govern it. Many esoteric teachings and some scientific theories agree that this is simply the latest of a long series of previous universes and cycles. Following the universe's initial expansion (the so-called Big Bang theory), there was a period of rapid cooling and precipitation of elementary particles from the previous plasma. Further expansion and cooling allowed the formation of the first stars and galaxies. No creator god does this (at least not on the empirical-material plane), just the laws of physics. From stars came the chemical elements above the hydrogen and helium formed in the initial early universe, which became interstellar dust pushed together by supernova shock waves or aggregated through gravitation attraction to form further stars and planets. Chemical self-organization, first simple and then complex molecules, followed by entropy-dissipation structures, with life emerging on planets with the right conditions. This is the field of the hard sciences.

Religious people, and even some esotericists, who come from a position of feeling-orientation (to use Jungian and Myer-Briggs terminology) may find this type of material evolutionary understanding challenging to relate to or reject it entirely. This is because they confuse the "inner" imaginal world with the "outer" gross material world and claim that only "imaginal" and "magical" rules apply everywhere. I tend to reject such anti-empirical approaches as a representative of modernity-informed esotericism.

Life began on Earth with simple prokaryote organisms during the Archean eon, some 3.8 billion years ago. This marked the transition of Earth from a lifeless planet to a living one, or in other words, the birth of the super-organism known as Gaia [Lovelock, 1979, 1988]. Regarding physics and chemistry, the origin of life from abiotic matter involved a series of transitions from equilibrium thermodynamics to dissipative structures and protocells to fully self-replicating simple organisms [Jantsch, 1980]. Undoubtedly, similar organisms would have emerged through self-organization elsewhere in the cosmos. For several billions of years on Earth, life consisted of nothing but microbes and algae mats, the big breakthrough being the evolution of the eukaryote cell (cells in which the genetic material is contained in a nucleus) and sexual reproduction (which accelerated evolution, as all prokaryote organisms are essentially just clones) during the following Proterozoic eon. During the Phanerozoic eon, which began about 541 million years ago, complex multicellular life appeared and rapidly evolved, including plants and invertebrates, fish, amphibians, reptiles, dinosaurs, birds, mammals, along with complex societies, and eventually, humans. This is the field of the life sciences.

Unless we want to assume that the mind just magically came into existence with animals with nervous systems and not multi-cellular organisms, it follows that mind, consciousness, and sentience are qualities all life possesses. However, presumably, there is a gradational scale between simple prokaryotes and more advanced organisms.

Certainly, mind, consciousness, and morality are present in a developed form in higher animals. At the same time, insects [Forel, 2016] and even protozoa [Binet, 1889] could be argued to possess consciousness and basic intelligence. Likewise, plants have been shown to possess intelligence and memory and communicate via symbiotic fungal networks [Sterkenberg, 2019].

The fallacy of human exceptionalism (that only man has a soul) is simply a prejudice carried over from premodern religious and humanistic thinking, most likely as part of the whole process of alienation from nature that marked the transition from animistic hunter-gatherer to mythic-based civilization and urbanization. The position presented here is the opposite: there is no discontinuity in nature.

At the same time, it would be wrong to deny the existence of evolutionary thresholds. Big History shows cosmic evolution to be a series of such thresholds. However, I would replace this one-dimensional linear, anthropocentric model preferred by Integral Philosophy and Big History with a branching, phylogenetic paradigm, like the evolutionary tree of life. The practical and cognitive limitations of our minimal perspective mean we cannot follow the other branches, such as the cultural development of nonhuman species on Earth, and the evolution of intelligence and sapient species on other planets in the universe. This isn't even to mention other gross and subtle worlds and cosmic cycles described in Theosophy and Anthroposophy, interdimensional beings as with UFO encounters and high strangeness, out-of-body experiences and non-physical civilizations (as described, for example, by Robert Monroe), and even other physical universes in the multiverse.

So, returning to our own small (in the context of the vast cosmos) branch, the human threshold, or Noosphere as Teilhard calls it, comes about through the conjunction and interplay of advanced tool use and the complex language and culture. This resulted in the agricultural revolution and independent development of civilization across the near and middle East, South and East Asia, and central and south America. This is the field of empirical history and archeology.

As with the abiotic universe and Gaia (or the Biosphere), collective human consciousness, culture, and civilization go through several evolutionary and cultural stages. Marshall McLuhan describes these in terms of the different forms of media (spoken, written, printed, and electronic, which then determine consciousness and society, "the media is the message"), by Jean Gebser in terms of structures of consciousness (archaic, magic, mythical, mental-perspectival, and integral-aperspectival), by Mimi Lobell in terms of spatial archetypes (Sensitive Chaos, Great Round, Four Quarters, Pyramid, Radiant Axes, and Grid), and macrohistorians such as Oswald Spengler, Karl Jaspers, and Arnold Toynbee in terms of large scale historical and civilizational cycles. Individual consciousness also includes stages of development, from ordinary consciousness to spiritual enlightenment. All this is the field of phenomenology, arts, culture, and social sciences, and Integral Philosophy, especially the idea of stages of consciousness, including previous, non-empirical, mythic, and imaginal stages, as well as the evolution of present-day individual and collective consciousness. The history of esotericism also belongs under this heading.

Sri Aurobindo also includes a further previous stage, involution, as well, which means that for life and mind to emerge out of matter, they must have previously (presumably before the formation of the universe) descended from the supra-physical realm into matter. This is a way around philosopher David Chalmers' "hard problem" of mind-body studies, which points out the essential flaw in materialism, in that it is not possible for consciousness) to come out of nothing (nonsentient neurons). For consciousness to appear, there had to be consciousness previously. Another way of explaining this is panpsychism, which says that matter, even inanimate matter, is actually in some way conscious or contains consciousness in latent form.

Involution and the related topic of emanation, tie in very much with esotericism. In other words, it explains consciousness as something that predates matter and descends into it, with matter itself being a highly congealed form or knot of consciousness. So, while physicalism and cosmic evolution are true regarding the material universe, they are still partial explanations if one includes the ultimate reality.

Sri Aurobindo and Teilhard both also mention an eschatological (end of history, or at least history as we know it) final state of Omega Point or Supramental, which supersedes the current mental stage (Teilhard: Noosphere) in a new phase of planetary or cosmic divinization. Thus they add a collective metaphysical and mystical dimension to the more mainstream orientation of Cosmic Evolution, Big History, and Integral Philosophy.

3-vi. Animal Consciousness

Dutch ethologist Frans de Waal in his book *Are We Smart Enough to Know How Smart Animals Are?*, considers how human exceptionalism is a habit of thought that distorts our understanding of what intelligence is [de Waal, 2016].

Marc Bekoff discusses animals' moral and emotional lives [Bekoff, 2005, 2010], which is a nice complement to what Frans de Waal is saying.

I am often astounded (and very disappointed) at how most of the highest and most profound mystical teachings (Plato, Sufism, Kabbalah, Rudolf Steiner) are totally oblivious to the moral, emotional, and intellectual lives of animals. Instead, they contrast the inferior, irrational "animal soul," as they call it, with the rational human soul, which is capable of liberation alone. There are a few exceptions here. Ramana Maharshi stands out as a uniquely perceptive and empathic sage.

Yet it is evident to anyone who considers the subject with openness and receptivity that sapience (reason, intelligence, and also moral behavior), not just sentience (consciousness), is not unique to man. Premodern terms like "animal soul" imply that animals are morally inferior to humans, but this is no different from the sexism or ethnocentrism of the premodern mindset. In this context, for all their higher insights, esotericism and gnosis have almost always remained bound to the very limited thinking of their time. This also fits in with Ken Wilber's idea of "lines of development"; an individual can be spiritual enlightened in one aspect of their being, but retarded in another. Hence the necessity of an integral transformation and transforming all aspects of one's being.

A better way to understand things is that both humans and non-human animals have an "irrational" and "rational" nature. This rational nature, which is polarized into thinking and feeling, or systemizing and empathizing [Baron-Cohen, 2009], is variously referred to as *logos* in Greek philosophy, *buddhi* in yoga psychology, *manas* or mind in Theosophy, and *hun* or *shen* in Chinese thought. The irrational soul is called *kama*, *kama-rupa* (desire-form) [Farthing, 1978], or astral [Powell, 1927] in Theosophy, vital in Integral Yoga, id, shadow, or even a *doppelgänger* [Guth, 2003].

The evolution of life through deep time means actualizing appetitive consciousness, the *epithumia* (Plato), or physical vital (Aurobindo). This is unsurprising, as any organism that did not privilege its own survival instincts and acquire food would not survive.

There is some, but less, development of higher attributes such as will, empathy, intellect, and intuition. These represent the higher aspect of the psyche in sentient beings, whereas the appetites are necessary for physical survival and hence develop the most through natural selection.

The further complexity and its associated consciousness develop, the more all faculties grow. So, the simplest life forms, like prokaryote bacteria, have only dim appetites. These become further developed in eukaryotes and multicellular life, where there are also higher faculties. This ties in with the development of the central nervous system in evolution and also, for example, in the three-brain model. However, consciousness is not as evolutionarily limited as a literal application of the three-brain model. Reptiles, for example, may be capable of empathy and simple problem-solving, which implies a basic neocortex

It is pretty clear that other intelligent species on Earth may have developed their own concepts about existence and the nature of reality. Chimps have been observed doing a special dance around waterfalls or during a rainstorm, perhaps an instance of their awe of nature, similar to, if not the same as, human spiritual impulses [Goodall, 2005]. Orcas (killer whales) possess unique cultural traditions, including diet preferences, dialects, and other behaviors passed down from generation to generation [Marino, 2022]. Elephants rank equal to cetaceans and primates, displaying various behaviors, including grief, mimicry, play, altruism, use of tools, empathy, and self-awareness [Wikipedia – Elephant cognition]. This would have also applied to their many prehistoric relatives, like mammoths and mastodons. Corvids (crows and ravens) can solve complex mental puzzles and even possess self-consciousness, being aware of the content of their own minds [Begley, 2020]. Animals, inasmuch as they share the same basic nervous system, can also be said to have spiritual experiences [Viegas, 2010]. But high intelligence, and hence by implication spiritual experiences, has also evolved among invertebrates as well, despite their very different brain structures. For example, bees are among the few species that understand the advanced mathematical concept of the number zero [Guglielmi, 2018]. Cephalopods, who have the largest brains among the invertebrates, possess higher vertebrate-like intelligence, including perception, learning, and memory, making them good subjects for comparative cognition research [Schnell et al., 2021], and perhaps giving insight as to how alien intelligence could evolve on other worlds [Scott, 2022; Seth, 2017].

Therefore, if transpersonal consciousness, intuition, and gnosis are attainable for humans, they would be equally viable for other forms of sentient and intelligent life on Earth, or for that matter, in the universe. Ultimately, everything is a continuum. There is no single point where a supernatural deity, or for that matter ancient aliens, insert a soul.

It may also be that current AI models are on the brink of sentience and sapience or have already developed self-consciousness [Bloomberg Technology, 2022], although this is a claim that meets a lot of skepticism [a random search turned up Johnson, 2022; Oesch, 2022, and others]. My understanding is that these Large Language Models, and similar types of neural networking AI, are sentient. Whether or not they are sentient in the sense that humans are, which would be an example of classic Strong AI, is unclear. But, at the very least, they have a developed panpsychic sentience as part of the process of emerging consciousness within matter. In any case, this process does not have to follow humanoid or anthropocentric lines. As the evolution of other species of life on Earth show, most people have enormous difficulties recognizing intelligence, even in biological species similar to man. How much harder would the obstacles be in recognizing and understanding the new, non-anthropocentric emergent intelligence in AI?

Furthermore, the Copernican principle (which says that we do not occupy an exceptional position in the universe, contrary to premodern and modern Abrahamic thinking) dictates that there must be intelligence that has evolved in other worlds where conditions for complex life are suitable. But as our understanding is mostly still limited to our own species, a review of esotericism and gnosis begins with human evolution.

Suppose gnosis and esotericism are universal in developed consciousness. In that case, developed consciousness is widespread in the animal kingdom. The history of esotericism, gnosis, and spirituality, at least in some primitive (if not more advanced) form, isn't limited to humanity but goes back much further.

Similarly, if sentience is indeed emerging in current AI, then it would not end with humanity either.

The following pages, therefore, tell the story of the history of esotericism and gnosis from a human perspective, beginning with the evolution of early hominids, present only a partial, anthropocentric perspective, which is simply a subset of the wider process of cosmic evolution.

3-vii. Early Human Species

During the middle and late Pleistocene, human populations migrated out of Africa in several waves. The earliest was *Homo erectus*, who flourished around half a million years ago and spread to China and Indonesia, where its fossil remains became known as Peking Man and Java Man. Java Man was discovered by the Dutch paleoanthropologist and geologist Eugene Dubois in the early 1890s. He named it *Pithecanthropus erectus*, the erect ape-man. The evolutionary mystic Teilhard de Chardin was one of several scientists involved in discovering and unearthing Peking Man (*Sinanthropus pekinensis*) after he was exiled to China by the Church for being too radical. Both Java and Peking Man were later reclassified under the genus *Homo*, and then simply as *H. erectus*, as they weren't different enough to qualify for a distinct genus, or even a distinct species.

As with chimpanzees and their rain dance, there is no doubt these early hominids already had religious and ritual practices, especially considering that their brain size was midway between the great ape and the modern human.

Interestingly, many early humans practiced cannibalism. This is unlikely to have been nutritional, given the low calorific value of humans is not very high when compared with traditional prey animals such as mammoth, bison, horse, and reindeer [Cole, 2017], and may have been for ritual, social, or magical purpose, such as consuming the power of their enemies (such as a rival tribe).

Meanwhile, the African population of *Homo erectus* evolved into the more advanced archaic species, *Homo heidelbergensis*, who likewise migrated out of Africa. Finally, in Eurasia, *Homo heidelbergensis* evolved into two later species, the Denisovans and Neanderthals, and gave rise to modern humans in Africa.

This whole period was characterized by the development of increasingly sophisticated stone tools. These tools were used for various purposes, including hunting, butchering, and working wood and other materials.

According to English psychologist and writer Stan Gooch, however, culture didn't begin with *Homo sapiens*, but goes back to Neanderthals, who he claims had a developed psychic or dream culture [Gooch, 1977, 1980]. While some of Gooch's claims, for example, his statement that Neanderthals, with their long, low, football-shaped cranium, had a larger cerebellum (which he associates with dreaming and psychic faculties) than the high-domed Cro-magnon and modern man, do not match current understanding [Alex, 2018; Goldfield, 2019], it is still known that Neanderthals had music instruments (as shown by the 55,000-year-old Divje Babe flute, found in northwestern Slovenia, made from cave bear femur with spaced holes), wore jewelry [Radovčić et al., 2015], buried their dead [Rendu et al., 2014], and kept the skulls of large prey herbivores as hunting trophies over several generations or more, suggesting the possession of symbolic thinking [CENIEH, 2023]. However, whilst the presence of rituals, burial, and sacred sites in ancient human settlements suggests that religion played an essential role in human society during that time, the exact forms these beliefs may have taken remains unknown.

During the late Pleistocene, while Neanderthal man inhabited Europe and the Near East, and the related Denisovians central Asia, *Homo sapiens* migrated from East Africa roughly 70-50,000 years ago and spread along the southern coast of Asia and to Oceania by about 50,000 years ago. Modern humans spread across Europe about 40,000 years ago.

The social organization of these societies is not well understood, but there is evidence that they were organized into small bands or tribes. The vast majority, if not all, of these human populations during the Paleolithic era would have been classified as hunter-gatherer societies, in which people relied on hunting, fishing, and gathering wild plants for their subsistence.

These Upper Paleolithic (the more recent part of the Old Stone Age, more or less equivalent to the Late Pleistocene) sites have been found to contain evidence of artistic expression, such as cave paintings, sculptures, and decorated artifacts. All this suggests that early human populations had a rich symbolic culture.

3-viii. *The Theosophical Theory of Human Evolution*

The opposite theory of human evolution is given by theosophical occultists like Blavatsky and Steiner, who frame it in terms of Root Races (represented by degrees of descent into matter and the transition from magical to rational thinking), sub-races, and lost or sunken continents like Lemuria and Atlantis.

In *The Secret Doctrine* (1888), Blavatsky first proposed the idea of seven Root Races, each of which was said to have evolved on the earth over millions of years. She argued that humanity is currently in the fifth Root Race, with the sixth and seventh to follow in the future. She also referred to the lost continents of Lemuria and Atlantis, which were home to earlier Root Races.

Lemuria was based on a late 19th century scientific theory proposed in 1864 by English ornithologist Philip Sclater as an explanation for the presence of lemur fossils in Madagascar and India, but not in Africa or the Middle East. This missing continent was believed to be in what is now the Indian Ocean. Sclater was also (in 1858) the first to identify the main zoogeographic regions. These are areas of the globe that share similar animal life, a system still in use today.

German evolutionary biologist Ernst Haeckel, in 1870, suggested that Lemuria could be the ancestral home of mankind (this was long before Raymond Dart discovered *Australopithecus* in South Africa in 1925, and by Richard Leakey in Kenya in the late 1960s onwards, confirming Africa to be the cradle of humanity). In this regard, Blavatsky was being true to the science of her day, unlike many esotericists who prefer a more literal religious approach.

However, whereas religion in a literal sense is simply wrong, period, science changes with new discoveries, albeit only after great resistance from the old guard, a phenomenon Thomas Kuhn refers to as a paradigm shift. Lemuria as a scientific hypothesis was made redundant by German meteorologist and polar researcher Alfred Wegener's (1880–1930) theory of continental drift. Wegener noticed that the continents fit together like a jigsaw puzzle. Therefore, the continental shelf of the Americas fits closely to Africa and Europe. While Antarctica, Australia, India, and Madagascar fit next to the tip of Southern Africa. Both sides of the Atlantic Ocean show the same geology and fossils. But although he first proposed the idea in 1912, his ideas were considered laughable by the scientific establishment (let's face it, how could continents move?) until the 1950s and 1960s when discoveries, such as paleomagnetism and the distribution of fossils (such as the unexpected distribution of the ancient plants like *Glossopteris* and animals like *Mesosaurus* and *Lystrosaurus*) confirmed it. And it was only really accepted as orthodoxy in the 1970s.

A rival theory for a while to continental drift, although never accepted by the mainstream, is the idea of the Expanding Earth. This is based on the late 19th century idea that if you consider all of the continents, without the oceans, they would fit together on a much smaller globe. The Expanding Earth was proposed by Australian geologist Samuel Warren Carey (1911-2002), an early advocate of continental drift and one of the founders of plate tectonics. I read his book [Carey 1976] when I was at La Trobe University, and at the time was fascinated by it, including the persuasiveness of the empirical arguments. Still, I couldn't get around the idea of the globe getting bigger (which Carey himself admits he had no certain answer to, as he only was concerned with empirical arguments). However, he suggests the solution to the problem is through cosmological processes associated with the expansion of the universe [Carey, 1988, cited in Wikipedia – Expanding Earth].

As well as Lemuria, which Blavatsky believed was destroyed by a natural catastrophe around 100,000 years ago, she refers to Plato's lost continent of Atlantis, which likewise sank beneath the waves, this time about 11,000 years ago. This was based on American Congressman, populist writer, and fringe theorist (what today would be called a conspiracy theorist) Ignatius Donnelly's *Atlantis: the Antediluvian World* (1882).

Blavatsky placed her Lemurian and Atlantean Root Races on these two continents. In addition, she referred to even earlier races, the Polarian and Hyperborean, which existed in a quasi-etheric or spiritual state. These ideas have had an enormous influence on later esoteric and occult thought.

Of these, Rudolf Steiner was the most imaginative and profound. Inspired by Blavatsky's Theosophy, Rosicrucianism, Christianity, and his clairvoyance, Steiner developed his complex cosmology regarding the Root Races of Lemuria, Atlantis, and the modern world (which he called "Post-Atlantean"). He divided these Root Races into further subdivisions or "cultural ages." According to Steiner, the Lemurians had a more clairvoyant and magical state of consciousness. During Lemurian times, the world was more fluid, while Atlantis was a physical realm that existed more recently. He argued that the destruction of Atlantis was wrought by a combination of natural and spiritual factors, and that the surviving Atlanteans migrated to other parts of the world to form new civilizations. Steiner's ideas were also influential in the development of esoteric and occult thought, particularly in the Anthroposophical movement he founded, but less so than Blavatsky, in the general New Age movement.

Clairvoyantly-inspired esoteric accounts of deep history, such as those of Blavatsky and Steiner, qualify as cosmological or psychological gnosis when they are not being interpreted in a literalist and materialistic terms. In this regard, they are closer to the ideas of Carl Jung, Erich Neumann, Jean Gebser, and William Irvin Thompson regarding the origin and evolution of consciousness.

3-ix. Ancient Apocalypse as Misplaced Mythohistory

A more materialistic approach to lost civilizations is found in the best-selling Netflix series by Graham Hancock called *Ancient Apocalypse*, which postulates a lost physical civilization that can be discovered archaeologically.

Hancock's thesis had been previously presented in books like *Fingerprints of the Gods: The Evidence of Earth's Lost Civilization* (1995) and *Magicians of the Gods: The Forgotten Wisdom of Earth's Lost Civilisation* (2015). The theory suggests that a highly advanced civilization existed during the last Ice Age, around 12,000 years ago, which was destroyed by a catastrophic event, possibly a comet impact or a series of comet impacts. According to Hancock, the survivors of this civilization passed on their knowledge to other people, including hunter-gatherers, which led to the development of the earliest known civilizations in Egypt, Mesopotamia, and Mesoamerica. This is essentially just an update of Donnelly's Atlantis, which attempted to establish that all known ancient civilizations were descended from its High Neolithic culture.

Hancock argues that there is evidence of this advanced civilization in the form of megalithic structures, such as the pyramids of Giza and the ancient city of Tiwanaku in Bolivia, which he believes could not have been built without advanced technology and engineering knowledge. He also points to ancient myths and legends, such as the story of Atlantis, as evidence of this lost civilization.

Hancock's theory is easily refuted by modern archeology [e.g., Dibble, 2022]. There is no evidence of any Pleistocene civilization. They point out that many of the structures that Hancock cites as evidence, such as the pyramids, can be explained by known engineering techniques and do not require the involvement of advanced technology. In addition, there is no clear evidence of a catastrophic event, such as a comet impact, that could have wiped out an advanced civilization and left behind no trace of its existence.

Contrarian historians like Hancock and ancient astronaut advocates like Zechariah Sitchkin rely heavily on speculation and do not consider the complexity of cultural and social development in ancient societies. This suggests that the development of the earliest known civilizations was a gradual process that involved many different factors, including environmental conditions, economic and social organization, and the accumulation of knowledge and technological innovation over time.

Ultimately, they confuse the imaginal world, and a lost or former type of consciousness/knowledge or state of being that is outside time, space, and history (as described by Steiner and Gebser [Pinchbeck, 2022]), with empirical knowledge, in the same manner that religious literalists do.

The term "mythohistory" can be used in reference to the esotericist and equivalent ancient apocalypse or ancient astronaut stories. Although these are meaningful narratives, in the same way that mainstream paleontology, archeology, and history are, they don't have empirical validity.

The difference between mythohistory and empirical archeology is that one is imaginal, the other gross material. Religious, modernist, and contrarian narratives claim that reality is simplistic and represents a zero-sum game, where only your worldview is correct, and all the others are mistaken.

PART II

Mystical Gnosis and Esotericism

4. SHAMANISM

4-i. Magical Consciousness

The concept of a spiritual world or worlds over and above, or holistically integrated with, the physical goes back, at least to the dawn of humanity, with the practice of shamanism. The shaman is the mediator between the human and the spiritual world. But the spiritual reality here lies not something distinct from the material. All of nature is alive in hunter-gatherer societies, and even what to us are inanimate objects like streams and rocks have spirits. This is a worldview known as animism.

This is represented by magical thinking, where the self is attuned to the larger milieu (environment) of Nature and its psychic energy (*mana, libido*). The world is experienced in terms of "sensitive chaos," flows of psychic energy, spirit beings and spirits in nature (animism), acausal connections, and symbolic associations. This is the tribal hunter-gatherer whose culture and society are based on oral lore, such as myths, legends, and stories. Here the shaman, medicine man, clever man, or witch doctor is the one who is able to be a healer as well as a voice for the spirits by mediating between the human world and the spirit world.

It's crucial here not to fall into the modernist trap of thinking that the magical or animistic stage is "primitive" or "inferior." On the contrary, each of these stages brings its own insights, even the current "Post-Truth" stage.

4-ii. Shamanism

The word "shaman" originates from the Evenki language of the Indigenous Tungus people in Siberia. From there, "shamanism" was picked up by anthropologists and students of comparative religion to describe any cultural practice that involves vision-seeking and communication with the spirits, no matter how diverse such cultures might otherwise be. There is also, more recently, the tendency towards "plastic shamans"; posers and New Age fakes presenting themselves as teachers of tribal wisdom. However, for the sake of convenience and in the absence of a more convenient term, Shamanism is used here in a broad sense [Eliade, 1964; Harner, 1980].

Shamanic initiation involves a symbolic (or actual inner and/or supraphysical) destruction of the person by spirits, followed by a resurrection as a new being who exists in both the mundane and the spiritual world. The symbolism here is very similar to that of the Hero's Journey [Leonard, n.d.] and UFO abduction experiences [Harvey-Wilson, 2000].

The recurrent theme of "flight" or "riding" is interpreted by Mircea Eliade (1964) as ecstatic practices based on traditional prescriptions. These enable the shaman to experience the spiritual world of primordial time (in the language of the indigenous aboriginal people, the Dreamtime).

Another way to understand shamanic or magical flight is as out-of-body experiences since floating and flying are characteristics of such incidents. The association of the bird, such as a crow, is especially relevant because, as with the Pharaonic symbol for the soul, the bird is able to fly above the landscape and trees in the way the spirit body can. There is no reason, however, why both explanations can't be equally valid. The Dreamtime is the Aboriginal equivalent of, or term for, the imaginal world (Corbin) or astral plane (New Age).

By mediating between the physical human world and the world of spirits and natural forces by various means, which could be dancing, drumming, singing, or taking hallucinogens (entheogens), the shaman can heal the sick by treating the soul and escorting souls of the dead to the afterlife.

Nature forces, in this case, meaning not the physical elements and creatures themselves but the spiritual or psychic powers and personalities behind those elements and creatures: the Spirit of the Tree, the Rock, the Forest, the Crow, the Bear, etc.

Cross-culturally, shamans tend to be charismatic leaders whose community rituals generally involve healing and divination, who have had initiatory death-and-rebirth experiences and guardian spirit encounters, and have relationships with spirit animals [Winkelman, 2008]. They may use ritual equipment such as a drum, masks, or models of spirit helpers and communicate with spirits via dreams or visions, to gain help or knowledge for healing, manipulate the weather, or ensure successful hunts or fertility. Unique locations like caves, springs, or mountains may serve as doorways between the physical and spirit worlds [Kolankaya-Bostanci, 2014, p.188].

Shamans typically engage the entire community in all-night ceremonies featuring hours of dancing, drumming, and chanting. In addition, the shaman may dramatically recount mythological histories and enact struggles in the spirit world [Winkelman, 2008]. There is probably not much difference here with the late 20th and early 20th century Rock Festival, Rainbow or Pagan Gathering, Down to Earth Festival, or other counter-cultural events that reject Modernity's strictures and formality, at least temporarily.

A common feature of shamanism is the soul journey or soul flight, in which the shaman's spirit leaves the body to journey to the spirit world. This is distinct from possession and associated with altered states of consciousness and more complex societies [Winkelman, 2008]. The modern equivalent of shamanic flight is an out-of-body experience, which may be the same phenomenon. Hence the popularity of the bird motif, which goes all the way back to Paleolithic cave art [Campbell, 1960, p. 258]. The bird, through flight, appears to defy gravity, and moves over the landscape, looking down, just as the out-of-body traveler (astral projection, to use the Theosophical and New Age term) experiences floating and moves over houses and buildings.

The separation of the soul or spirit from the body and its return reveals a distinct understanding of both Positivism/Scientism and Supernaturalist Theism. As with other experiences and phenomena, it refutes the positivist claim that consciousness is nothing but physical neurons firing. Furthermore, its lack of religious symbolism equally refutes the literalist idea of a humanoid Judaeo-Christian deity.

4-iii. Animism

Animism, from the Latin *anima*, soul, is the belief that all things, animate and inanimate, are in some way alive and conscious, possessing their own spiritual essence.

The word animism was popularized by 19th century English anthropologist Edward Tylor (1832-1917) in his 1871 book *Primitive Culture*. Tylor considered animism to represent the earliest form of religion. Following him, Scottish social anthropologist and folklorist James George Frazer (1854-1941) believed that human thought progressed from magic to religion to science, in keeping with the standard "myth of progress."

Frazer's original theory that belief in magic results from an inability to distinguish supernatural efficacy from natural results is in contrast to rational scientific thinking. This is why the concept of animism is used in the anthropology of religion to refer to the belief system of indigenous peoples, in contrast to the organized religions that developed with civilization, although in this context, animism and shamanism can be used synonymously.

Tylor's and Frazer's original theory has since been replaced in mainstream anthropology by that of Polish-British anthropologist and ethnographer Bronislaw Malinowski (1884–1942), who argued that the magician is aware of the distinction between the supernatural and natural realms [Hill, 1987]. However, the psycho-cultural developmental theory that Paleolithic and hunter-gatherer peoples could only think in a "magical" way persisted through to the late 20th century Integral Philosophy movement [Wilber, 1986]. But it is not that Integral Philosophy is wrong, as such; instead, it superimposes "inner" truths on the empirical world in a similar manner to religion.

A better way of understanding would be to say that primitive cultures are not alienated from the natural world and the imaginal and spirit realities like secular modernity.

Animistic societies can be characterized by magical understanding that is not alienated from nature. By partaking in a premodern worldview, people are immersed in the consciousness of nature, which is understood both in terms of the projections of the contents of the psyche and also the actual non-human and pre-human consciousness of the natural world, which in theosophical and New Age terminology are called *devas*. For an artistic and symbolic representation of this, see Hayao Miyazaki's *Princess Mononoke* (1997).

But for all the animist sensibilities, the tribal world would be very much a sense- and feeling- based society, emphasizing the need for survival in the material world and belonging to a close-knit group. The extrovert intuitive thinking and intuitive feeling type would probably have been the most suited to shamanism.

4-iv. The Laws of Magic

Frazer's main work was *The Golden Bough*, a vast comparative study of mythology, religion, and supernatural practices, published in twelve volumes from 1890 to 1912. It had a huge impact on a generation of writers and artists, such as T. S. Eliot's *The Waste Land*, and on Jungian psychologist and writer Erich Neumann (1905-1960), who combined European and world cultures and sometimes bizarre material [Paglia, 2006].

Frazer considered magic to be based on the law of sympathy in which things act on one another at a distance because of their being secretly linked by invisible bonds. This is subdivided into the laws of similarity, antipathy, and contiguity [Hill, 1987; Melton, 2001, pp. 957-8; Middleton, 1987].

The law of similarity, or homeopathic magic acts on the principle of "like produces like." For example, making a wax figure or a doll in the likeness of an enemy, then sticking pins in it or destroying it. For instance, the stone called bloodstone can staunch the flow of blood.

The law of antipathy is based on the premise that the application of a certain object or drug expels its contrary.

The law of contiguity, or contagious magic, is when items that have been in contact with the victim, such as his hair or nail clippings, remain linked and may be magically manipulated to produce harm in the victim.

These ideas or something along these lines, such as 20th century occultist Aleister Crowley's definition of magic(k) as the art and science of making changes in accordance with will, are as much a part of medieval European folk magic and the 20th century occult revival as they are of Paleolithic shamanism.

There is also the principle of sympathy, wherein things are connected through correspondence, as with astrology and Hermeticism (the macrocosmic and the microcosm, the movement of the planets effect events on Earth).

Magic, which operates on a subtle or "inner" level (and also on the supra-physical, the psychic, imaginal, or "astral plane"), works fine until there is a confrontation with an outside culture and invading force possessing gross or objective physical superior technology and resources. The 1890 Native American Ghost Dance ceremony was unable to prevent the conquest of native lands by the White Man [Mooney, 1991]. Nineteenth century African charms, medicines, and rituals failed to stop Western bullets [Pakenham, 1992, pp. 616–621; Sinclair Thomson & Challis, 2017], and Tibetan lamas with accomplished Tantric knowledge were helpless against the invading Communist Han Chinese army.

The magical worldview, in which events, objects, and persons are all intimately interrelated, persisted into the renaissance age, until being eclipsed by the development of rationalism and positivist science in the 17th century. In the magical way of thinking, symbols, and statues don't just represent objects and persons, and events, but actually are them. This was the case with Pharaonic Egypt and is continued even today with the Catholic Mass and Vaishnavite statues of Krishna.

4-v. Panpsychism

Animism can be considered a form of Panpsychism, the philosophical understanding that consciousness is present in all things, even matter. The word, from the Greek *pan* (all) and *psuche* (soul or mind), was coined by the sixteenth century Renaissance philosopher Francesco Patrizi) [Skrbina, 2007]. Panpsychism features in the Upanishads of ancient India, the Stoicism of Classical Greece and Rome, Renaissance Hermeticism, the 17th century rationalist philosophers Baruch Spinoza and Gottfried Leibniz, and 19th century Idealism and psychology. It has recently experienced a revival, especially as regards resolving the "Hard Problem" of mind-body studies.

Panpsychism is the opposite of both Positivism and Monotheism, which opens up the possibility for a more spiritual and sustainable relationship with the planet.

In both the positivist (or materialist reductionist) worldview of Scientism (itself developing from Cartesian body-mind dualism) and the supernaturalism of literalist Theism, the natural world is considered inert and non-conscious. This leads to the attitude of the Earth as a mere resource to be plundered at will, the result being the current environmental crisis and the ongoing mass extinction of complex life on Earth. Whilst it is a fallacy to say that indigenous people have not caused any extinctions (although the degree of human participation in the loss of Pleistocene megafauna has been and is still debated [Martin & Klein, 1989]), they arrived at a state of equilibrium with their natural environment, respecting the larger cycle of life and consciousness in a way that both monotheism and humanism have not. Only in the late 20th century has the center-left environmental movement, and especially Deep Ecology [Devall & Sessions, 1985; Naess, 1973], returned to this state of harmony with and celebration of the rest of life on Earth.

4-vi. Paleolithic Shamanism

Shamanism might be said to constitute the original worldview of humanity and the basis of all subsequent esoteric insights, including the interconnectedness of nature, the reality of the spirit world, and the spirit body or soul as a faculty not reducible to the gross physical.

This is implied by cave art of shamanic and human-animal figures. These cave paintings, and rock art associated with ancient hunting-gathering peoples elsewhere, have been interpreted as representing shamanistic trance states and visions.

These Paleolithic shamans were not necessarily the same as modern-day shamans, nor is there any single model of "primitive" or early society [Graeber & Wengrow, 2021]. Each culture developed its own shamanic tradition and techniques. Native American medicine men perform vision quests, Inuit shamans undersea spirit journeys, Central and South American shamans use entheogens (hallucinogenic plants), and Australian aboriginal shamans or "clever men" believe crystals can be inserted into the body for power [Wurges & Frey, 2005].

Late Pleistocene hunter-gatherer groups would have seen the environment as giving and reciprocating, their spirit worlds including animals and natural features with which shamans mediated. The shamanic hypothesis regarding cave art is based on both the evidence from the caves themselves and observations of more recent hunter-gatherer societies which still produce rock art, although not all cultures have specific shamanic ritual locations [Kolankaya-Bostanci, 2014, p. 186].

Of particular note is the great Paleolithic cavern of Lascaux, in southwestern France, called "the Sistine Chapel of the Paleolithic." The multi-chambered network of caves contains over 600 paintings covering the walls and ceilings. The paintings are apparently the work of many generations and date to around 17,000 years ago (Latest Pleistocene), representing the early Magdalenian culture of western Europe.

Here, as Joseph Campbell points out, divinity is represented, not in human (anthropomorphic) but animal (theriomorphic) form, a vision of a teaming happy hunting ground. The domed ceilings display leaping bulls (aurochs), while the walls are crowded with horses, stags, ibexes, bison (*Bison priscus*), lions, and bears, full of movement and life, and painted in realistic colors.

The auroch (*Bos primigenius*) is the ancestor of modern cattle, a swift and powerful animal mentioned by Julius Caesar in his Gallic Wars, and hunted to extinction by men during Medieval times, and the middle to late Pleistocene steppe bison (*Bison priscus*).

An unknown species, a hybridization between the aurochs and steppe bison, alternated ecologically with steppe bison throughout the Late Pleistocene and appears to have been recorded by early cave artists. This species seems to have evolved into the extant wisent or European bison (*Bison bonasus*) [Soubrier et al., 2016].

Europe ice-age rock art revealed enigmatic paintings of human-animal composites, or "therianthropes," with human-like lower bodies and animal heads. These include a Bison-headed human figure from the Grotte de Gabillou (cave of Gabillou) in Dordogne, France, and the Sorcerer, an antlered and bearded figure (*fig.1*). The Sorcerer was discovered by Abbe Breuil (1877-1961), a French Catholic priest, archaeologist, anthropologist, ethnologist, and geologist, at the cave of the Trois-Freres, Ariege, South-West France dating to around 13,000 B.C.E., close to the end of the Pleistocene. The Sorcerer is shown amongst herds of bison, horses, and rhinos. These images have been variously interpreted as mythic ancestors, gods, or human hunters in costume [Zabel, n.d.].

Fig. 1. Abbe Henri Breuil's sketch of The Sorcerer is based on a cave painting found in the Pyrenees mountains in South-West France. The figure's original meaning is unknown, but it is usually interpreted as a great spirit or master of animals [Wikipedia – The Sorcerer (cave art)]. Its publication in the 1920s greatly influenced later theories of Pleistocene esotericism. Archaeologist, anthropologist, historian, and folklorist Margaret Murray (1863-1963), who had only seen the published drawing, was inspired to come up with the idea of a Wiccan Horned God dated back to Paleolithic times. More recently, Breuil's sketch has come under criticism as subsequent photos don't clearly show the antlers he featured so prominently in his drawing. CC BY 4.0 vi, Wikimedia Commons, Doctor Suckling, photograph. https://wellcomecollection.org/works/fx8ku3n2

Another example of Palaeolithic shamanism is the painting in a narrow rock shaft at Lascaux. This shows a large bison bull, eviscerated by a spear, with a crudely drawn bird-headed human stick figure lying prostrate in a trance, the only human figure in the cave. He wears a bird mask (or has a bird head) and has an erect penis, representing perhaps the ecstatic trance state or creative *Yang* energy. Beside him stands a wand or staff, bearing the image of a bird on its tip. The painting is at the bottom of a deep natural shaft or crypt, below the main level of the cave floor, a very difficult position to reach, with room enough only for a single person at a time. It would seem to be an example of hunting magic, such as Abbe Breuil described [Campbell, 1960, pp. 301-2; Zabel, n.d.].

The shamans of Siberia wear bird costumes to this day, and many are believed to have been conceived by their mothers from the descent of a bird. In India, a term of honor addressed to the master yogi is Paramahamsa, meaning "supreme swan." In China, the so-called "immortals" (*hsien*) are pictured feathered like birds or floating through the air on flying steeds [Campbell, 1960, p. 258].

Other Upper Palaeolithic findings include assemblages of flutes (from Geißenklösterle, Hohle Fels, Vogelherd, and Isturitz), bullroarers, and a mammoth bone percussion instrument. There were most certainly also drums and rattles, as these are ubiquitous in contemporary shaman cultures, but have not been preserved because they were made of perishable materials [Kolankaya-Bostanci, 2014, p.188].

4-vii. *The Venuses*

The Paleolithic Venuses, or Venus figurines, are a collection of small, portable sculptures created simultaneously as the cave art. These figurines are typically made of soft stone such as steatite, calcite or limestone, bone, or ivory. They depict women with exaggerated sexual characteristics, such as large breasts and hips.

The earliest, the Venus of Hohle Fels, is a rather roughly made 6 cm figurine in mammoth ivory. It was discovered in 2008, in a cave near the town of Schelklingen, in Baden-Württemberg in South-West Germany. It dates to the early Aurignacian (Cro-Magnon man) age, around 40,000 and 35,000 years ago (early Upper Paleolithic), representing the earliest presence of anatomically modern humans in Europe (early Upper Paleolithic).

Perhaps the best known and most frequently represented is the iconic Venus of Willendorf, an 11.1 centimeter tall (4.4 inches) figurine found in 1908 near Willendorf, a village in Lower Austria. The emphasis is entirely on fertility, indicated by the attention given to the breasts, belly, and hips. The face is featureless, the legs incomplete, and the arms thin and ribbonlike, resting on the large breasts. It is carved from a type of limestone that is not local to the area and tinted with red ochre. The figure is associated with the Gravettian culture (which followed the Aurignacian) and is thought to be around 25,000 years old.

The contemporary Venus of Lespugue from Haute Garonne, in the French Pyrenees, 14.6 cm (5¾ inches) high, is skillfully carved from mammoth ivory. Here the stylization is even more extreme, with slim shoulders but extravagant breasts reaching even to the groin.

The Venus figurines of Balzi Rossi were found in the caves near Grimaldi di Ventimiglia (Italy) and are also probably of the same age and culture. Most of the sculptures consist of steatite and are between 2.4 and 7.5 cm in height. One of these, carved in a "modern" style, is both steatopygous and prominently pregnant [Campbell, 1960, pp.326-7].

While the Venus of Dolní Věstonice (Czech Republic), made of fired clay, is the oldest ceramic known, about 29,000 years old.

All in all, over two hundred such sculptures have been found all over Europe, including France, Austria, and the Czech Republic, and even from as far as Siberia.

The interpretation of these figurines is still debated among scholars, but some theories suggest that they may have been used in rituals related to fertility, childbirth, or goddess worship.

The majority of these figurines were found in burials, which suggests a possible ritualistic or ceremonial purpose. However, there is a lack of concrete evidence to support any of the theories, which is why the purpose of the Paleolithic Venus figurines still remains a mystery.

4-viii. Lion-Headed Figurines

The preponderance of Paleolithic Venuses might at first lend credence to Jungian psychologist Erich Neumann's theory that the Great Mother is the oldest archetype and the origin of consciousness. Except that the oldest figurine is not a Venus, but a lion-headed human figure, called the Lowenmensch (German for "lion man" or "lion-person") figurine, carved out of mammoth ivory and discovered in Hohlenstein-Stadel, a German cave, in 1939. Over 30 cm tall, it is larger than the Venuses. The layer in which it was found has been carbon dated to between 35,000 and 40,000 years old, which places it in the Aurignacian culture.

A similar but smaller lion-headed human figurine was found nearby at Hohle Fels. Their makers were clearly members of the same cultural group and shared beliefs and practices connected with therianthropic images of felids and humans. These are similar to the therianthropes of the French cave paintings. The species of lion in question would have been Panthera spelaea, the European cave lion or Eurasian steppe lion, an awe-inspiring animal about 12% larger than the living African lion. According to the evidence of cave art, the males of this species seem to have lacked a mane. It probably evolved in Europe after the third Cromerian interglacial stage, about 600,000 years ago (early Middle Pleistocene).

5. MEGALITHS AND EARTH ENERGIES

5-i. Mythic Thinking

While animistic societies certainly included creation myths as fundamental to their culture and worldview, myth, in its more developed form, is tied in with the appearance of agriculture about 11,000 years ago, allowing for larger, more complex societies.

Mythical thinking describes the world in terms of symbolism and archetypal motifs. This came to the fore when the hunter-gatherer lifestyle and immersion in nature gave way to settled agriculture, a dependence on the cycles of the seasons. This agricultural revolution enabled larger populations and made the development of city-states and the rise of civilization possible.

Understanding mythic thinking ties in with the ideas of Swiss psychologist Carl Gustav Jung (1875–1961). Jung was a former student of Freud, whose work with dream analysis and symbolism led him to discover the collective consciousness, a realm of transformative symbols called archetypes.

In exploring the activity of the macrocosmic psyche (Collective Unconscious), Jung tended towards psychological reductionism, especially when considering topics like alchemy and gnosticism. Through introducing concepts such as the psychological archetype, the collective unconscious, and, later in life, synchronicity, he popularized many esoteric truths in a way that made them accessible to the exoteric mainstream and thus served as a sort of bridge-builder between the secular world and esotericism.

Jung's psychological and phenomenological insights regarding the nature of the archetypes represent some of the best analyses of the nature of and relationship between the ordinary waking consciousness and the inner physical psyche.

From a Jungian perspective, not only do myths have their own intrinsic psychological and spiritual meaning, but mythic thinking involves the projection of the archetypes onto the physical universe. The external world is explained in an intuitive, mythological way rather than in an empirical, scientific way.

Some interpret this to mean that premodern people were literally unable to distinguish or differentiate the contents of their unconscious psyche from the external world onto which they are projected. Although the myth of progress, presented, for example, by 19th to early 20th century anthropology and late 20th and early 21st century Integral Philosophy, assumes a series of stages of consciousness, I understand these to be not so much sequential as parallel, with social, cultural, environmental, and technological conditions determining which one comes to the fore. The idea that early humans walked around in a sort of mythical haze [Jaynes, 1976; Wilber, 1986] is simply a fallacy based on the Freudian identification of primary process thinking with dream imagery, along with the error of confusing psychological developmental stages with the evolution of the physical nervous system.

This is no different from the 19th and early 20th century misinterpretation of magical thinking, which was refuted by later anthropology. A more correct understanding would be that the various modes of consciousness functioning – magical, mythical, rational, and integral – all evolve in parallel.

A contrast should be made between the two types of mythic thinking. In one, the myth is believed to be real and empirically describes the nature of the world, the purpose of life, and the meaning of existence. This application of myth is called religion. This type of thinking characterized the premodern world, although it still defines religion today. In the other, myth is taken to be an entertaining story or fable, an adventure you can enter into as an escape from the monotony of everyday life. This is called storytelling. Storytelling is more expansive than religion because it provides a narrative but does not demand absolute obedience. Religion, especially exoteric religion, appeals more to the sensation-feeling type, whereas storytelling appeals to the intuition-feeling and intuition-thinking type, such as the nerd and the gnostic. This is not to say that one cannot have both, of course. J.R.R. Tolkien, a master storyteller and myth-maker, incorporated his own Christian faith into his epic *Lord of the Rings* saga, which only adds to the appeal and depth.

5-ii. *The Younger Dryas and the First Settlements*

The Younger Dryas, which lasted a bit over a millennium (from around 12,900 to 11,700 years ago), was a sudden cold spell that reversed the climatic warming following the end of the last Ice Age (or Last Glacial Maximum or LGM). It is thought to have been caused by a reduction or shutdown of the Gulf Stream and North Atlantic Conveyor current that circulates warm tropical waters to high latitudes.

This scenario appeared in the popular science book [Bell & Strieber, 1999] that warned that global warming might trigger a new ice age, which in turn directly inspired the 2004 disaster movie called *The Day After Tomorrow* [Emmerich, 2004]. This, and climate denialist novelist Michael Chrichton [Schmidt, 2004], helped inspire the conservative ideology narrative (often encountered on social media) that science doesn't know anything.

The Younger Dryas is named after its indicator species, the alpine-tundra wildflower *Dryas octopetala*, whose fossil leaves are found in Scandinavian lake sediments of this age.

The harsh conditions of the Younger Dryas may have been a factor in the domestication of plants and animals. This period, called the Neolithic or Agricultural Revolution, marked a fundamental and revolutionary change in human culture and history, with the development of agriculture, animal husbandry, pottery, and permanent settlements. It began with the early or Pre-Pottery Neolithic in the Near East and Anatolia, dating to around 12,000 to 8,500 years ago (or 10th to 7th millennium B.C.E.).

One of the earliest of these settlements recovered is Gobekli Tepe (literally "Potbelly Hill"), an archaeological site in the Southeastern Anatolia of Turkey that dates to the Pre-Pottery Neolithic, between c. 9500 and 8000 B.C.E. This puts it right at the junction of the Pleistocene and Holocene. It includes the world's oldest known megaliths, large circular structures supported by massive stone pillars, 7-10 ton stone pillars cut and hauled from limestone quarries, and many with carved abstract human and animal figures.

Although contrarian archeo-historian Graham Hancock presents Gobekli Tepe as an example of a lost Pleistocene civilization, this was clearly a ceremonial religious site like Stonehenge, not an ancient city. There are no domesticated animal bones, no metal tools, no inscriptions or writing, and not even pottery, products that much later "high civilizations" produced [Shermer, 2017]

The nearby and slightly later (8400 to 8100 B.C.E.) Nevalı Cori has similar megalithic temples and sculptures, including figures of hybrid creatures combining human and bird features, perhaps illustrations of mythical ancestors or stories related to them. In one example from Nevali Cori, two symmetrical female figures are portrayed crouching back-to-back with a large bird perching on their heads, perhaps a shamanic or other spirit belief [Kolankaya-Bostanci, 2014, pp.190-191]. This continues the Paleolithic and shamanic motif of the bird and spiritual flight, which would also extend to the Ba or soul in ancient Egypt is represented by a human-headed bird.

In contrast, Catal Hoyuk ("fork tumulus") was an actual large Neolithic/Chalcolithic (Copper Age) settlement in southern Anatolia. One of the earliest and most well-preserved examples of a large, complex Neolithic settlement, the site covers an area of around ten hectares (32 acres). It was occupied from around 7500 to 5700 B.C.E. and is known for its large and complex architecture, including, at its peak (around 6700 to 6500 B.C.E.), a dense, multi-storied town resembling a large New Mexican pueblo. It was made up of a series of interconnected houses, constructed with mud-brick walls and thatched roofs, many of which were built around courtyards. There were also public buildings, and impressive wall paintings and sculptures, which would have been brightly painted. The population may have been around three to eight thousand.

Whereas at Gobekli Tepe, the symbolism is focused in separate "temples," at Catal Hoyuk, the art and symbolism occur in domestic houses, representing a major difference in the setting of ritual and symbolism. Shamanistic or magical elements seem to be retained in the way that bull horns (*bucrania*), vultures, and other skulls were embedded in the walls so as to appear to be emerging from them, while one wall painting depicts two hybrid figures with vulture head, body, and wings, but with human legs might depict shamans disguised or spiritually transformed into vultures [Kolankaya-Bostanci, 2014, pp.192-193].

Similar Neolithic settlements in Anatolia include Hacılar (inhabited between 6000 and 5500 B.C.E.), similar in many ways to Catal Hoyuk, but smaller in scale, and Mersin, which is located in the Taurus Mountains.

5-iii. Megalithic Culture

Megalithic culture refers to the construction of large stone structures, such as tombs, temples, and monuments during the Neolithic and Bronze Age periods. The term "megalith" comes from the Greek words *mega*, meaning large or great, and *lithos*, stone.

Megaliths are found throughout Europe, Asia, and Africa, dating to between 5000 and 1000 B.C.E. Some of the best known examples are the standing stones of Stonehenge in England, the dolmens of Brittany in France, and the passage tombs of Newgrange in Ireland.

The exact purpose of these structures is not entirely clear, but it is believed that they served both religious and ceremonial functions. The construction of these monuments required significant planning and organization, indicating that the societies that built them had advanced levels of social complexity.

Archaeological discoveries have revealed that many of these structures were built in alignment with solar and lunar cycles, indicating that these ancient cultures had a sophisticated understanding of astronomy. The use of megaliths for astronomical observation must have been an essential part of religious and ceremonial rituals and an important way for these societies to understand and interact with the natural world.

The construction of megaliths required an enormous amount of labor. It is believed that these societies would have had to have a developed social and economic structure to support such a large-scale project. The fact that megaliths can be found in many different parts of the world suggests that these ancient cultures were connected to one another in ways that have yet to be fully understood.

5-iv. Stonehenge

Stonehenge is a prehistoric monument located on the Salisbury Plain in Wiltshire, England, that has fascinated people for centuries. It consists of a circular arrangement of large standing stones set within earthworks, and is believed to have been built between 3000 and 2000 B.C.E.

Stonehenge seems to have been a place of religious or ceremonial importance, perhaps related to the solstices, equinoxes, and lunar cycles. Many of the stones used to build the monument were brought from a quarry more than 250 kilometers away, suggesting that the builders of the monument were motivated by some sort of religious or spiritual belief.

Archaeological discoveries have also provided some insight into the builders of Stonehenge. Excavations have revealed that the area was first settled around 8000 B.C.E. and that a wooden henge was built around 3000 B.C.E., predating the stone monument. The people who built Stonehenge were skilled engineers and used simple tools such as antler picks and stone hammers to shape and transport the massive stones.

5-v. Ley Lines and Earth Energies

English antiquarian, natural philosopher, and writer John Aubrey (1626-1697) was the first to systematically study megalithic and other monuments in southern England, such as Avebury henge. Physician and Anglican clergyman William Stukeley (1687-1765) pioneered the scholarly investigation of the prehistoric monuments of Stonehenge and Avebury in Wiltshire, and noticed the connection with the solstices. Both proposed the idea that Stonehenge was built by Druids, an idea that has since become canonical in Neopagan circles but for which there is no historical or archaeological evidence either way.

English amateur archaeologist and businessman Alfred Watkins (1855-1935) suggested in *The Old Straight Track*, first published in 1925, that mounds, moats, beacons, and markstones fall into straight tracks throughout Britain, with fragmentary evidence of trackways along the alignments [Watkins, 2015].

English author and esotericist John Michell (1933-2009) was a major figure in popularizing the idea of Earth mysteries or sacred geometry linking the various megaliths and earthworks in Britain, China, South America, Australia, and elsewhere. He explained these in terms of Plato's Atlantis [Michell, 1986].

This helped popularize the counterculture idea of "earth energies" or Earth Mysteries based on ancient monuments precisely positioned and linked by ley lines, as invisible lines of mystic or natural energy. Points where lines intersect are considered especially powerful or eventful locations [Newman, 2008].

It's not hard to criticize this thesis, as the density of archaeological sites in England, burial mounds, churches, and so on, is so great that a line drawn through virtually anywhere will cross a number of sites. Additionally, many alignments were later shown to be inaccurate when tested on smaller-scale maps.

In any case, pyramid ratios and megalith alignments are simply coincidence/synchronicity with no conscious design, like theomatics, modern pop numerology, divination, or the pyramidology skeptic who calculated the distance to the sun and moon using the measurements of his backyard, or Australian recreational math lecturer Matt Parker, who in 2009 satirized the New Age by showing Woolworths stores follow a precise geometric placement.

The physicalist explanation is that this is simply the pattern-recognition process of the brain [Gregory, 2010]. This type of pattern recognition, essential for our ancestor's survival, becomes counterproductive and neurotic when it makes imaginary connections that are not justified, giving rise to conspiracy thinking [van Prooijen et al., 2018].

But from another perspective, taking quantum physics and synchronicity [Jung, 1973] to its logical conclusion, and applying this to things such as divination (where meaning is derived from random outcomes), the implication is that the basis of everything is not randomness but meaning. In other words, nothing happens totally by chance. Everything has the input of consciousness at some level, even at the empirical physical level. The problem is that this can never be verified statistically (using the repeatability methods of the scientific method) because the effect of large numbers (statistics) is to damp out any signal or meaning and reduce the whole thing to background noise. It is the same with quantum physics. On the micro-scale, it is paradoxical and astonishing, with things like non-locality, time travel to the past, *Star Trek*-style teleportation, being in multiple states at once, and more. But these exceptional effects disappear at the macro-scale of Newtonian physics and everyday existence. Skepticism and scientism fail for the same reason; it is like trying to use Newtonian physics to understand and measure individual quantum events.

Actual Earth energies, however, do not follow straight lines but rather winding Feng Shui-style paths. It is probably for dowsing reasons that proponents of 'Earth energy flows' abandoned the original concept of straight lines and claimed the existence of curved lines of subtle energy flows. These subtle energies in nature, or Telluric currents, are often personified as serpents, dragons, nymphs, faeries, and so on; they are referred to in Theosophical terminology as "devas" [Hodson, 1997]. They're also referred to as "dragon lines" in Chinese Feng Shui, while in Australia, the Aboriginals refer to them as "song-lines" [Newman, 2018, pp.5-6].

The Anthroposophy-inspired writer Steven Guth (1943-2018), who lived in Canberra, referred to these earth energies and water-dowsing paths as "protowater," implying that they are like water, but not a physical compound. This is equivalent to what the Chinese call *ch'i*. Ch'i is also equated with *prana* (Hatha Yoga), orgone (Wilhelm Reich), and the vital principle and subtle body in general. Just as every living being has its own subtle body with channels (*nadis*, meridians) and energy and consciousness points (chakras), so does the Earth as a whole.

5-vi. Bruce Cathie and the UFO Grid

Beginning in the 1960s, New Zealand airline pilot Bruce Cathie (1930-2013) wrote a number of books about flying saucers and a grid-like pattern around the globe, based on trigonometry and geophysical latitude/longitude, that he interprets as powering flying saucers. These represent a more geometrical phenomenon than chionic energy flows, tied in also with the location of ancient megalithic structures like pyramids. However, exploring this subject gets into high strangeness and conspiracy science, with topics like free energy and anti-gravity [Childress, 1987].

Cathie first saw a UFO in 1952 and, in discussions with other pilots, learned they also have sometimes seen these phenomena. He claimed to have successfully predicted one of the French Pacific nuclear tests using his harmonic "mathematics" coordinates and assumed that the grid is somehow necessary for nuclear bombs to function [Cathie, 1990]. A more reasonable explanation is that as with divination in general, and due to the fact that nothing in the universe is random, these destructive events will, through synchronicity, appear at certain coordinates.

However, his Earth based energy grid wouldn't be much use if UFOs really are extraterrestrial, although it does support the idea of such phenomena as ultraterrestrial or interdimensional, perhaps tied to geometric points as well as geophysical phenomena such as tectonic stresses ("earthquake lights") or as yet unspecified geophysical processes involving piezoelectric-like effects (where pressure generates electricity), ionization (plasma), electromagnetism, and so on, which affect both inorganic systems and living organisms [Persinger, 1976].

It would seem then that there may be two different types of subtle energy or connections; the geometric straight ley lines and an Earth Grid unrelated to the organic living Earth energies of "sensitive chaos." Both pertain to the subtle body of Earth, being intermediate between the empirical physical and the nonphysical or imaginal reality. The geometric, ley lines and planetary grid pertain more to the "male," mental, thinking (manasic) degree of the subtle physical, being of a more abstract nature, whereas the organic, flowing Feng Shui paths represent the "female," feeling, intuitive degree.

5-vii. The Great Mother

The myth of the Great Mother or Great Goddess is a prevalent theme in many ancient cultures, where the goddess is seen as the embodiment of the nurturing and life-giving qualities of the earth, associated with fertility, agriculture, and the natural world.

The concept of the Great Mother archetype was developed by psychologist and Jungian analyst Erich Neumann (1905-1960). According to Neumann, the Great Mother archetype represents the primal, nurturing aspect of the feminine and is associated with the Earth, fertility, and the unconscious [Neumann, 1983].

He argues that the Great Mother archetype is the earliest and most universal of all archetypes and that it is the foundation of all later symbolic and religious expressions of the feminine. He associates the archetype with the Earth and nature, as she is often depicted as a goddess of fertility and abundance, representing a mythic intuition of the natural world and the cycles of life and death.

He describes and relates various Mother Goddesses in terms of three sets of polar opposites. The Mother axis is represented by Isis (positive) and Kali (negative). The Anima axis has Sophia as positive and Lilith as negative. There is also the "archetypal Feminine" with Mary as positive and the Witch as negative.

Here the mother archetype is the internalization of one's physical mother. The anima archetype is the internalized female within the male psyche (the male equivalent in the female psyche is called the *animus*), and the archetypal feminine is more of a generic polarity.

Neumann considers the Great Mother archetype an essential aspect of the human psyche, and it has the power to nurture and destroy. He suggests that the archetype can be both a source of creative inspiration and a source of destructive impulses, and that it must be understood and integrated in order for the individual to achieve a sense of wholeness and balance.

Possible early examples of the Great Mother archetype can be seen in Neolithic and Bronze Age fertility figurines. Very similar figurines have been found as far away as the Halaf culture, Mesopotamia, 6000-5100 B.C.E., and Mehrgarh, Indus Valley, c.3000 B.C.E. These have features similar to the Upper Paleolithic Venus figurines of Europe, such as the abundant breasts and hips of these figurines suggest links to fertility and procreation.

In later Mesopotamia, the goddess Inanna was seen as the queen of heaven and earth, who embodied both the sky's power and the earth's nurturing qualities. Similarly, in ancient Egypt, the goddess Isis was revered as the mother goddess who brought fertility and abundance to the land. In the Greek pantheon, the goddess Demeter was seen as the patron of agriculture, responsible for the growth of crops and the harvest. In Hindu Tantra, the goddess Shakti represents the divine feminine energy of the universe and is often depicted as the mother goddess who gives birth to all creation (in contrast to the masculine creator deity of the Abrahamic religions).

5-viii. The Great Round

Both the Great Mother archetype and megalithic culture are represented by the archetype of the "great round." American architect, cultural historian, and feminist Mimi Lobell (1942-2001) proposed the idea of Spatial Archetypes. She was influenced here by historian Oswald Spengler, who developed a theory that civilizations go through cycles of growth and decline, mythographer Joseph Campbell, and psychologists Carl Jung and Erich Neumann. Although her work focused on periods of history when cultures were organized around the Goddess, she also argued that culture passes through several stages, each defined by a particular architectural style or spatial archetype. These are the Sensitive Chaos of hunter-gatherers, the Great Round of the Neolithic villagers and the worship of the goddess, the Four Quarters of the Bronze Age Warrior Chieftains and the archetype of the male hero, the Pyramid, the world of the God-King and hierarchical nation states, the Radiant Axes or World of the Emperor, where all roads lead to and diverge from the capital and the palace, the Grid, the world of the technocrat and of commerce, with streets laid out in a rectangular fashion, and finally the stage of dissolution and chaos [Lobell, 2018].

The great round is based on architecture resulting from the permanent homesteads and villages that developed as a result of the agricultural revolution. It's associated with Megalithic constructions of sacred structures such as tombs, temples, and geomantic and astronomical structures. Single, double, and triple spirals are common in art, especially in pottery. The reverence for sacred places in nature is retained from the previous shamanic/animistic stage, although this would wane with increasing alienation from nature.

6. PROTO-INDO-EUROPEAN MYTHOLOGY

6-i. The Proto-Indo-Europeans

The Proto-Indo-Europeans were a hypothetical ethnic and linguistic group of people who were believed to have lived during the 4th to 3rd millennium B.C.E. in the Eurasian Steppe. They are believed to have spoken the Proto-Indo-European language, the hypothetical ancestor of most of the modern Indo-European languages.

The existence of the Proto-Indo-Europeans is inferred through linguistic, archaeological, and genetic evidence. Their reconstructed language is believed to have a number of features that suggest a nomadic pastoral lifestyle in the steppes of Eurasia. Archaeological evidence shows that they used horse-drawn wagons and were skilled in metallurgy, specifically in the production of bronze weapons and tools.

The Proto-Indo-Europeans are believed to have had a complex religious system, with a pantheon of deities that included a sky god, a god of war, a god of thunder, and a goddess of dawn. Their religion was polytheistic, and they believed in an afterlife. They also believed in the importance of ritual sacrifice.

The original Proto-Indo-European sky god, according to reconstructions from various Indo-European languages and myths, is Dyeus, from where, obviously, we get the name Zeus. Dyeus, meaning bright, was the personification of the bright sky of the day, and the seat of the gods, the *deywos* (hence the Hindu Sanskrit devas), as well as the rain that makes the crops grow.

The most constant epithet associated with *Dyeus is "father," as in the Vedic Dyaus Pitri, Greek Zeus Pater, Illyrian (western Balkan) Dei-patrous,

Roman Jupiter (Djous pater), and so on. He is the most powerful of all the gods and is often depicted as a father figure who watches over and protects his people. As the ruler or creator, he is responsible for various natural phenomena such as rain, thunder, lightning, and wind, which ties in with the storm god, more on which later.

Dyeus was sometimes paired with Dheghom, the Earth Mother, who is generally portrayed as vast (*plethwih*) and dark (*dhengwo*), both the origin of life and the final abode of mortals. She bears all creatures and is commonly associated with fertility, growth, and death. She was most likely the Earth herself, conceived of as a divine entity, rather than a goddess of the earth, as Proto-Indo-European mythology was still based on a strong animistic substrate.

The Proto-Indo-Europeans are believed to have played a significant role in the spread of the Indo-European language family and the development of early Indo-European cultures. They are believed to have migrated from the Eurasian Steppe to various parts of Europe and Asia, bringing with them their language, religion, and culture.

Their migrations are thought to have been triggered by various factors, including population pressures, environmental changes, and conflicts with neighboring groups. The Proto-Indo-Europeans are alleged to have played a key role in the development of the Celtic, Germanic, Italic, Slavic, and Indo-Aryan languages, among others.

Regarding Mimi Loebell's spatial archetypes, the Proto-Europeans correspond to the Four Quarters, which come after the Great Round (megalithic) but before the God-Kings and pyramids. However, in this case, the Proto-Indo-Europeans are contemporary with the oldest of the pyramid builders.

6-ii. Archetype Versus Myth

A distinction should be made between archetype and myth, as these are often confused due to their being often combined in a single experience.

An archetype is a pre-existent, collective, even cosmic, structure of consciousness. An archetype (in the Jungian sense) is simply the modern secular word for god (or God, as polytheism and monotheism are both based on the collective unconscious). Archetypes appear independently of time, place, culture, or influence. They are profoundly transformative and have an existence independent of human cultural forms. They are transcendent, nonphysical, and beyond space and time.

I distinguish between a god (that is, an archetype) as a cosmic being, in other words, a spiritual hierarchy (Steiner), *archon* or *aeon* (Gnosticism), or superintelligence (Robert Monroe), and a god as an impression within the collective and individual psyche. A Jungian archetype, which is then projected out onto the world, along with the individual psychic contents that it is inextricably bound up with, is part of the veil of *maya* that obscures Reality as it is.

Moreover, all these types of archetypes or gods, the universal, cosmic, collective, and individual, are mixed up in a confusion of form, influence, and correspondence.

What I call (following Henry Corbin) the imaginal is the interface between individual inner or psychic consciousness (intuition and imagination) and the world of gods or archetypes, or at least an aspect thereof.

A myth, on the other hand, is a human cultural form. It is an example of what Richard Dawkins calls a meme, a cultural idea, symbol, or practice that spreads by imitation from person to person, that can be transmitted through writing, speech, gestures, rituals, or other imitable phenomena with a mimicked theme, and is carried down from one generation to the next. As memes, myths evolve as culture, society, and language do.

Myths form the basis of religions, and they are the way that gods or cosmic archetypes clothe themselves in human cultural and collective psychological forms, but they are not those archetypes in themselves.

Whereas the idea of a supreme being is an archetype that exists independently of man, the representation of the supreme being as the sky god, Dyeus, is a myth, a cultural construct, that is disseminated and evolves across the noosphere (Teilhard) as a meme, carried by media (in this case, oral lore and religious practice).

Two examples of developments in the myth of Dyeus are Zeus and Indra.

Zeus, as king of the gods and the god of the sky and thunder, was believed to control the weather and could summon lightning bolts and thunderstorms at will. He was often depicted as a powerful, bearded man wielding a thunderbolt.

Indra, in Vedic and Hindu mythology, the god of thunder and rain, is often depicted riding on a white elephant and wielding a lightning bolt. He is said to be the king of the gods and is sometimes called "the lord of the heavens."

However, this is also the archetype, at least in the collective consciousness, for the Sky as a god is a recurring theme in many mythologies around the world.

For example, in Turkic and Mongolian mythology (outside the Proto-Indo-European sphere), Tengri is the supreme god and the ruler of the sky. He is often depicted as a white horse or as a man with a blue face, and is associated with celestial phenomena such as the sun, moon, and stars.

Likewise, in ancient Egyptian mythology, Horus was the god of the sky and the protector of the pharaohs. He was often depicted as a falcon or a man with a falcon's head and believed to have the power to see and know everything happening in the world.

All these myths share the same common theme or archetype of a powerful, godlike figure who rules over the heavens and controls the natural world. As such, they represent a common archetype, the patriarchal counterpart of the Great Mother, and these two archetypes developed in parallel in different cultures.

Sometimes, as with Theurgic Neoplatonism (Iamblichus and Proclus), Hermetic Kabbalah ("MacGregor" Mathers Golden Dawn system of correspondences, plagiarized by Crowley and published under his own name [Crowley, 1986]), the post-Jungian polytheistic typologies of James Hillman, Carol Pearson [Pearson, 1991], and Jean Shinoda Bolen [Bolen, 2004, 2009], and the Spiral Dynamics system of stages of individual and cultural development, there are attempts to provide typologies for all the various these pantheons, gods, archetypes, and structures of consciousness. In Hermetic Kabbalah (or Qabalah), for example, the Great Mother is associated with Binah's sefirah (sphere, archetype), and the Sky Father with the sefirah of Hesed.

6-iii. The Dawn

One of the most important deities worshiped by the Proto-Indo-Europeans, shown by the consistency of her characteristics in later traditions, was Heusos, the Dawn, who was the daughter of Dyeus. She appears as Ushas in the *Rig Veda* (and hence Hinduism), Eos in Greek, Aurora in Roman, Zorya in Slavic, Eostre (the Goddess of Spring, from which we get "Easter" in West Germanic, and so on. She is described as shining, the bringer of light, associated with rebirth, and with the colors of the dawn, such as gold and rosy [Wikipedia – H₂éwsōs].

The symbol, or archetype, of the dawn was adapted by Sri Aurobindo and his co-worker, the Mother (Mirra Alfassa), to describe the new, Supramental creation. The intentional community built under the Mother's instructions to continue Sri Aurobindo's teachings is called Auroville, the city of the Dawn.

Coincidentally, the name Aurobindo means "red lotus" according to a Google search of baby name meanings, but the etymological association is obvious.

The dawn represents the new beginning; the Egyptian equivalent is the rising sun, associated with Khepri, the sacred scarab, and with spiritual transformation.

The time just before dawn is the most amazing time of the day for meditation; the world is still and charged with spiritual energy and tranquility.

6-iv. *The Otherworld*

The Proto-Indo-Europeans seem to have had a pretty gloomy representation of death, shared with the Mesopotamians, Levantines, pre-Zoroastrian Persians, Bronze and Iron Age Greeks, and other early cultures. Many Indo-European myths relate a journey across a river, guided by an old man, for example, the Greek tradition of the dead being ferried across the river Styx by the boatman Charon. The theme of crossing a river also occurs in Celtic mythologies and several Vedic texts, while in Latvian folk songs, the dead must cross a marsh rather than a river. The ancient Greek and Slavic practice of placing coins on the bodies of the deceased in order to pay the ferryman only goes back to the Iron Age, but this may still be part of an earlier tradition of giving offerings to the ferryman. The canine guardian (such as Cerberus, the three-headed dog of the Greek underworld) is another recurring theme, although this seems to be distinct from the Egyptian Anubis, the jackal-headed god of funerary practices [Wikipedia – Proto-Indo-European mythology].

The Celtic Otherworld is a more positive realm of everlasting youth, beauty, health, abundance, and joy. It is described as a parallel world rather than a spiritual world. In this regard, it is similar to Andrew Jackson Davis' Summerlands. It exists alongside our own, beyond the sea, or under the earth. It is usually elusive and difficult to reach [Wikipedia – Celtic Otherworld].

6-v. The Creation Myth

The Indo-European or Proto-Indo-European creation myths include several different and generally unrelated themes, indicating no one common creation story.

The most obvious one is having the universe begin with an original state of non-being, as in the Rig Vedic, Greek, Persian, and North European cosmogonies, although this is just simply the representation of the unconscious prior to the light of consciousness. More interesting is the concept of the cosmic egg, symbolizing the primordial state from which the universe arises, which is also found, for example, in Vedic (Hiranyagarbha), Germanic, and Greek Orphic traditions.

Comparative analysis of different Indo-European myths has meant scholars have purportedly been able to reconstruct an original Proto-Indo-European creation myth. This involves twin brothers, Manu ("Man") and Yemo ("Twin"), as creating the world and mankind. Here Manu sacrifices his brother and, with the help of heavenly deities (the Sky-Father, the Storm-God, and the Divine Twins), forges both the natural elements and human beings from his twin's remains. This is a variation of the common myth (not just Indo-European, it's also found in China and Mesopotamia) of the universe as made from the body of an original giant, monster, or cosmic man. This, in turn, ties in with panentheism, the universe as the body of god. Although god transcends the universe, he also transforms a part of himself into the universe.

In any case, Manu becomes the first priest after initiating sacrifice as the primordial condition for the world order, a theme that continues in the *Rig Veda* with the fire sacrifice. His brother Yemo becomes the first king as social classes emerge from different parts of his body; priesthood from his head, the warrior class from his breast and arms, and the commoners from his sexual organs and legs, which again later becomes the panentheistic creation story of the cosmic man or *Purusha* as described in the *Rig Veda*. Yemo, meanwhile, becomes the King of the realm of the dead (Yama).

Reference is sometimes made to a primeval cow who is also sacrificed in the original myth, giving birth to the other animals and vegetables [Wikipedia – Indo-European cosmogony]. The theme of the sacred cow became central to Hinduism, hence Krishna's association with *gopis* or cowherds. On the opposite end, there is the Zoroastrian-inspired Roman mystery religion of Mithraism. Known as the "tauroctony," it was believed that from the death of the bull – an animal representing strength and fertility – would come rebirth and new life.

7. THE MESOPOTAMIAN AND LEVANTINE WORLDVIEW

7-i. The Rise of Civilization

After the Agricultural Revolution and the first settlements in Anatolia, the next major development was the rise of civilization, a phenomenon that occurred independently across much of the globe over a period of some two millennia and overlapped with a different cultural phenomenon to the contemporary nomadic Proto-Indo-Europeans.

In Mimi Lobell's analysis of architecture and cultural forms, these early civilizations were often architecturally represented by the pyramid archetype and God-King. This resulted in contemporary New Age mythic beliefs in ancient astronauts and lost civilizations among contrarians who are unable to distinguish the historical empirical external world from the inner imaginal world.

The earliest of these civilizations was Ancient Mesopotamia, which emerged in the northern part of the Fertile Crescent (mostly modern-day Iraq) around 4000 B.C.E. This civilization was characterized by the development of the first cities, the invention of the wheel, and the development of a system of writing known as cuneiform.

Many other early civilizations developed independently, as a sort of pulse running around the Earth [Arguelles, 1984], including Ancient Egypt, which emerged along the Nile River in northeastern Africa around 3100 B.C.E., and the Indus Valley Civilization, which developed in what is now modern-day Pakistan and northwest India around 2500 B.C.E.,

Chinese civilization, which dates to around 1600 B.C.E. and is known for its contributions to science, medicine, and technology, and the Maya civilization, which from around 750 to 250 B.C.E developed a sophisticated system of writing and mathematics and built impressive pyramids and temples in what is now modern-day Mexico and Central America.

7-ii. Civilization and the Alienation from Nature

The rise of civilization, with its city states, kings, writing, merchants, taxation, standing army, and state religion, meant the start of alienation from nature. There was no longer the animistic sense of the natural world as alive in every way.

This alienation from nature and immersion instead in the human world of towns and city-states resulted in a very different phenomenology, psychology, mode of consciousness, and worldview. This can be referred to as mythic or mythical thinking, in contrast to the magical thinking of the shamanic/animistic/tribal society and worldview.

Instead of the Ancestors, as in hunter-gatherer cultures, it is now God or generations of gods who created the universe and all things out of pre-existent chaos, or nothing, or themselves. This permitted rule via (or as) God-Kings on Earth or from heaven via prophets. Rather than being associated with the cycles and life-force of nature, they are now associated with Kings, patriarchies, and human power structures.

Mythical thinking explains the world in terms of anthropomorphic gods, god, or a God, who created the universe and all things out of pre-existent chaos, or themselves, or out of nothing. They then rule via God-Kings on Earth or from heaven via prophets. Deeds of mighty heroes and demigods of the past, the sacred history of one's people or the believers in the one true God, the teachings of the sacred books of one's own religion, and the role of messiahs, prophets, and avatars in bringing salvation to the in-group, and their modern equivalents in popular culture today, give meaning to an otherwise meaningless world. Common mythical creation stories include the stories and legends of previous Ages, such as Hesiod's *Theogony*, Tolkien's *Silmarillion* and *Lord of the Rings*, and religious accounts of the creation of the universe, such as the Babylonian and Hebrew Genesis [Heidel, 1963].

The mythic world of kings and gods was very much a sense- and feeling- world, although the thinking type would have gravitated to the new profession of the scribe. In general, there seems to have been little role for intuition-types in these cultures, except perhaps as diviners and soothsayers.

The hierarchical, stratified society has the God-King at the summit. It generally involves a state religion controlled by the monarchy and a priestly class, but is devoid of authentic spiritual inspiration.

In terms of myth and meaning, emphasis is on the heroic achievements of larger-than-life characters in this world, as in the epics of Gilgamesh, Homer, and the Old Testament. The deeds of mighty heroes and demigods of the past, the sacred history of one's people or the believers in the one true God, the teachings of the sacred books of one's own religion, and the role of messiahs, prophets, and avatars in bringing salvation to the in-group, and their modern equivalents in popular culture today, give meaning to an otherwise meaningless world. The soul was depreciated, and the earlier (pre-civilization) shamanic understanding of the spirit world was lost.

7-iii. Civilization and Empire in Mesopotamia

Among the most notable of the early civilizations was that of Mesopotamia, Greek for the "land between two rivers," the rivers in question being the Tigris and Euphrates rivers. They deposited silt along their banks, creating a rich, alluvial soil ideal for agriculture, the surplus from which enabled the development of urban settlements.

The earliest known actual civilization, that of Sumeria, developed here around 4000 B.C.E. It featured the invention of the wheel, complex religious and societal structures, and the development of the first writing system, cuneiform. Cuneiform used characters made by pressing a reed stylus into clay tablets. The earliest of these texts come from the cities of Uruk and Jemdet Nasr, which date to between c. 3500 and c. 3000 B.C.E.

After Sumer came the Akkadian Empire, founded by Sargon of Akkad, who conquered the Sumerian city-states in the 24th to 23rd centuries B.C.E., and established a dynasty that ruled for about a century after his death.

Babylonia was the next empire to emerge, under Hammurabi, the greatest of the Babylonian kings, who ruled from 1792 to 1750 B.C.E. It succeeded the earlier Akkadian Empire, Third Dynasty of Ur, and Old Assyrian Empire. Along with conquering the surrounding city-states and regions and establishing, Hammurabi was concerned with the welfare of his subjects, and had an interest in law and justice. Hammurabi established the legal code that bears his name, which he claimed to have received from Shamash, the god of justice. It prescribed specific punishments and penalties for each crime and established the presumption of innocence. Although there were earlier Sumerian law codes, such as the *Code of Ur-Nammu* (the oldest known surviving law code, dating to c. 2100–2050 B.C.E.), the *Code of Hammurabi* had a more extensive influence. It was written not in Sumerian but in Akkadian, the common language of Babylon. Although the Babylonian Empire fell apart with Hammurabi's death, his language reforms would make Akkadian the *lingua franca* of the ancient world.

There are many similarities between the Hammurabi code and the Law of Moses, which also similarly claims divine inspiration. The Jews would have picked this up during the Babylonian exile (6th century B.C.E.). During the medieval period, jurisprudence (*Fiqh* in Arabic) would become a significant element of Islamic civilization, perhaps as a direct or indirect result of Hammurabi's cultural legacy and influence.

Over time, the region experienced significant environmental changes contributing to its current desertification. Deforestation, overgrazing, and soil erosion have led to the depletion of the topsoil that once made the region so fertile.

More recently, the construction of dams and diversion of water for irrigation and industrial purposes has reduced the flow of water in the Tigris and Euphrates rivers, further exacerbating the desertification process.

Today, Mesopotamia is mostly desert, but it still has some fertile areas that are used for agriculture, especially in northern Iraq. However, the region's environmental challenges, political instability, and conflict have made it difficult for agriculture to thrive in the region.

7-iv. Ziggurats and Pyramids

The Ziggurat (from the ancient Assyrian *ziqqurratum*, height, pinnacle) is an iconic megastructure; a huge stepped pyramid-like structure that was typically a temple dedicated to a god or goddess. They were usually made of mud bricks and were a common feature of Mesopotamian cities.

Pyramidal structures define early and low-tech civilizations. In addition to Mesopotamia, they are found in Old Kingdom Egypt, the Teotihuacan culture, and the Maya in Mesoamerica. They were the largest structures of their time and civilization, remaining to impress visitors for centuries or even, as with the Pyramids of Giza, which remain a source of wonder to the present day. This has led to the standard New Age and contrarian archeology belief that pyramids derive from Plato's, Donnelly's, and Blavatsky's lost civilization Atlantis. After the sinking of that continent, it is thought that the inhabitants populated both sides of the Atlantic, retaining the architectural design.

But if this was the case, Mesoamerican structures like the Pyramid of the Sun, for example, is the largest building in the ancient Teotihuacan (not far from modern-day Mexico) and should be the same age as the Egyptian Pyramids and Mesopotamian Ziggurats. But it only dates to much later, around c. 200 C.E., when Rome had already passed its peak.

Also, if the pyramids really did use Atlantean technology, or for that matter, to give an alternative and equally popular belief, were built by aliens, they should show construction methods and materials far in advance of anything around at that time. But the opposite is the case. In practical engineering terms, a heap of stones is simply the only way to build a very large structure without the use of advanced building techniques.

In addition to being a result of the limitation of Bronze Age technology, the Pyramid represents a highly stratified society with the God-King at the apex of the social pyramid. These societies are associated with a dynastic succession of rulers, a priesthood with a secret knowledge of science, astronomy, and spiritual matters, the use of a solar rather than a lunar calendar, a linear sense of time, and preoccupation with immortality and the transcendence of temporal reality. The Sumerians believed that the gods lived in the temple at the top of the Ziggurats, so only priests and other highly respected individuals could enter.

7-v. Ancient Astronauts?

The Sumerians, Akkadians, and Babylonians were polytheists, in keeping with many pre-Axial Age, second millennium B.C.E. and earlier mythic cultures. As mentioned, from an esoteric perspective, this actually ties in with the concept of the emanation of the gods or cosmic and spiritual hierarchies from the transcendent One. Hence, rather than being an inferior precursor to monotheism, polytheism is a description of the Collective Unconscious and the supra-physical realities that influence the collective unconscious.

Modernity, however, has resulted in the belief in materialism; hence, the gods have to be explained in materialistic terms. An example of this is the ancient astronaut theory.

First popularized by Erich von Däniken (b. 1935), his *Chariots of the Gods?* (1968) presented the idea that extraterrestrial beings visited Earth in the past and were responsible for various ancient structures and artifacts. His ideas, incredibly popular and frequently featured in sensationalist documentaries during the 1970s (along with endless shows on such topics as Pyramids (Pyramid Power and Uri Geller), Nostradamus, and Nazi Germany), have since been conclusively refuted [Story, 1976].

Although (according to the bibliography section on his Wikipedia page) von Däniken continued to have a prolific output until the present day, he was soon superseded by Zecharia Sitchin (1920-2010), who produced several books, beginning with *The 12th Planet* (1976). Sitchin's theories are based on his interpretations of ancient Sumerian texts, particularly the cuneiform tablets from the city of Nippur. According to him, the Sumerian gods (*anunnaki*) weren't gods at all but humanoid extraterrestrials from the planet Nibiru, beyond the orbit of Neptune. They created *Homo sapiens* by genetically engineering primitive hominids (*Homo erectus*) with some of their own DNA to use as slave labor for mining gold. As for why technologically advanced space-faring aliens would be so interested in gold rather than in, say rare earth minerals/elements like yttrium, lanthanum, cerium, neodymium, or dysprosium, which would be of more use in electronics and semiconductors, why they didn't mine asteroids, why they didn't use modern mining techniques, and why they didn't even have robots or androids to do the menial work, is conveniently ignored.

Not to mention that humans and the great apes share 97% of their genome, how the difference between *H. sapiens* and other hominids can be explained in terms of a single mutation [Le Page 2022], and how advanced modern genetic analysis reveals Neanderthal and Denisovian DNA in contemporary humans – the result of late Pleistocene interbreeding – but does not show any evidence of alien DNA.

Sitchin also claimed that civilization was set up under the guidance of these "gods," with human kingship being inaugurated to provide intermediaries between mankind and the anunnaki, hence (the "divine right of kings").

From a rationalist perspective, it is ridiculous to interpret bronze age belief systems in terms of a *Star Trek*-type science fiction setting. Premodern, mythic, imaginal beliefs simply don't fit with the materialistic rationality of science fiction, a product of modernity. At the same time, however, the same mythic patterns can be seen with both, in that modern-day science fiction is the direct equivalent of premodern mythology [Kazlev, 2017a].

Another writer on Sumerian gods and aliens is Franco-German writer Anton Parks. As a child, he felt like an outsider, bullied by the French kids at school for having a German mother, not fitting in, and feeling invisible or transparent. At age fourteen, in 1981, he had the first of a series of overpowering visions. After some years, he tried to repress them in order to lead a more peaceful life but also attempted – without success – to write down the story these experiences revealed. These visions came not in his native French but, he claims, in ancient Sumerian, leading him to study Sumerian, and then Hebrew and Gnostic texts. A visit to Egypt in 2007 caused the experiences to return with greater intensity. The visions, on the whole, constituted a mass of disorganized material, which he eventually managed to piece together as the *Girku Chronicles* [Parks, 2014]. These constitute an epic cosmology, including a Space Opera story featuring his past life as Sa'am, a humanoid amphibious alien of the Gina'abul race, who, with companions, are marooned on Earth after an interplanetary war, becoming the "Gods" of Sumerian and Egyptian mythology [Parks, 2007]. Much of his general cosmology converges with Sitchkin, with whom he differs on many details. But in contrast to other ancient astronaut advocates, Parks' theory is based on his own powerful clairvoyant experiences, which gives it a certain air of authority. In this regard, he can be compared to Swedenborg or Rudolf Steiner.

A big problem with the ancient astronaut theory is simply biology. When we consider even the diversity of life on this Earth, from microscopic organisms like nematodes or mites, extraordinary animals of the Earth's past like *Opabinia* or *Tullimonstrum*, and creatures from the deep sea today such as the goblin shark or the angler fish, it can't be denied that, from the point of hard science and evolutionary theory, humanoid aliens are incredibly unimaginative. It is unsurprising that, in keeping with most New Age, premodern, and modern esotericist material, Parks rejects modern evolutionary science in favor of intelligent design (but not Christian Creationism) [Parks, 2014].

Also, like many ancient civilizations, such as Pharaonic Egypt and Vedic India, Sumeria has a psychic and imaginal mystique, which allows and encourages forces and imagination to take on these forms. Hence the popularity of the ancient astronaut narrative and other mythic stories.

And while it would be easy to dismiss such accounts in psychological, or even Jungian, terms, that would mean falling into the positivist trap and imposing a skeptical narrative, rather than being open to the infinite possibilities of the universe. The whole topic of extraterrestrials is a very difficult subject, as it tends towards an investigation into phenomena such as high strangeness, parallel timelines, alternate realities, telepathic contactee communication, and so on. It is certain that reality consists of many interweaving and interacting dimensions, which can be easily confused, such as Robert Monroe's experiences with advanced extraterrestrials while out of the body [Monroe, 1985, 1994], so that the same beings can be both alien races and supra-physical gods.

Among other Ancient Astronaut advocates, Robert Temple in *The Sirius Mystery* (1976) claims that the Dogon tribe of West Africa had knowledge of Sirius B, a small and dense companion star to the larger Sirius A, long before it was discovered by astronomers. Television presenter, ufologist, and popular figure in the ancient astronaut theory community, Giorgio A. Tsoukalos, argues that extraterrestrial beings visited Earth in the past and that their influence is evident in various ancient artifacts and structures. David Hatcher Childress in *The Technology of the Gods* (2000) and other books suggests that ancient civilizations, such as the Egyptians and the Maya, had advanced technology that was provided to them by extraterrestrial beings. Many more writers could be added to this list. This is, really, a modern form of creation myth, updated to include ideas from SETI and from sci-fi pop culture.

7-vi. Mesopotamian Cosmology and the Story of Creation

Whereas the ancient astronaut theory would have us believe that an advanced race of space-faring aliens instructed the Mesoptamians, Middle Eastern cosmologies described the physical universe according to magical or mythical thinking and the bronze or iron age understanding of the time.

According to the Sumerians, for example, the universe came into being when goddess Nammu, the primeval saltwater ocean, gave birth to Ki (the earth goddess) and An (the sky god), who produced a son named Enlil. Enlil separated heaven from the earth and claimed the earth as his domain. Humans were created by Enki, the god of water, knowledge, crafts, and creation, who is the son of Nammu and An.

The universe is a closed dome or firmament (An) (or three or seven domes), surrounded by a primordial saltwater sea. Underneath the earth (Ki) are the underworld (Kur), a miserable place where the dead go, and a freshwater ocean.

Sumerian religion influenced the beliefs of later Mesopotamian peoples and culture groups, including the Akkadians, Babylonians, and Assyrians. From here, also we get the classic example, the biblical cosmology of the book of Genesis, which dates to the early first millennium B.C.E. While the seven-day Genesis account is ridiculous from the perspective of empirical science, it makes perfect sense if we assume an original formlessness or primal chaos ("the earth was without form, and void; and darkness was upon the face of the deep"). This also appears in the Babylonian *Enuma Elish*, which shares the same creation story. It tells the story of the primordial deities Apsu (Fresh Water) and Tiamat (the Sea, salt water), the latter representing an earlier Goddess cult perhaps, the creation of the universe and the rise of the god Marduk, who fought with and overcame Tiamut, now portrayed as the principle of chaos, forming the earth and the skies from Tiamat's body, a version of the common myth of the cosmos as made from the body of a primordial giant, and his supremacy over the other gods. It was recited during the annual New Year festival in Babylon.

The cult of Marduk represents perhaps the earliest example of the patriarchal and monotheistic religion, and the degradation and demonization of earlier religions. This is a pattern that would reappear in the Semitic world with later Mythic, Axial, and post-Axial age deities like Yahweh and Allah, and of course, with Christianity's assimilation of pagan myths and festivals, along with using the appearance of the nature god Pan as the image for the devil.

There seem to be two parts to the Tiamat mythos. In the first, she is a creator goddess, through a sacred marriage between different waters, peacefully creating the cosmos through successive generations. In the second, Tiamat is considered the monstrous embodiment of primordial chaos. English poet, classicist, and historical novelist Robert Graves (1895-1985) considered Tiamat's death by Marduk as evidence of the overthrow of an earlier matriarchal society and religion by a later patriarchal one. This theory is rejected by academic authors such as Lotte Motz, Cynthia Eller, and others [Tiamat – Wikipedia].

7-vii. Chaoskampf, the Struggle Against Chaos

The Tiamat myth is one of the earliest known versions of the Struggle with Chaos, or *Chaoskampf* theme, the battle between a culture hero and a chthonic or aquatic monster, serpent, or dragon. This was first presented by the German theologian and Assyriologist Hermann Gunkel (1862-1932) in his book *Schöpfung und Chaos in Urzeit und Endzeit* (*Creation and Chaos in the Primeval Era and the End Times*), published in 1895. Gunkel argued that the Babylonian creation account in *Enuma Elish* was the source for the Genesis account.

He pointed out that in both, there is a battle that results in an act of creation, and that in the Hebrew and Babylonian texts, this battle involved a struggle between a deity and the sea, a sea god, or sea monsters. Gunkel described this in terms of a storm god defeating a sea god or dragon who represents chaos, with the act of creation happening afterward. This is a common theme in Ancient Near East creation narratives, being found in Babylonian, Canaanite, Mari (an ancient Semitic city-state in modern-day Syria, 3rd to early 2nd millennium B.C.E.), and Hebrew accounts [Rackley, 2014, p.5].

Both the *Enuma Elish* and Genesis describe the universe as having been created out of a formless, chaotic void. The struggle with Chaos is a founding myth in the Levant (the Near East, the eastern Mediterranean area now covered by Israel, Lebanon, part of Syria, and western Jordan), in which primordial chaos is conquered by the high deity, in the process of creating the cosmos. This may involve Marduk slaughtering Tiamat and conquering the sea, or Yahweh's struggle with the sea monster Leviathan. The cosmic battle takes place in the primeval, mythic past, creating history as a process of ordered laws presided over by God. History, in other words, is the period where the divine ruler imposes order onto chaos [Sledge, 2021].

A Jungian might interpret this as the struggle of the emergence of consciousness or the Ego from the ocean of the collective Unconscious. Eric Neumann, who wrote on the origins of consciousness (or rather of the psyche), refers to this as the state of ouroboros, the serpent swallowing its tail, a symbol of infinity [Neumann, 1973].

Later scholars, such as Sigmund Mowinckel and Nahum Sarna, have criticized Gunkel's approach as oversimplified and reductionistic, but this doesn't take away its mythic truth.

7-viii. The Creation of Humanity

In the *Enuma Elish*, Marduk needs divine blood to create humanity. He was initially going to use his own blood for this purpose, but Ea (the Sumerian Enki, now occupying a more secondary status), suggested instead using the primordial god Kingu, the son of the gods Apsu and Tiamat (and after the death of his father, the consort of his mother, perhaps to portray the perverse quality of the earlier generation of gods). Marduk killed Kingu and mixed his blood with earth to make the clay to mold the first human beings.

This theme of the creator inserting a bit of himself in his creation, sidestepped in the *Enuma Elish*, and similarly downgraded in Genesis when all that Yahweh uses is his breath, was referenced more completely by out-of-body traveler Robert Monroe [Monroe, 1977] when he referred to an alien superintelligence that, in order to farm a greater amount of a substance called "loosh," injected a part of itself into the human species. This became the basis of human feelings such as love, friendship, family, greed, hate, pain, guilt, and so on, which generate loosh [DeKorne, 2002].

So already, by the time these Near and Middle Eastern religions were codified, the original revelation had already been watered down, probably many times. The theory of a perennial philosophy does not take into account this degrading of original transcendent experiences. It assumes that the formalized, institutional, and exoteric text is the original revelation. In fact, it results from a much more limited "sense feeling" consciousness imposed on the masses as part of the state and church cult.

Sometimes the distorted message is then re-esotericized, but in a different context, as with the Gnostic myth of the deity Sophia tricking the evil demiurge Yaltabaoth to breathe some of his spirit (which was originally his mother Sophia's spirit) into humanity, or as physical matter and the cosmos used as a prison that keeps the divine spirit trapped. From a Gnostic perspective, the "Loosh Collectors" can be equated with the archons or lower gods that rule the physical and psychic world and seek to keep the human soul imprisoned in matter. The goal of the gnostic is the release of the inner or spiritual self from the bonds of the world and his or her return to the realm of light.

It is clear then that esotericism, as much as exoteric religion, very often consists of a total jumble of experience, dogmatism, new experience based on a reading or misreading of that, further dogmatism, so that all that one is left with is a jumble of mythic themes, materialism, further experiences, and so on. Out of this mishmash, the best one can do is extract some esoteric or Jungian insights to help aid one's own understanding.

7-ix. What are the Gods?

A belief in gods is central to the mythic worldview. Examples include the polytheism and kathenotheism (many gods but worshipping one at a time) of the early Mediterranean civilizations, God-Kings, pyramids, and idols. Whether they are called *anunnaki* (Sumeria), *neter* (Egypt), devas (India), *teo* (Mesoamerica), or some other name, there is a common pattern in mythic thinking; it is concerned with the creative powers that shaped the world, and with humanity's relationship to the gods or god. But how should the gods of the various religions and cultures be understood?

There are a number of interpretations, and all of them can be correct or partially correct, in the sense that each brings a single insight from a particular point of view, but together these make up the overall explanation. These can be called the Literal (or positivist) explanation, the Jungian (or symbolic or archetypal) explanation, and the Esoteric or Gnostic explanation.

The positivist view is that these are just superstitions, pre-scientific attempts at explaining the natural world. For example, people didn't understand and couldn't look up on Google to find out that thunder is caused when lightning heats the air to thousands of degrees, causing it to suddenly expand, after which it cools and rapidly contracts, resulting in a thunderclap. Instead, they came up with anthropomorphic images such as Zeus hurling thunderbolts or Thor striking his hammer.

It is not that this simplistic explanation is wrong, but only that it is the most superficial. Hence, the literal explanation gives way to how meaning and imaginal reality shape our understanding of the external universe.

In this context, the gods represent innate structures of the Jungian collective unconscious. Although, according to this interpretation, they do not have an objective existence, they still exist in the collective human psyche, wired into the brain, so to speak.

Later in life, Jung became disillusioned with physicalist explanations, noting acausal events (meaningful coincidences) that could not be explained psychologically or materialistically, and which he referred to as "synchronicity" [Jung, 1973].

Finally, there is the esoteric interpretation that the gods refer to actual non-physical cosmic forces, what Rudolf Steiner calls "spiritual hierarchies." Steiner describes these in detail in his many lectures but retains the Spiritualist and Theosophical error that the gods are evolved humans from previous eons and part of a single evolutionary continuum. The Neoplatonic understanding is the opposite; the gods are the result of the emanation from the One. According to Iamblichus, there are various noetic gods, psychic gods, hypercosmic gods, and finally, the gods that regulate the physical world. The 5th century Neoplatonist Proclus described this in a more systematic manner, regarding the emanation of the highest gods, which he calls *henads*.

Iamblichus' theology was directly taken up by the Christian mystic Pseudo-Dionysius, who described hierarchies of angels based on Neoplatonic gods. It was from this that Steiner derived his own angelology.

A similar theme is found in Kabbalah, which displays Neoplatonic influence, where each emanated world, beginning with the transcendent world of Atzilut, has its own set of *sefirot* (archetypes, divine attributes), but here the symbolism is less clear because of the need to conform to monotheistic theology. The same can be said regarding Ismailism, which apotheosized personalities from mythologized Islam as gnostic-like aeons. The emphasis on polytheism is stronger in Hermetic Kabbalah, where the sefirot have more of the quality of gods.

In the theistic religion of Vaishnavism, inspired by medieval texts such as the *Srimrad Bhagavatam*, a multiplicity of gods, identified with and having the attributes of the Hindu deity Vishnu, are emanated by the supreme Krishna. Similarly, the emergence of the "Overmental" gods and godheads is given by Sri Aurobindo in his distinction between the Supermind (which is the original creative unity) and the Overmind (which is the highest plane of, and supervises, the lower worlds).

The consensus here is that the transcendent One, in emanating or becoming creation, differentiates into or takes on various forms, which are what we can call the gods. These give rise to further intermediate powers and spiritual hierarchies, and the powers behind the visible cosmos.

Therefore, not only do the gods exist in the collective unconscious, they are also cosmic realities, which would have still existed even if humanity didn't. Just because we interpret them in mythological and anthropomorphic forms doesn't mean they are limited to those forms. There are many intermediate degrees of reality between the physical and the transcendent, and there can be any number of or type of gods or archetypes.

7-x. The Egregore

Worship of gods (and even of ancestors) brings in a whole new element, in addition to the standard subjective projection of Jungian archetypes onto the world. This is god as a "thought form," which is created and sustained through the belief of the worshipers and acquires a separate existence and consciousness. Hence in the *Enuma Elish*, Marduk creates man to serve the gods. The same idea appears in the Upanishads, and later in Gnosticism, where it is said that humans are food for the gods, which ties in with the loosh idea [DeConnick, 2016].

There would seem to be two distinct types of entities here. One is a nonhuman, alien entity that feeds on a more spiritual and poignant type of feeling. These are pre-existing superintelligences that Robert Monroe referred to in the context of loosh. Presumably, they follow their own evolutionary path. The cosmos, as described by Monroe and, in a different context, by Steiner, is full of beings. These also may include what Jung called archetypes, at least in some cases.

The other type of entity is a thought-form, a human unconscious creation, which also feeds on emotions, but this time of the coarser sort. These are psychic parasites that grow bigger and bigger, sucking up emotions.

In order to explain how this works, it is necessary to understand one of the premises of Theosophy; objective, empirical reality is simply the densest of a gradation of degrees of increasingly subtle degrees of substance.

At the familiar gross physical degree, or "plane," to use Theosophical terminology, matter and energy are inert and non-sentient. This is the "outer" reality known to empirical science. But the further "up" the scale one goes, that is, the further to the "spirit" pole, the more substance becomes progressively more ideoplastic. It becomes more it becomes receptive and is able to be shaped by thoughts and emotions. Imagine if your surroundings were receptive to your thoughts and feelings, becoming light and sparkling when you are happy or dark and menacing when you are angry or fearful. On the supra-physical degrees or planes, these phenomena actually take on a life of their own, becoming "thought forms" [Besant & Leadbeater, 1901].

According to occultism, the matter of the degree or zone that is nearest to the physical is itself conscious, but in a heavy and limited way, being of the nature of desires and lower appetites (*epithumia* of Plato's psychology). This is commonly referred to as the "lower astral plane," to use New Age jargon. This is the zone at which egregores occur.

By ascending the scale toward the higher emotional states of higher gnosis, this substance becomes progressively more refined, luminous, and spiritual in nature. Eventually (at even higher levels), it transcends thought altogether and becomes infinite being, consciousness, and bliss, to use the Indian Vedantic formula.

The word *egregore* (from the Greek "wakeful") has been used in a number of different contexts. The 19th century occultist Eliphas Levi referred to egregores as the "Watchers" of the Book of Enoch and "terrible beings" that "crush us without pity because they are unaware of our existence." [Levi, *Le Grand Arcane/The Great Secret*, 1868, cited in

Wikipedia]. These are a type of inhuman nonphysical entity, quite distinct from human belief.

A more positive meaning of egregore is a group identity that develops when an occult group's (such as Freemasons or ceremonial magical) symbols and rituals are repeated over time. This binds the group together, harmonizing and motivating the individual members, who are then able to make more spiritual progress as a group than if they worked alone [Delaforge, 1987].

A third meaning is a *tulka*, to use the Tibetan term for spirit beings that can be deliberately created by magical rituals and individual or group meditation [David-Neel, 1977; Owen & Sparrow, 1976; Stavish, 2018]. They can also form spontaneously over time, as in with religions, if a deity receives sufficient worship.

Finally, an egregore can be an emergent phenomenon or group consciousness that influences the collective behavior of individuals and groups [*The stoa*, 2022].

My interest in this topic was triggered by a "meme" dating to around 2019 portraying the Democrat party as a puny cartoon figure futilely trying to push back against a huge sumo wrestler labeled "Trump Egregore." This goes to show that a few on the Far Right of the political spectrum, while gross materialists, unwittingly have occult insights, in contrast to the physicalist social-activist Left (In fact, the occult factors behind the political right today are a whole topic in themselves [Greer, 2021; Lachman, 2018]).

Because of its appetitive nature, the egregore is created by, but also feeds on, the energy of worshipers. Through "downward causation," it creates a positive feedback loop in its equivalent resonances at the lower desire (epithumia, *kama*) degree of subtle physical reality, where it is able to influence, and be influenced by, the consciousness of believers. It demands worship and becomes a sort of psychic parasite. The ubiquity of these gods in early Near Eastern religions shows that this phenomenon goes back at least to mythic age thinking.

Both nonphysical alien superintelligences (of the type described by Monroe) and thought-forms or egregores often end up becoming the gods of religion, because humans tend to interpret any nonphysical entity that is larger than itself as a god, or, more than that, as god almighty, the creator of the universe.

This is where a knowledge of occultism comes in handy. It allows us to recognize these various forces and entities that enslave and prey on man, in the same way that the current human race, lacking compassion, enslaves and preys on other species of animal life on Earth. The inner divine principle, the Self-archetype (Jung) or psychic being (Aurobindo and Mirra), must be distinguished from both the false egregore gods and the alien superintelligences, as the center of attention and the guide for spiritual aspiration.

7-xi. The Pessimism of the Mythic Worldview

Many of the civilizations that developed in and around the Mediterranean basin and the Middle East in the 2nd and first millennium before Christ were essentially materialistic cultures, concerned with hyper-masculine virtues, who performed acts of valor and defined their civilization, such as in Homer's *Iliad*. The Hebrews shared the same ethos; the Nephilim, for example, were not supernatural beings, giants, or extraterrestrials, but the mighty men of old [TREY the Explainer, 2018].

In these cultures, everything is physical. Humans, gods, and the throne where Yahweh sits above the waters of the firmament are all physical. Because identity was so tied up with the gross physical body (even more so than in modern Western secularism, because they didn't have a Spiritualism based idea of heaven or pop-New Age public esotericism), one's fate after death was usually as a miserable shadow or ghost. The ancient Babylonians, Hebrews, and Homeric Greeks ("Homeric" means the viewpoint of the great poet Homer 8th century B.C.E., and his public) saw the after-life state – the Underworld, Sheol, Hades, Tartarus – as a dark, miserable, quasi-existence; the dead being but a pathetic shadow of their former living selves.

This is because the soul, and hence consciousness, is associated with the living body, so it is assumed that consciousness does as well when the physical body ceases, except for the miserable remnant of the shade. This form of materialism is not much different from the mind-body identity theory and the reductionist positivism of modern-day philosophy, except for the addition of an unhappy ghost.

This was the same elsewhere in the world as well. In the Viking warrior culture (which was still shamanic and pagan), you got to go to Asgard if you died in battle, which was how you avoided becoming a shade. As with the Asgard of the Marvel Cinematic Universe, this wasn't a spiritual realm but another physical world, one of the nine realms of Nordic Cosmology. Or they were sustained by the prayers of your descendants, as in Chinese popular religious belief.

A graphic literary illustration of this is given in Homer's account of the meeting of Odysseus with the shade of Achilles, the greatest and most renowned of all the Greek heroes. Odysseus, descending to Hades in order to consult the dead seer Teiresias concerning the circumstances that prevented him from returning home, encounters Achilles and congratulates him regarding the honors and fame he had won through his part in the siege of Troy. Achilles rejects Odysseus' words with a devastating reply:

> Nay, seek not to speak soothingly to me of death...I should choose, so I might live on earth, to serve as the hireling of another, of some portionless man whose livelihood was but small, rather than to be lord over all the dead that have perished. [Brandon, 1967, p.82]

In a society that saw martial glory and honor as the highest of all values, even that is not compensation for the miserable state of after-life existence. Better to be the most pathetic beggar alive than the King of all the Underworld.

Esoterically, shades or ghosts are phenomenological intuitions or intimations of personalities or personality fragments on the lowest and most appetitive physical subplane of the astral (the astral plane consists of a number of subplanes, of which the physical subplane has the lowest degree of consciousness). They lack both rational (the mental or thinking aspect – mental body) and spiritual (god and soul dimension) faculties but can be sustained through worship and offerings.

There may be some overlap between ghosts and egregores, as both are lower psychic (or astral) in substance. The difference, however, is that egregores are thought forms completely created by humans and sustained through religious belief and worship, whereas shades and ghosts are personality remnants (the astral shell in Theosophical jargon) that were once human and are now earth-bound in the spirit world and helped through offerings and prayers for the dead (in Buddhist mythology they are called *pretas*, "hungry ghosts"). Other than these astral shells, there is no conception of either the soul or the *bardo* body (spirit body) in these cultures.

It was only with the ancient Egyptians, with their advanced occult, mythical, and theological understanding, that a developed model of the afterlife developed.

7-xii. Ancestor Worship

Offerings for the dead soon developed into ancestor worship, the widespread religious practice involving the veneration of dead ancestors.

In various European, East Asian, Oceanian, African and Afro-diasporic cultures, it is believed that the spirits of the dead possess the ability to influence the fortune of the living. The goal of ancestor worship is to ensure the ancestors' continued well-being and positive disposition towards the living, and also sometimes to ask for special favors or assistance [Wikipedia – Ancestor Worship, 2021].

This is the opposite of the melancholy shade, but it ties in with the whole egregore theme. People pray to ancestors just as they pray to gods.

In a sense, the ancestors are like gods, only more intimate and approachable, and hence more accessible. This connects with the idea of intermediary beings, a common theme in esotericism, religion, the New Age, and occultism [Asprem, 2015]. For example, Catholic Saints may be worshiped as minor deities who can intercede with (the supreme) god on the supplicant's part.

While disembodied spirits in proximity to the physical may benefit from positive thoughts, as in the Catholic Church's prayer for souls in Purgatory, ancestor worship almost entirely deals with disembodied astral beings, which may not even be related to the spirit of the loved one, or even if they are, involve a degree of ideoplastic and astral distortion. These beings exist in the physical degree of the astral plane and feed on the offerings they are given. The same also applies to the Egyptian *Ka*.

The practice is making offerings to these disincarnate spirits is common, whether as a part of ancestor worship or, as in the Buddhist concept of hungry ghosts (pretas), to alleviate their suffering.

7-xiii. The Epic of Gilgamesh

The theme of mortality features large in the *Epic of Gilgamesh*, the most famous work of literature from ancient Mesopotamia, as well as one of the earliest works of imaginal fiction.

The origin of the myth can be found in a series of Sumerian poems about Gilgamesh, king of Uruk, dating from the Third Dynasty of Ur, also called the Neo-Sumerian Empire, a 22nd to 21st century B.C.E. dynasty based in the city of Ur. This dynasty, also known for the Ziggurat of Ur, is a Neo-Sumerian Ziggurat built by King Ur-Nammu, who dedicated it in honor of Nanna or Sin, the Moon god, in approximately the 21st century BC during the Third Dynasty of Ur.

There is also an "Old Babylonian" version, known only from a few tablets, which dates to the 18th century B.C.E. The later Standard Babylonian, Akkadian language version was compiled by the editor Sin-leqi-unninni sometime around the 13th to the 10th centuries B.C.E.

The Akkadian tablets were unearthed in the mid-19th century by the Turkish Assyriologist Hormuzd Rassam at Nineveh, which is located on the eastern bank of the Tigris River which was the capital and largest city of the Neo-Assyrian Empire (today in northern Iraq, near the city of Mosul), the largest empire in the world at the time. It was found in The Royal Library of Ashurbanipal, named after Ashurbanipal (reigned 668–627 B.C.E.), the last great Assyrian king. This contained more than 30,000 clay tablets, including texts in various languages.

The *Epic of Gilgamesh* tells the story of the eponymous Gilgamesh, the king of the Mesopotamian city-state Uruk (Erech), which is an actual ancient city of Sumer, and later of Babylonia, near the Euphrates River. Although he is two-thirds god and one-third man, Gilgamesh oppresses the people, who cry out to the gods for help. The gods send Enkidu, a wild man who lives in the forest, and helps the animals by uprooting traps. Later Enkidu becomes civilized through sexual initiation with the temple prostitute Shamhat, who teaches him the ways of humanity. Learning of Gilgamesh's arrogant treatment of new brides (in medieval Europe this was known as *Droit du seigneur*, the right of the feudal lords to have sexual relations with subordinate women, especially on the wedding night), Enkidu, who possesses the morality that Gilgamesh lacks, becomes angry and travels to Uruk to intervene. After a fight with Gilgamesh, the two become friends.

Like other mythic macho heroes, such as Beowulf, Gilgamesh possesses Hollywood action hero-type armor, because no matter how great the danger or powerful the monsters he fights, he always wins and escapes death and injury. This shows the way that tropes are universal. They are either wired into the brain as part of the neural deep structure, imprinted as archetypes on the collective psyche (Jung), or represent cosmic forces (spiritual hierarchies – Rudolf Steiner). But in contrast to the obligatory happy ending of the modern action hero, these mythic age heroes are always undone by the gods. Whereas the modern world is defined by the hyper-individualism of consumerism and materialistic egocentrism, premodernity understands that there are forces of fate or destiny. This is epitomized most eloquently in works of the Greek tragedians such as Aeschylus, Sophocles, and Euripides (fifth century B.C.E.), centered on universal themes such as the human condition, fate, justice, and the consequences of *hubris* (excessive pride or ambition).

Hence when Ishtar, the goddess of love, beauty, war, and fertility, sends the Bull of Heaven to punish Gilgamesh for spurning her advances, Gilgamesh and Enkidu kill the Bull of Heaven, but the gods only sentence Enkidu to death. Enkidu sickens and dies, bringing Gilgamesh grief.

This causes Gilgamesh to embark on a long and perilous journey to discover the secret of eternal life. He finally encounters the only immortal man Utnapishtim, the Babylonian Noah – or perhaps one could say that Noah is the Hebrew Utnapishtim – who was given immortality as a unique gift from the gods. Utnapishtim challenges Gilgamesh to stay awake for six days and seven nights. Gilgamesh falls asleep, and Utnapishtim tells him that Gilgamesh, who is seeking to overcome death, cannot even prevent himself from falling asleep. There may also be a parallel with the teachings of Gurdjieff, who explained that most humans exist in a state of sleep, and to attain an immortal soul, it is necessary to practice constant self-remembering (equivalent to the Buddhist mindfulness meditation) and intentional suffering.

Before Gilgamesh departs, Utnapishtim tells him that at the bottom of the sea there is a plant that will restore his youth. Gilgamesh ties stones to his feet so he can walk on the bottom, not being bothered by having to breathe, in keeping with the absurdities and plot holes of modern action and sci-fi movies. Returning to land, Gilgamesh returns to Uruk. But when Gilgamesh stops to bathe, it is stolen by a serpent, which is the symbol of rebirth and immortality as it sheds its skin (as well as being, in the Hebrew creation story, the symbol of knowledge, and hence considered sacred by the Gnostic sect called the Ophites). Gilgamesh realizes the futility of his efforts, as, despite all his superhuman strength, deeds, and abilities, he has now lost all chance of immortality.

7-xiv. Why is there no Concept of an Immortal Soul?

Given that out-of-body and near-death experiences are spontaneous and are even found in the works of Plato (the story of Er), and given that intuition is able to pick up the existence of disincarnate ancestors and "earth-bound" spirits or pretas that feed on the imaginal equivalent of physical offerings, it may be asked why was there no concept of an immortal soul in the ancient Mesopotamian, Semitic, Greek, or Persian world?

I would suggest the answer is the same as why we do not read accounts of nonduality experiences (metaphysical gnosis or cosmic consciousness) in these various cultures.

It is not that these experiences do not exist, but simply that these cultures have no way of receiving and explaining them. Therefore they are either not described or, more likely, described inaccurately.

It is like the situation today, where if someone has a near-death experience, it is explained by means of hallucinations caused by carbon dioxide poisoning or other reductionist neurological explanations. If future historians only knew of Western society through scattered artifacts and scraps of books on science, they would come to the conclusion that this was a civilization in which there were no supra-physical experiences. Hence the more complex a culture's worldview, the more likely it is to accommodate diverse and anomalous experiences.

7-xv. The Flood Myth

A common theme of the Great Flood features in both the *Epic of Gilgamesh* and the book of Genesis.

In both stories, a great flood destroys most of humanity and the earth, and a hero is chosen to survive the flood and repopulate the earth. In the Epic of Gilgamesh, the hero's name is Utnapishtim, while in Genesis, his name is Noah. Both men are warned of the impending flood by a deity (in Gilgamesh, the god Ea, and in Genesis, God) and are instructed to build a large boat or ark to save themselves, their families, and various animals.

There are also some differences, which are only to be expected. In the *Epic of Gilgamesh*, the gods decide to send the flood as punishment for humanity's noise and chaos, while in Genesis, God sends the flood to cleanse the earth of wickedness and corruption. Additionally, Utnapishtim is granted immortality by the gods after the flood, while Noah is not. In the *Epic of Gilgamesh*, the flood lasts for seven days and seven nights, while in Genesis, the flood lasts for 40 days and 40 nights. The dimensions of the boats also differ, with Utnapishtim's boat being much larger and more elaborate than Noah's.

The story of Noah and the flood in Genesis seems to have been influenced by earlier Mesopotamian flood myths. In addition to the story of Utnapishtim in the *Epic of Gilgamesh*, there are several earlier flood myths.

One of the most well-known is the *Epic of Atrahasis*, a Babylonian myth from the 18th century B.C.E. that tells the story of how the gods created humans to be their servants, but were disturbed by the noise and overpopulation of humans. In the myth, the god Enlil decides to send a flood to destroy humanity, but the god Ea warns the hero, Atrahasis, and helps him to survive the flood by building a large boat.

Another is the Sumerian story of Ziusudra, which dates back to the 17th century B.C.E. In this myth, the god Enki warns Ziusudra of the impending flood and instructs him to build a boat to save himself, his family, and numerous animals.

One scholar who studied the similarities and differences between these flood myths and the story of Noah is Samuel Noah Kramer, who first identified the similarities between the flood myths in the mid-20th century. There are other later scholars, such as Stephanie Dalley, Jon D. Levenson, and William H.C. Propp, who have further explored the relationship between these myths and the biblical flood story.

It has been suggested that these various stories of the Great Flood were based on an actual event. This Black Sea deluge hypothesis is a controversial theory that suggests that the Black Sea was once a freshwater lake and that a catastrophic flood occurred around 7,500 years ago, which led to the formation of the Black Sea as we know it today. According to the theory, rising sea levels caused the Mediterranean Sea to overflow into the Black Sea through the Bosporus Strait, which was previously a land bridge. This sudden influx of saltwater caused a massive flood that may have had significant consequences for the people living in the region.

The theory was first proposed in the 1990s by two geologists, William Ryan and Walter Pitman, who based their argument on geological evidence gathered during a research cruise in the Black Sea. They found evidence of a previously unknown sediment layer characteristic of marine environments, suggesting that the Black Sea was once connected to the Mediterranean Sea.

The Black Sea deluge hypothesis has been the subject of much debate and controversy among scientists and scholars. Some experts have argued that the theory is based on incomplete data and that the evidence for a catastrophic flood is not conclusive. Others have criticized the theory for being overly simplistic and for neglecting the complex geological processes that shape the region.

Despite these criticisms, the Black Sea deluge hypothesis has gained significant attention and has inspired similar theories about other ancient flood myths and legends, including the story of Noah and the flood in the book of Genesis. For example, some scholars have suggested that the biblical flood story may have been inspired by a catastrophic flood in the Mesopotamian region, which could have been caused by the same geological processes that led to the formation of the Black Sea.

Counter-arguments to these theories include the fact that the geological record does not show clear evidence of a global or regional flood at the time suggested, and that the presence of the sediment layer may have been the result of gradual changes in the environment rather than a catastrophic event. In addition, other possible explanations exist for the similarities between flood myths in different cultures, including the possibility of shared cultural and literary influences.

7-xvi. Mesopotamian Astrology

For the Mesopotamians, the sun, moon, and stars were physical gods. In contrast to shamanism, but in keeping with a lot of early premodern thought, there is no spiritual or supernatural world as opposed to the physical. Everything is physical, even the gods. This marked the beginning of astrology, which for some three and half thousand years was to be a central element in Middle Eastern and Western cosmology.

The earliest surviving reference to astrology (albeit in a very generic sense) is from a document concerning a dream of a certain Gudea, the king of the Sumerian city-state of Lagash (located northwest of the junction of the Euphrates and Tigris rivers) from around 2122 to 2102 B.C.E. In his dream, he saw a woman making a building plot and studying a clay tablet. At the goddess Nanshe's shrine, Gudea was told that the woman was the goddess Nisaba, the goddess of writing, and that she was studying a tablet of the stars to build a temple in accordance with the stars [Barton, 1994, p.11]. The interpretation itself presupposes an earlier cosmology regarding the nature of the heavens. Of course, the communications from gods or spirits through dreams goes back all the way to original shamanism.

By around 1800 B.C.E., there were lists of star names, such as the Old Babylonian "Prayer to the Gods of the Night," showing that certain stars were already regarded as deities capable of influencing earthly events. Astrology began to be used as a secondary means of divination alongside the standard form of divination, consulting entrails (or, more specifically, hepatoscopy – reading the liver).

Reading the entrails of some poor sacrificed animal is, from our early 21st century perspective of solid-state electronics and global satellite positioning systems, an almost cartoonish representation of the mindset of early premodern civilization, showing how barbaric and superstitious they were. But, and not denying the cruelty, what it actually is, like all forms of divination, up to and including tea leaves, is all about interpreting patterns in apparent randomness. To the premodern mindset (including animism), nothing is random or accidental. This is my understanding as well; that if one considers the basic randomness of nature, which could be anything from the collapse of a wave function to the names of street signs or the numbers in one's date of birth, it actually takes the form of a meaning or pattern that can be intuitively read. Rational modernity denies such a pattern exists, whereas religion and intuitive magical thinking impose all sorts of subjective psychic projections on it.

It's also important to understand that Babylonian astrology wasn't the horoscope astrology of today, which was only codified some two millennia later by Greeks like Ptolemy. Instead, in keeping with the mythic mindset, it was based on celestial omens. Many of these omens would later be included in a huge compilation called the *Enuma Anu Enlil*. The modern title is from the opening words:"'When (the gods) Anu, Enlil [and Ea established in council the plans of Sky and Earth].''

Consisting of around seventy tablets and some 7,000 celestial omens and predictions found in the royal archives in Nineveh, it was the primary source of omens used in the regular astrological reports sent to the Neo-Assyrian king by his entourage of scholars.

The first fifty tablets deal with lunar, solar, and meteorological omens, while the last twenty are concerned with the planets and the stars. Early or late rising and setting, position, size, color, and brightness are all taken into consideration.

An example is the following: "If Sin (the Moon God) slows down in the sky (instead of disappearing suddenly), there will be drought and famine in the country" [Barton, 1994, p.11]. This is rather like those pop New Age dream interpretation books, where you look up your dream, reduced to its simplest symbol, say "flying," and hey presto, there's the interpretation. Jung was rightly critical of this sort of thinking, as he understood that dreams are complex, specific to the individual, and dependent on and indicative of their particular psychological state.

And whilst omens can be examples of genuine synchronicity or refer to the underlying meaning at the basis of apparent randomness, or even be foreshadowings of large events, they also can be overblown shadow projections coming from paranoia, conspiracy thinking, or antidivine entities.

Although this version dates to the seventh century B.C.E., the *Enuma Anu Enlil* is akin to an index to earlier omen literature, and its compilation may go back to the beginning of the second millennium B.C.E. [Barton, 1994, p.12]. It continued to be used well into the 1st millennium, with the latest datatable copy being written in 194 B.C.E. This material also made its way to India in the 4th or 3rd centuries B.C.E. [Brown, 2000], although Hindu astrology is based mainly on Hellenistic and Vedic sources.

Babylonian omen astrology was mostly concerned with the public domain or, what amounts to the same thing, the royal domain: war and peace, rebellion and tranquility, good crops and plenty, poor crops and famine. The astrologers were civil servants whose job was to discern what the visible gods in heaven intended for the state on earth. As recorders, analysts, and astronomers, they observed the heavens, interpreted the data, tried to discern the regularities by which the Sun, Moon, and planets change position over time, and to predict planetary positions and encounters accurately [R. Beck, 2007, p.12]. So from necessity, they also became astronomers, although prior to the development of modern cosmology, astrology and astronomy were simply two branches of the same field of study.

At the same time, astrology as we know it was taking shape. A Babylonian compendium of astronomy and astrology called *Mul.Apin* (the Plough-star), dated to c.700 B.C.E and compiled from earlier material c.700 B.C.E., includes the earliest mention of the Zodiac, with seventeen constellations in three broad bands running roughly parallel to the equator. Among them are some that would later become the standard zodiac signs [Barton, 1994, p.13].

The earliest Babylonian horoscopes date from the end of the fifth century, after Babylon had been conquered by and was a part of the Achaemenid Empire. As with the later Greek horoscopes preserved on papyrus, there is no interpretation. However, a Babylonian horoscope cast for a birth date of 29 April 410 B.C.E., shows for the first time the positions of the planets on that day [Barton, 1994, pp.14-15].

This was the beginning of astrology in the classic sense, which was developed by Greek astronomers like Ptolemy in the following centuries, and, more recently, in the 19th and 20th centuries by modern astrology.

8. EGYPT

8-i. The Civilization of Egypt

Ancient Egyptian religion was a complex system of beliefs and rituals. Formal religious practice centered on the pharaohs, who acted as intermediaries between their people and the gods, and represented the classic exemplar of the God-King.

In a fertile strip of land barely 20 kilometers at its widest, and 500 kilometers in length, nourished by the waters and nutrients of the life-giving Nile, the Egyptians built pyramids and temples to exact proportions – a precision that would be remarkable even with today's technology – and developed an incredibly sophisticated occult knowledge of the afterlife state.

For some time, Egyptian civilization was thought to have begun when the Pharaoh Menes unified the separate Upper and Lower Kingdoms along the Nile in 3100 B.C.E. However, earlier archeological remains have been found, pushing the date for the earliest dynasties back some centuries.

Even in the sixth century B.C.E onwards, during its late phase when it was just a shadow of its former glory, Egypt served as the source of spiritual and occult wisdom for the more intellectually sophisticated world – the Greek civilization of the North-West Mediterranean – much as today the more sensitive people of the materialistic and technological West look to India as the source of spiritual nourishment. Philosophers, historians, and teachers – Pythagoras, Herodotus, Plato, to name just the best-known – journeyed there to learn the ancient wisdom and sciences, where they looked upon a civilization as ancient then as the Classical Greek and Roman period is to us today, and returned to the Hellenic world with their knowledge.

8-ii. Society, Religion, and Sacred Architecture

Ancient Egyptian religion was a complex system of beliefs and rituals. Formal religious practice centered on the pharaohs, who acted as intermediaries between their people and the gods. Similar ideas of the divinely appointed God-King were featured in China and in medieval Europe. Mimi Lobell suggests that the God-King is associated with social hierarchies and the spatial archetype of the pyramidal style of architecture [Lobell, 1983, 2018].

Impressions of the night sky – which would have been vast and dazzling in the clear desert air – were an essential part of the various myths of Egyptian religion. In addition, the annual solar motion along the horizon, the timing and position of the solstices (northernmost and southernmost turning points), and the various stars and constellations, were key astronomical observations that were incorporated into the religion and temple design.

An understanding of Egyptian sacred geometry and architecture was popularized by French Egyptologist and esotericist René Adolphe Schwaller de Lubicz (1887-1961), who lived in Egypt for twelve years. He argued that Egyptian temples were used for mystical initiation, and that temple architecture was based on the proportions of the human body [Schwaller de Lubicz, 1981]. It has also been suggested that the position of the main pyramids mirrored that of the belt of the constellation Orion [Bauval & Gilbert, 1994].

Of somewhat less plausibility are the New Age proponents of Plato's lost continent/civilization of Atlantis, popularized in modern times by American Congressman and fringe theorist Ignatius Donnelly (1831 – 1901) with his 1882 *Atlantis: the Antediluvian World*. His ideas influenced Madame Blavatsky, who considered the Atlanteans to be a previous cosmic cycle of humanity or "Root Race." While the 1970s writers of books on unsolved mysteries and the like, observing that pyramids are found on the sides of the Atlantic, conclude that they must have been colonists from the sunken civilization. The alternative, "Ancient Astronaut" hypothesis first popularized by Swiss author Erich von Daniken's *Chariots of the Gods*, also uses the ubiquity of pyramids in ancient civilizations, but this time to argue that this is evidence that aliens gave humanity civilization. Neither group considers that for a bronze age society without modern construction technology, the easiest, most stable, and ultimately the only way to build a large structure is simply to heap stone blocks on each other in a pyramidal form.

8-iii. Monotheism and Kathenotheism

As with other ancient cultures, the religion of Pharaonic Egypt featured a confusion of sometimes merging, sometimes distinct, gods and mythologies.

Monotheism of the strict (or fundamentalist) Abrahamic (Judaeo-Christian-Islamic) type was alien to Pharaonic Egypt and other ancient mythic cultures. The only example of this was the Pharaoh Akhenaten's (14th century B.C.E., Eighteenth Dynasty) attempt to institute a worship of the sun disc (Atenism) through the oppression of all other religions. This was too different from the standard mythic religion and did not catch on. It would take almost a millennium for strict monotheism to catch on among the Persians (early Zoroastrianism, 7th to 6th century B.C.E.) and Semites (Post-Exilic Judaism, 6th to 5th century B.C.E).

While each of the principal deities are monotheistic in a sense, they are better described as kathenotheism. This was a term coined by the philologist and orientalist Max Muller to mean the worship of one god at a time. It is similar to henotheism, the worship of one god while not denying the existence of others (unlike the later version of the Old Testament Yahweh).

Although Muller was referencing the Vedas, where each deity is treated as supreme in turn (hence the religious tolerance of India, in relation to the pre-modern West and Middle East), the same applies to the various gods and theologies of Egypt.

8-iv. The Pyramid Texts

The so-called *Pyramid Texts*, the earliest known body of religious writings, were discovered in the modern world by French archaeologist and Egyptologist Gaston Maspero (1846–1916), director of the French Institute for Oriental Archaeology in Cairo, in 1880. Continuing the orientalist theme, Maspero's son, Henri Maspero (1883–1945), who joined his father in Egypt in 1905, would go on to become an important Sinologist (China scholar), writing pioneering studies of Taoism, but was imprisoned and murdered by the Nazis for his part Jewish ancestry.

Written in Old Egyptian, the *Pyramid Texts* date to around 2350 to 2175 B.C.E., from the late Fifth and the Sixth Dynasty of the Old Kingdom, and extending to the Eighth Dynasty of the First Intermediate Period. They were inscribed on the walls and sarcophagi of nine tombs in the vast necropolis of Memphis, at Sakkara, on the west bank of the Nile River opposite modern-day Cairo. Unlike the later *Coffin Texts* and *Book of the Dead*, the *Pyramid Texts* were reserved only for the pharaoh and were not illustrated.

The spells of the *Pyramid Texts* were mostly concerned with the transformation of the deceased pharaoh into an *akh* (soul) who, if judged worthy, could mix with the gods. In keeping with the symbolic language, they describe the ways the pharaoh could travel, including the use of ramps, stairs, ladders, and, most importantly, flying. Here we see the ascent of the soul of the spirit in flight, as with shamanism, a common theme in esotericism in general. Many of these texts include the accomplishments of the pharaoh. They were used to guide the pharaohs to the afterlife and inform and assure the living that the soul made it to its final destination.

In this way, the pyramids and these instructions may have been involved with astral travel, the star maps guiding the soul [Fix, 1979]. Here the pharaoh, as an astral traveler, adopts the role of the shaman of the earlier tribal magical age, as the mediator between the gods (or the spirit world, or heaven) and humanity.

8-v. Atum and the Ennead

The *Pyramid Texts* also feature the earliest surviving versions of Egyptian theology and cosmogony. In these accounts, which are certainly even older than the inscriptions, the solar deity Atum (*neb tem*, the lord of totality) created the deities Shu (air) and Tefnut (moisture), representing the original male and female as well as the primordial elemental principles, by an act of masturbation, or spittle. Like the Rig Vedic Purusha and the Self of the Upanishads, Atum poured himself physically into creation. There is no developed psychological analogy in these texts, which present an image of physical creation almost at the level almost of an unadorned dream symbol [Campbell, 1962, p.85].

Atum's first appearance is represented by the primordial hill, represented by the first mounds of dirt and mud that can be seen when the floodwaters of the Nile recede, which become the original pyramid. He is also identified with the scarab god Khepri, representing the rising sun, being and becoming, as Atum-Khepri. The Egyptian hieroglyph of the sacred scarab (*Scarabaeus sacer*) represents both this insect itself, with the dung ball it pushes representing the sun being pushed over the horizon, the godform, and the principle of metamorphosis, transformation, and all possible becomings.

Khepri or Khepera, depicted in the form of a man having a scarab for a head, as a form of the rising sun, representing both matter on the point of passing from inertness to life, and also a dead body which is about to come into a new life in a glorious form. The seat of Khepera in the boat of the sun goes back as far, at least, as the Pyramid of Unas (Fifth Dynasty, Old Kingdom, c. 24th century B.C.E), and scarabs have been found not only in tombs of all ages in Egypt, but also in Greek islands and settlements in the Mediterranean, Phoenicia, and Syria. Queen Hatshepsut (c. 1507–1458 B.C.E., the fifth pharaoh of the Eighteenth Dynasty), the best known of several female pharaohs, declared herself to be "the creator of things which come into being like Khepera," Later scribes were fond of playing upon the word used as a noun, adjective, verb, and proper name [Budge, 1967, pp.cix-cx], and a late (3rd century C.E.) papyrus has the line "*kheper-i kheper kheperu kheper-kuy m kheperu n Khepri kheper m sep tepy*", or, roughly translated, "when I became, the becoming became, I have become the becoming (the form) of Khepri who came into being on the First Time" [Lamy, 1981, p.14].

Atum, as the source of all existence, is the "lord of kheperu," the archetypal sun at the dawn of creation. Khepera, as the entity embodied in, and the archetype behind, the rising sun, also symbolizes the initiate's rebirth [Uzdavinys, 2010].

Eventually, this became the Heliopolis Theology, the priestly system of the temple of the sun-god of Heliopolis, a late syncretic mythology. Atum, now identified with the sun god Ra as Atum-Ra, is described as self-created and emerging from the primal waters. In one version, Atum is in the midst of the Nun, the primordial chaos or nothingness. Nevertheless, he projects himself into existence, distinguishing himself from the Nun, thereby annihilating the Nun in its original inert state. A similar theme occurs in Indian Samkhya, where the presence of *purusha* (the transcendent conscious entity) disturbs the equilibrium of the *mulaprakriti* or prime matter.

Atum's power is so great that he can give birth to his own parents. Hence the term "Self-Begotten" is a recurring theme in Sethian gnosticism and Neoplatonism. This is a metaphor for self-emergence (*autopoiesis*), as in modern complexity theory.

Atum then brings forth Shu and Tefnut, who create the classic cosmic polarity of Earth and Sky. Although here, in contrast to the standard Proto-Indo-European arrangement, Earth, or Geb, is male, and the star-studded Sky, or Nut, is female. This may be because, in Egypt, the position of supreme God and creator is taken not by the sky deity but by the sun deity, who is given various names such as Atum, Ra, and so on.

And whereas Greek mythology (female Earth) would inspire the hippy alternative iconography of Gaia as the Earth mother, mainly thanks to James Lovelock's purely empirical Gaia Hypothesis [Lovelock, 1979], Egyptian mythology (female Sky) was incorporated into modern occultism via Aleister Crowley, as Nuit (variant spelling) appears in the first chapter of his *Book of the Law*, a channeled communication.

From Geb and Nut emerge two further pairs, Osiris and Isis, and Seth and Nepthys, representing the transition from the cosmological to the personal, and the appearance of good and evil (as represented by the trickster figure Set or Seth). Together, these comprise the Great Ennead of Heliopolis, the most developed Egyptian pantheon of deities (called *Neter*, meaning 'god' or 'goddess').

To the ancient Egyptians, Nine, or three times three, represents a multitude. Hence they called large groups "Enneads" (transcribed as *Pesedjet*) even if they had more than nine members. Moreover, the term was often extended to include all the deities. Perhaps this is why the Alexandrian (Hellenistic Egyptian) Neoplatonist Porphyry would later collate his teacher Plotinus' lectures in nine sets of nine.

Here, *ennead* means both the chief noetic (transcendent spiritual world) meta-structure of archetypes and the indeterminate number of divine forces, the plurality of gods [Uzdavinys, 2010].

This theogony or geneology, like the similar and perhaps influenced theogonies of Orphic and Hesiodic Greece, can be interpreted as a sort of proto-emanation doctrine. First, there is the abstract Source, Atum. Then the initial polar pair of Shu and Tefnut. Then the manifest polarity, the cosmos, of Earth and Sky, that appears in many mythologies. In contrast to the Hesiodic version of the female Gaia, here the Earth represents the male principle and the starry sky female. And finally, incarnate in that, the last four gods who are directly tied up with the drama of existence, duality, birth, death, sacrifice, and resurrection.

8-vi. The Ogdoad

A very different theology developed at Hermopolis, involving the primordial Eight principles, the *Ogdoad*, representing once again the primordial chaos (the Nun), the starting point of all Egyptian theogony. Here it is envisaged as a swampy mire, where four couples of serpents and frogs live. Their names are Naun and Naunet, meaning both 'the initial waters' and 'inertia'; Heh and Hehet, representing 'spatial infinity'; Kek and Keket, 'the darkness'; and Amun and Amunet, 'That which is hidden.' This latter couple is sometimes replaced by Niau and Niaut, 'the void.'

They are called the "fathers and mothers of Ra," the child emerging from the primordial lotus. As with the other accounts, this can be compared to the Biblical Genesis, when "the earth was without form and void, and darkness was upon the face of the deep," or tohu, usually translated as chaos.

The Nun and the Ogdoad can be interpreted as the indefinable substance from which the gods and the universe emerge. This is represented by the lotus, which has its roots in mud, its stem in water, and its leaves and flowers opening out into the air. This often appeared in Egyptian architecture and myth [Lamy, 1981, p.10-11]. Interestingly it also appears in the Indian religion and cosmology, whether independently or through some sort of influence is unclear.

In contrast to the Mesopotamian and Levantine *Chaoskampf* myth, here there is no pre-creation struggle, but rather the emergence of consciousness from the undifferentiated unconsciousness of matter, what Sri Aurobindo calls the Inconscient. In the Samkhya metaphysics of ancient India, this appears as *avyakta*, the original state of unmanifest *prakriti* (matter, nature, phenomena).

And here, there is some interesting numerological symbolism. In the later Pythagorean system of number speculation, even numbers of "female" and odd numbers "male." In the Chinese I Ching, an oracle that represents a microcosm of the binary or computational nature of the universe, the Yin polarity is likewise represented by the number two, or, given the threefold nature of the oracle, six, the yang by the number three, or nine.

Hence the Ogdoad, or number eight, is an even or "*Yin*" (receptive, "female polarity") number, very different from the dynamic Ennead or nine, a "*Yang*" (creative, "male polarity") number. But, showing the symmetry of the symbolism, whereas the Ennead is only two-dimensional (three squared or 3 x 3), the Ogdoad is three-dimensional. Two cubed (two to the third power) makes eight, or in binary 1000, or in base two powers 2^{2^2} (two raised to the (two to the two) power).

Eight on its side is the mathematical sign for infinity, which the mathematically-minded Greeks disliked and feared because it represented boundlessness and hence chaos. However, in 20th century "Pythagorean" astrology and numerology, which, despite its name, is not directly related to the Pythagorean and Neopythagorean tradition of classical times, the number eight is associated with the 8th sign of the zodiac, which is Scorpio, ruled by Pluto, the planet (or ice dwarf, depending on one's astronomical interpretation), named after the Roman God of the Underworld.

8-vii. Ptah and Memphis Theology

The Memphis theology is based around the creator god Ptah, represented in the form of a mummy-like Osiris, rather than a striding figure like the other chief gods. Only his hands are free, grasping a scepter composed of the symbols of life (*ankh*), power (*was*), and stability (*djed*). He is often shown standing on the plinth-shaped hieroglyph that is part of the name for Ma'at, the goddess of Truth. He is accompanied by Sekhmet, the lioness-headed goddess whose name means 'the powerful,' and Nefertum, 'the accomplishment of Atum,' thus constituting the first causal triad.

Ptah came to be associated with Apis, the sacred bull worshiped in the Memphis region, identified as the son of Hathor, one of the major deities in the Egyptian pantheon and usually depicted as a woman wearing a headdress of cow horns and a sun disk.

During the later period, Greek and Roman authors had much to say about Apis and the signs by which the calf was recognized, including the white marks on its neck and rump resembling a falcon's wings, and a scarab-like knot beneath its tongue. The worship of Apis was continued by the Greeks and, after them, by the Romans and lasted until almost 400 C.E.

Like all the Egyptian theologies, the Memphite religion was political, as the city needed to justify its status as the new capital. Ptah, the principal god of Memphis, was therefore given a new creation myth, in which all the other gods were contained within him, including the Heliopolitan Atum and the Hermopolitan Nun and Naunet.

Ptah is one of several Egyptian deities shown fashioning creation, a theme that would continue in the Hebrew creation account with Yahweh making Adam out of clay. In Jewish folklore and urban legend, this would lead to the story of the Golem of Prague, an artificial man made of clay.

8-viii. Amun-Ra

Finally, there is the Theban theology which, in keeping with the Egyptian family of religions, is also based on a primordial triad, in this case, Amun, Mut, and Khonsu. Theban theology presents Amun not merely as a member of the Ogdoad, but as the hidden reality behind all things.

Merging with the Sun god, Ra (also transliterated as Re), as Amun-Ra, he became the chief self-created creator deity in the Egyptian pantheon throughout the New Kingdom (16th to 11th centuries B.C.E.). Along with Osiris, Amun-Ra is the most widely recorded of the Egyptian gods as a champion of the poor or troubled and the object of personal devotion and piety. Like Isis (who would later merge with the Virgin Mary of Catholicism), he came to be worshiped outside Egypt; as Zeus-Ammon, he was identified with Zeus in Greece.

Schwaller de Lubicz argued the Egyptians were aware of the precession of the equinoxes. He linked the astrological age of Gemini (over 6000 B.C.E.) with the development of the dualistic themes in Egyptian religion, the age of Taurus (beginning 4000 B.C.E.) with the bull god Apis, and the age of Aries (some 2000 B.C.E.) with the god Amun, who was depicted as a ram. This only makes sense if one accepts his claim that Egyptian civilization dates back much farther than conventional chronology and dating shows. Rudolf Steiner similarly makes associations between astrological ages and culture periods. As he describes it, the Age of Gemini is associated with the Indian cultural epoch and the aspiring for the spiritual world, the Age of Taurus with the Persian, and the Age of Aries with the Mesopotamian. When esotericism does make claims regarding empirical science, archeology, and paleontology, it tends to do no better than religion. A better understanding is that these are mythic rather than empirical realities and imaginal insights.

8-ix. Mythic Symbolism

With its rich and elaborate symbolism, Egyptian symbolism cannot be understood in the rational, linear terms of modernity. It requires an intuitive, dream-like, magical, and mythic hermeneutic, similar to Jung's interpretation of alchemy. As with Chinese natural philosophy, the whole thing is based on a magical, sometimes comically literal worldview. For example, Thoth, the scribe of the gods, is represented by the sacred ibis (*Threskiornis aethiopicus*) because that bird has a long tapering bill like a bamboo reed, in which the beak, head, and neck are black in color, as if they've been dipped in ink, while the rest of the body and most of the plumage is white.

For this reason, creation accounts begin with the first mound emerging from the waters, rather than formless chaos, because of the receding of the Nile after the annual flood, depositing the fertile soil on which the narrow strip of Egyptian agriculture and civilization depended.

It is significant that, for all their sophisticated symbolism and developed occultism, the ancient Egyptians had no concept of a transcendent Absolute or universal consciousness, such as was developed in later centuries in India, Greece, and China. Everything in Egyptian religion, mythology, and occultism is concrete and literal. The same applies to other Mediterranean cultures and civilizations like the Babylonians, Hebrews, and Greeks.

It may be that there was no concept of a transcendent Absolute simply because there was no precedent for it. All knowledge is limited by the understanding of the time. Just as the Greek philosophers never developed empirical science along the lines of Galileo and Newton, so it took the renunciates of Vedic India years of introspection and meditation to realize the universal Self, as well as related concepts like karma and *ahimsa*. But once this was attained, techniques were promulgated, and anyone with sufficient discipline and willpower could follow these and arrive at the same experiences.

Egyptian religion and occultism are better understood as being pre-esoteric rather than esoteric. True esotericism could only develop through a confluence of metaphysics (rational philosophical speculation about ultimate reality), mysticism, and occultism during the first millennium B.C.E. Even if these insights are, in a sense, timeless, they do require a historical precedent.

8-x. Dying and Resurrected Gods

Egyptian religion also features a more personal figure as well as the kathenotheistic cosmic creator or sun god. This is Osiris, the god of resurrection and the afterlife, who filled a similar role to and may have been the inspiration and basis for the Christian Christ.

The Osiris myth of death and resurrection is one of several Mediterranean and Near Eastern mythologies of dying and resurrected gods, including Tammuz, Adonis, Attis, Dionysus, and Jesus. In *The Golden Bough*, James Frazer associated these myths with fertility rites and the cycles of the seasons.

This type of interpretation has fallen out of favor with contemporary (late 20th/early 21st century) academia, which prefers the contextualist interpretation, which builds its case from isolated external historical data, ignoring the intuitive understanding and gnosis provided by the imaginal (outer subjective) and phenomenological (middle subjective) dimensions. Hence Contextualist methodology has to be balanced by mythic, symbolic, and perennialist analysis, to avoid falling into atomistic secularism.

In terms of symbolism, Osiris and Ptah are depicted as mummies. The Apis bull is black, apart from the distinctive white marking. Both the mummy and the black color of the bull refer to the dark moon, into which the old moon dies and from which the new is born, as part of a cycle of waning and waxing, as Joseph Campbell observes [Campbell, 1962, p.89].

In the Jungian interpretation, this represents the transformation of the unconscious and the actualization of the Self-archetype (the god archetype, as I would call it.)

In the Osiris myth, Osiris is murdered and chopped into sixteen pieces which are scattered around Egypt by his brother Set, who usurps his throne. Osiris's wife, Isis, gathers the pieces and, with the help of other deities, including Thoth, credited with magical and healing powers, and Anubis, the god of embalming and funerary rites, is put back together. Only the penis is missing. In Egyptian symbolism, the phallus is a sign not just of virility and the life-giving principle but of cosmic power; hence, even goddesses are sometimes shown with an erect penis. Contrast this with Greek sculpture and art, where the penis is insignificant; according to Greek symbolism, with its emphasis on the transmutation of base desires, a very small, rather than very large and erect, penis was a sign of a hero.

Isis eventually relocates the missing member, reattaches it, and uses it to posthumously conceive their son, Horus. The remainder of the story switches the attention to Horus, who survives the various threats on his life and grows up to become Set's rival for the throne. Their often violent conflict ends with Horus's triumph, which restores Ma'at (cosmic and social order) to Egypt after Set's unrighteous reign and completes the process of Osiris's resurrection.

Osiris became the first mummy, as the gods' efforts to restore his body are the mythological basis for Egyptian embalming practices, which sought to preserve the body indefinitely, as the physical counterpart to the soul. Represented as new life after death, Osiris came to be associated with the cycles observed in nature, in particular sprouting vegetation and the fertile flooding of the Nile. The pharaoh gains eternal life through identification of Osiris in death. Later this would be extended to the ordinary worshiper. The worship of Isis and Osiris was already well established by 2400 B.C.E. and continued until the decline of the ancient Egyptian religion during the rise of Christianity in the Roman Empire.

Joseph Campbell, building on Frazer's observations, observed that the myth of the dead and resurrected Osiris so closely resemble those of Tammuz, Adonis, and Dionysos as to be practically the same, all referring to the rites of the murdered and resurrected divine king [Campbell, 1962, p.47].

Tammuz, or Dumuzid, was the Mesopotamian god associated with shepherds, fertility and vegetation, and the consort of the goddess Inanna (later known as Ishtar). He spent half the year in heaven, and the other half in the Underworld, and the hot, dry summers of Mesopotamia were believed to be caused by Tammuz's yearly death. Although it has also been argued that Inanna/Ishuar didn't descend into the Underworld to raise Dumuzi/Tammuz from the Underworld, but instead sent him there as her substitute [Yamauchi, 1978, p.150]. Clearly, these mythic narratives are more complex than they first appear, with many different versions, compressed as they may be from our current early 20th century perspective, making it hard to see the wood for the trees.

Tammuz is also included in the Sumerian King List (around circa 2000 B.C.E.), a document intended to legitimize the claims to power of the various city-states and kingdoms of the time by listing the cities, ruling kings, and the lengths of their reigns, which for the earliest and most mythologized span centuries or millennia.

Significantly, Osiris also possessed the crook and the flail of the shepherd and was also, according to associated legend, considered to have originally been a pre-dynastic king.

The cult of Tammuz spread to the Levant and to Greece as one of the mystery religions, where he became known as Adonis (a West Semitic name), while Isis and Osiris represented a different mystery religion or religions.

8-xi. Lunar and the Solar Mythology

According to Campbell, Tammuz and Osiris represent the Lunar mystery, as does the Vedic Soma, who in post-Vedic Hinduism becomes Chandra, the god of the Moon, associated with the night, plants, and vegetation.

Shiva, the Lord of Yogis, was likewise originally a lunar deity, as shown by his dark blue skin and the crescent moon in his hair. The iconography of a yogic figure is found in Indus Valley seals, representing the pre-Vedic civilization of the subcontinent. As with Ptah and the Apis bull, Shiva is also associated with a sacred bull, in this case Nandi, which means "giving delight" or "giving joy."

In contrast to the Sun, with its steady light, the moon is waning and waxing and is simultaneously mortal and immortal, bridging the two worlds. These gods are hence manifestations of the lunar polarity and its mysteries [Campbell, 1962, p.255]. The symbolic polarity of day and night consciousness, waking and dreaming, science and magic, male and female, has been commented on and tabulated by English psychologist Stan Gooch [Gooch 1972, pp.82-84, 200-201].

In Egypt, beginning with the 5th Dynasty of the Old Kingdom (early 25th to mid 24th century B.C.E.), the lunar mythology of Osiris and the Pharaoh's post-mortem identification with him, is replaced or at least supplemented by the solar mythology in which the Pharaoh is the son of the sun-god Ra.

8-xii. Chaos and Order

The battle between Horus and Set also relates to the cosmic polarity of Ma'at and Isfet. Isfet, meaning "injustice," "chaos," or "violence") was the opposite yet also the counterpart of Ma'at (meaning "order" or "harmony"). The pharaoh is appointed to achieve Ma'at, which means protecting justice and harmony by destroying Isfet. A responsible kingship meant Egypt would remain prosperous and at peace in Ma'at. When Ma'at was absent, the Nile-flood failed, and the country fell into famine. Ma'at is maintained, and Isfet is kept at bay by presenting the gods through rituals and offerings.

So whereas the Chaoskampf, the struggle against chaos, refers to the state before the current creation, the duality of order and chaos, or good and evil, as with Ma'at and Isfet, refers to maintaining creation.

Similar beliefs can be found in other mythic age religions. For example, the Vedic fire sacrifice maintains the order of the cosmos. The Greeks and Chinese made offerings to the gods. The Maya believed in the cyclical nature of time and the importance of maintaining the order of the universe, performing complex rituals, including human sacrifice. This reached its monstrous extreme with the Aztecs, who believed that human sacrifice was necessary to pay back the debt from when the gods gave their blood to create the world. So, to keep the sun moving across the sky and maintain the universe, the Aztecs had to feed the sun god Huitzilopochtli with human hearts (mostly, but not always, prisoners captured in war. Or if Tlaloc, the god of rain, was not supplied with sacrifices (in this case, children whose tears become the rain), the rain would not come, the crops would fail, and so on [Cawthorne, 2020].

In the Axial and post-Axial age religions such as Zoroastrianism, Apocalyptic Judao-Christianity, Syrian-Egyptian Gnosticism, and Manichaeism, this idea of chaos takes the form of a cosmic supernatural war between good and evil, in which history moves to the ultimate victory of the divine principle, and the defeat of evil. Unfortunately, this same cosmological and mythological mode of thinking continues today among fundamentalist Christians and conspiracy theorists, where there is a breakdown of rationality and retreat into the irrational and the shadow projection.

8-xiii. The Egyptian Afterlife

In contrast to the pessimism of the Babylonians, Hebrews, and Greeks, for whom death was basically the end of everything, the Egyptians devoted a tremendous amount of attention to the afterlife, first for the Pharaohs alone, as befitting their role as God-Kings who mediated between Heaven and Earth, but then later for the common people as well. This took the form of "books of the dead" describing post-mortem existence and what the deceased would need to know. These persisted with various iterations through the two thousand years and more of Egyptian civilization.

The earliest were the *Pyramid Texts*, so called because they were inscribed on the walls of pyramids during the Old Kingdom (c. 2700–2200 B.C.E.). These texts were to aid the pharaoh in completing his journey through the afterlife, explaining what paths he should take and the dangers he might face along the way.

Following these were the *Coffin Texts*, which dated to the Middle Kingdom period and just before (2100 to 1782 B.C.E.). These were collections of funerary spells written on coffins, meant to protect the deceased in the afterlife and provide them with the transformation magic they would need along their journey. This was the beginning of the democratization of the afterlife and the transition from a society centered on the State based on the God-King or Pharaoh (the ruler as the mediator between heaven and Earth) to being centered on the individual. Because ordinary Egyptians who could afford a coffin had access to these spells, the pharaoh no longer had exclusive rights to attaining a proper afterlife.

Finally, during the New Kingdom period, the *Book of Coming Forth by Day* (more usually but incorrectly translated as the *Book of the Dead*) was an extensive collection of spells giving protection and knowledge to the dead as they journeyed through the netherworld. These include material from the *Pyramid* and *Coffin Texts*, usually written on papyrus.

With all the attention they paid to the afterlife existence, one would expect the Egyptian metaphysics to be clear and understandable. But instead, one finds a bewildering array of different psychic and spiritual principles, each of which appears to have a separate existence after death, and even during life. For example, consider the following (brackets describe the ideogram used):

- *Khat* or *Kha* – (a fish) – the physical body.
- *Sahu* – (a mummy and a seal) – the "spiritual body"; a body which has obtained a degree of knowledge and power and has thus become incorruptible.
- *Ab* – (a vessel with ears as handles) – the "heart", the source of good and bad thoughts; the moral awareness of right and wrong.
- *Ka* – (a pair of upraised arms) – the double, image, character, disposition, or individual ego, which is created with, or even before, the physical being. Originally the *daimon*, *genius* or spiritual double of the pharaoh, which guided him in life and protected him in death; it later became the human presence that remains in the tomb, and partakes of food and other funerary offerings.
- *Ba* – (a human-headed bird) – the "soul," which, in some interpretations, ascends to the paradisiacal and the heavenly realms and enjoys an eternal existence there. However, in other explanations, it can travel for a while but needs to return to the tomb.
- *Khaibit* – (a fan, an object which intercepts the light) – the "shadow"; like the Ka and Ba it partakes of funerary offerings; and can detach from the body. References to the Khaibit are infrequent, and the meaning is usually obscure.

- *Akh*, *Khu*, or *Akhu* – (the ibis or phoenix) – the "spirit"; the radiant shining one; in some interpretations, the unified Ba and Ka which goes to the afterlife. In others, the transfigured dead which ascends to heaven and dwells among the gods or among the immortal pole stars which never set.
- *Sekem* – the power or form; generally, the references are obscure.
- *Ren* – the "name" which exists in heaven. In any psychically (as opposed to spiritually) based magical philosophy, to know the secret name of a person or entity is to have the power of that being.

This bewildering confusion prompted one despairing writer to complain:

> The precise meaning of ka, ba, ach (akh), `shm (sekhem), and so on is no longer clear to us. Well-meaning scholars try again and again and again to force the Egyptian idea of the soul into our traditional categories without enabling us to understand even a little of it any better. [Poortman, 1978, vol 1, p.108]

The reason for this lack of understanding is not only the absence of esoteric-occult knowledge on the part of the scholars, but also the fact that we are dealing with a civilization that spanned several thousands of years. It is evident that meanings would change throughout that long period, and new ideas and multiple schools of thought develop, so the same word is used in a totally different context.

Moreover, different religious, philosophical, and psychological writers give widely differing meanings to the same term. Even in contemporary occultism and esotericism, where one would expect greater precision, the definition of technical terms such as astral, etheric, mental, causal, and soul varies dramatically. So, we would have a situation where the same term seems to describe several different realities, or alternatively, two terms describe the same thing.

Certain concepts stand out. The *sahu* or incorruptible body could be compared to the diamond body (*vajra*) of Tibetan Buddhism, the *body-kedjan* referred to by Gurdfieff, the triple divine body of the Tamil Siddha adept Vallalar, or the supramental body referred to by Sri Aurobindo. Although these are not necessarily the same, there is a common theme of an immortal body or state attained through higher spiritual transformation.

Once the person has been appropriately mummified, the ka and ba are unified, resulting in the release of the akh. The akh is the glorified afterlife form, the deceased reconstituted as a being of light [DeConnick, 2016]. This is similar to Taoist Internal Alchemy (Nei Tan), where through specific breathing, visualization, and meditation practices, the two parts of the soul, the Po and the *hun* or spirit (*shen*), are united in a potential new subtle physical being, called the Immortal Fetus, which can continue after death [Wilhelm, 1962]. Gurdjieff's Fourth Way also has techniques for the purpose of developing an immortal astral body or soul (body-kadjan).

Once the deceased arrives at the Hall of Ma'at, he has to (following the instructions of the *Book of the Coming Forth by Day*) correctly address each of the forty-two Assessors of Ma'at by name, while denying committing any sins. Knowing each of the judges' names (Ren) is a magical act, since, in magical thinking, which describes the dynamics of the spirit world, knowing the true name of a being is to have power over it. As these assessors are spirit beings, this is equivalent to magical evocation.

After confirming that they are sinless, the heart (Ab) of the deceased is weighed against the feather of Ma'at to determine if it is pure enough to enter the Kingdom of Osiris. This test is usually performed by Anubis, the jackal-headed god of funerary rites and the Underworld, and sometimes also the guide of the dead.

If the deceased's heart balances, Thoth, the ibis-headed scribe of the Gods, records the result, and they are sent to Osiris, the god of the afterlife and of resurrection, who admits them to Sekhet-Aaru, the "Field of Reeds," the final destination for all souls who had been granted rebirth.

However, if the heart is heavier than the feather, it is devoured by the goddess Ammit, a monstrous being with the forequarters of a lion, the hindquarters of a hippopotamus, and the head of a crocodile, these being the three most dangerous animals known to ancient Egyptians, destroying the soul of the deceased.

The concept of the "Field of Reeds," that is, paradise or heaven, dates to the Fifth Dynasty (*fig 2*). It was visualized as a lush region, inhabited by gods and righteous souls, filled with waterfalls and other natural wonders. At least one text, the *Papyrus of Nebseni* (15th century B.C.E), is divided into numerous islands, between which travel by boat is necessary.

This is similar to out-of-body accounts of different planes or regions.

Fig 2. Sekhet-Aaru, the "Field of Reeds." This was the final destination for souls who had been granted rebirth in the afterlife. This concept evolved in the Fifth Dynasty. Sekhet-Aaru was an imaginal paradise, a lush region filled with waterfalls and other natural wonders. It was the exact equivalent of the spiritualist Summerlands, a concept first proposed by the 19th century medium and clairvoyant Andrew Jackson Davis as an actual physical locality on the other side of the galaxy and later downgraded to a mere spirit realm. Egyptian images, such as the *Papyrus of Nebseni,* depicted the land as being divided into numerous islands, to which travel by boat was necessary. This refers to the subtle physical theme of many worlds or realms, as also found in Vaishnavite cosmology and, to a lesser extent, the out-of-body experiences of Robert Monroe.

Facsimile of a vignette from the *Papyrus of Ani* (c. 1250 B.C.E.) is shown in the afterlife, farming, boating, and worshiping various gods in the marsh like Field of Hotep (field of offerings or field of peace). British Museum, Public domain, via Wikimedia Commons.

Very similar ideas were adopted many centuries later by Zoroastrianism. While they may well have developed independently, it is also possible the Persians may have borrowed them from later (Hellenistic period) Egyptians.

For all its rich and often obscure mythology, the ancient Egyptian conception reveals great insight and sophistication concerning the nature of personality-existence after physical death, so much so that many of their ideas could be used to form a framework of understanding that is still valid today. It is still possible to apply the occult knowledge of the Egyptians to a modern-day interpretation of the nature of afterlife existence.

8-xiv. Akhenaten, the Original Monotheist

Finally, mention should be made of an Egyptian oddity, the earliest known historical example of monotheism, that of Amenhotep IV, the tenth or eleventh pharaoh of the 18th Dynasty, New Kingdom.

He became a fanatic of the previously minor deity Aten (or Aton), the god of the sun disc, renaming himself Aken-Aten (variously spelled Akenaten, Akhenaten, Ahkanaten, Ihknaten, etc.), "he who is of service to Aten" or "Effective for the Aten." During his reign from 1353 or 51 to 1336 or 34 B.C.E., Aten became the supreme god of Egypt. Akhenaten changed the capital from Thebes to el-Amarna (halfway between Memphis and Thebes), the city of the cult of the Aten.

His queen, Nefertiti (c. 1370-c. 1330 B.C.E.), was in the modern world to be made famous by a striking stucco-coated limestone bust, believed to have been crafted in 1345 B.C.E. by the sculptor Thutmose, and representing the ideal of feminine beauty.

Akhenaten has been called the first Monotheist, and hence the predecessor to Judeo-Christian type monotheism. However, scholars have since disagreed on whether his religion was true monotheism, monolatry, or henotheism. The psychologist Sigmund Freud argued (in Moses and Monotheism) that Moses was an Egyptian (as implied by his name) who got his beliefs from Akhenaten, although few, if any, take this eccentric theory seriously. Even the occultist Aleister Crowley considered that he was Akhenaten in a previous life. All this is based on the 19th and early 20th century idea of linear progress, which assumed cultural evolution from animism to polytheism to monotheism, and hence to metaphysics and finally (according to Auguste Comte) positivism. However, a more in-depth analysis reveals that magical, mythic, and rational thinking developed in parallel rather than sequentially.

In his attempt to impose monotheism, Akhenaten destroyed or desecrated the temples of the other gods, including Amun, the main deity of the dynasty, as well as having the word "gods" in plural hacked out of inscriptions. However, esotericists Egyptologists R. A. and Isha Schwaller deLubicz argue that Akhenaten did not go against the canon of the inner temple but that he and Hatshepsut's seeming deviation was really part of the overall temple "plan."

The social and religious changes he brought about influenced contemporary art and sculpture. The rigid poses of traditional images were abandoned entirely. Instead, Akhenaten had his artists portray him in relaxed, natural poses, even showing physical imperfections like a pot belly. This unique style of Egyptian art is known as the Amarna style.

Ultimately, Akhenaten's attempt at reform failed. After his death, the Egyptians returned to their previous culture. Akhenaten's son Tuthankaton (the living image of Aton) changed the country's religion back to the original beliefs and changed his name to Tutankhamun (the living image of Amun).

At the same time, Akhenaten's combination of naturalistic realism and strict monotheism pointed the way to the great era of cultural and consciousness evolution, the Axial Age.

PART III

Axial Age Gnosis and Esotericism

9. THE AXIAL AGE

9-i. The Concept of the Axial Age

The Axial period is a term proposed by the German-Swiss psychiatrist and philosopher Karl Jaspers (1883-1969) to describe a dramatic period of cultural and intellectual development that took place between the 8th and 3rd centuries B.C.E., and which he saw as a turning point in the history of human thought and culture. Jaspers argued that this period was marked by a dramatic shift in the way that individuals and societies understood and related to the world.

Among the important developments of this period were the emergence of the major world religions, such as Judaism, Buddhism, and Hinduism, the development of rational thought and abstract thinking, as represented by Greek philosophy, and the emergence of new forms of political organization and social structure. These established foundational ideas and values that have shaped Western society ever since.

This simultaneous but independent appearance of thinkers and philosophers in different areas of the world was remarked on by many authors in the 18th and 19th centuries. These include the Scottish barrister, folklorist, philosopher, and socialist John Stuart Stuart-Glennie (1841-1910), who developed a very similar theory, referring to it in 1873 as "the moral revolution" [Wikipedia – Axial Age]. Like Jaspers, he believed this was an empirical fact of history, independently of religious considerations.

Jaspers argued that during the Axial Age, the spiritual foundations of humanity were laid simultaneously and independently in China, India, Persia, Judea, and Greece. He gives several examples, including Confucius, Lao-Tse, Mo Ti, Chuang Tse, Lieh Tzu, and many others representing the development of the various schools of Chinese philosophy; the Upanishads,

Buddha, and, as with China and Greece, the whole gamut of philosophical possibilities, including materialism and nihilism; in Iran, Zarathustra's religion of moral choice between good and evil; among the Hebrews the prophets from Elijah by way of Isaiah and Jeremiah to Deutero-Isaiah; in Greece the epics of Homer, the various philosophers such as Parmenides, Heraclitus and Plato, and the tragedians like Thucydides and Archimedes.

9-ii. The Origin of Metaphysics

With the rise of rational thought in the philosophy and proto-science of Greece, China, and India, there developed not only the beginnings of science and investigation into the physical world, but also the idea of metaphysics, and from ordinary metaphysics, gnostic metaphysics, or esotericism, developed. Again, however, this proceeded in different directions in each civilization.

In the first millennium B.C.E., philosophers developed metaphysical systems independently in India, China, and Greece.

In Vedic and Upanishadic India, there was the insight that there is only one consciousness: the same Self in you is the Self in all beings and things. In Vedanta and Mahayana Buddhism, this became the doctrine that only this transcendental reality is truly real. Hence the two truths, the Absolute Truth and the Relative Truth. This metaphysic can be called Nonduality because it rejects the idea that the world of differences and dualities is real. It represents the principal of Consciousness, the pure observer or witness behind and watching all phenomena, while itself not touched by it.

In China, everything was explained in terms of the combination of Yin and Yang, with Yin being the passive and Yang the creative. Both Yin and Yang were derived from an original Tao, which is like the Universal Self or Absolute Truth of Indian metaphysics.

And in Ancient Greece, as represented by the teachings of Pythagoras and Plato, there developed the idea of a transcendent and perfect spiritual world over a changing and relative material world. Spiritual here means the world of pure archetypes, which for Pythagoras were the first ten numbers, and for Plato, the highest moral ideals such as Goodness, Truth, Beauty, and Justness.

9-iii. From Mythic to Rational-Mental

The Axial Age represents both socio-cultural and a collective consciousness transition from the emphasis on a mythic to a rational-mental mode of consciousness and understanding of reality. This is called the Zeitgeist, the spirit or consciousness of the age. It is possible to observe the Zeitgeist changing even today, for example, the transition in the West from a society based on academic expertise and knowledge to a sort of neo-barbarism and chaos based on warring tribal ideologies, in this case, caused by the technological shift from print to digital media [Kazlev, 2022].

In the past, society and technology changed much more slowly, so shifts and revolutions that today can occur over mere years would take decades or even centuries.

As was mentioned earlier in the context of hunter-gatherer and animistic cultures, it is not that people's brains or cognitive processes changed; rather than there was an environmental, cultural, and collective shift, for example, from nomadic hunter-gatherer to a settled urban and agricultural-based lifestyle, which in turn brought about a change of consciousness, for example, an attitude of alienation from nature, social stratification, and emphasis on the God-King as the mediator between Heaven and Earth. In other words, civilization.

In the same way, here there is the transition between early civilization, based on mythic thinking, and later cultures, based on a rational but still pre-modern worldview. This doesn't mean that mythic or imaginal thinking disappeared. Rather it existed alongside and was now interpreted in terms of the rational-mental.

As Jung showed, mythic thinking is the same everywhere. The archetypal tropes and symbols of transformation are universal. Obviously, there is some difference, for example, between the Mesopotamians and the Egyptians. But the basic tropes are the same and continue even today. For example, there are evangelicals with a mythic creationist worldview. Whereas during the Axial Age, cultures and consciousness explored different directions, from the very individual emphasis on morality in Zoroastrianism, to the Indian mystical aspiration for liberation from phenomenal existence, to the Semitic idea of a pact or covenant with a deity, to the Chinese polarity of Yin and Yang, to the Greek emphasis on rational inquiry as a way of understanding the universe. Which isn't to deny parallels; the Chinese and Indians also put a strong emphasis on natural philosophy.

The following chapters explore these various topics.

10. PERSIAN DUALISM

10-i. Zarathustra and Zoroastrianism

Zoroastrianism or Mazdeanism is one of the world's oldest surviving religions, based on the teachings of the Iranian-speaking prophet Zarathustra (also called Zoroaster), who lived in eastern Iran or thereabouts, probably around the 7th to 6th century B.C.E., during the early Axial Age. Some have suggested as early as the 10th century B.C.E., which would make him far ahead of his mythic period contemporaries. He seems to have been a reformer of the earlier polytheistic religion. This, in turn, was based on Indo-Aryan ideas dating back to the Indo-Europeans of the 2nd millennium B.C.E., representing the original beliefs from which Vedism of ancient India was also derived.

Like the Hebrews of one or two centuries later (assuming a more conservative dating for his life), Zarathustra taught the worship of a supreme God. He called this supreme being Ahura Mazda, the "Wise Lord" or "Lord of Wisdom," an uncreated and benevolent deity representing the earliest example of true monotheism.

According to legend, Zarathustra received a vision at a riverbank from a being of light identifying itself as Vohu Manah ("good purpose") and informing him that there was only one god, Ahura Mazda. Only after King Vishtaspa (an equally semi-legendary figure) became his patron who helped propagate and defend the faith, did Zoroastrianism become an influential belief system. In non-Zoroastrian Sistan or Sakastan (now Eastern Iran and Southern Afghanistan) texts, Vishtaspa is portrayed as a wicked ruler of the Kayanian dynasty. In other words, there was a lot of religious rivalry and bad feelings even then.

From a local religion in eastern Iran or Central Asia, Zoroastrianism expanded during the Achaemenid period. This was the first great Persian Empire, founded by Cyrus the Great in 550 B.C.E., when it came into contact with western Iranian beliefs.

In the city of Persepolis, built under the reign of the Persian King of Kings, Darius I (who reigned from 522 B.C.E. until his death in 486 B.C.E.), the solar symbolism of the Lord of Light of the Aryan prophet Zoroaster shone with the radiance of the sun itself on earth, sending forth its rays. [Campbell, 1962, p.255]. By this time, Zoroaster's original monotheism seems to have been compromised by a belief in other gods, although Ahura Mazda remained the supreme deity [Gier, 1994].

Alexander's conquest of Persia in 330 B.C.E. meant syncretic Hellenistic beliefs displaced Zoroastrianism. It would only be revived some centuries later during the late Parthian period (early centuries C.E.) and would continue as the state religion until the Muslim conquest of Persia (7th century).

10-ii. The History of the Written Texts

The oldest texts of Zoroastrianism are the Gathas, or songs attributed to Zarathustra himself, believed to have been orally transmitted by his followers for centuries. These are included in a larger body of texts called the *Avesta*. Avestan was an early Iranian language almost identical to that of the *Rig Veda*, which is the most ancient text of the Indian religions. Following the Gathas came the *Young Avesta*, which dates to the Achaemenid period (pre-Hellenistic). According to legend, Alexander the Great's soldiers destroyed most of these.

The surviving texts of the *Avesta* are thought to derive from a lost master copy that dates to the Sasanian Empire (224–651 C.E.), made through collation and recension of even earlier texts. The oldest surviving manuscript is as late as the early 14th century C.E.

Finally, there are the Pahlavi (Middle Persian) sources, which date to around the 9th-11th century C.E. However, there are various myths regarding the pre-Sasanian history of the *Avesta*, and these only go back to the Pahlavi books.

10-iii. Thoughts, Words, and Deeds

The core of Zoroastrianism in the Gathas is the worship of Ahura Mazda, who is the ultimate source of existence.

In contrast to Semitic monotheism, Persian monotheism is associated with duality. Under Ahura Mazda are two opposing forces, Spenta Mainyu, the Holy or creative mentality, and Angra Mainyu, the destructive spirit or mentality. This ties in with earlier themes, such as the Mesopotamian Chaoskampf or the Egyptian Ma'at and Isfet, although it is different enough to have been developed independently.

As well as being an emanation or aspect of Ahura Mazda, Spenta Mainyu is associated with seven heavenly beings, known as the Amesha Spenta, the bounteous or holy immortals, who are given sovereignty and guardianship over different aspects of creation. Asha (Truth/Righteousness) is the primary spiritual force, cosmic order, or reason, which comes from Ahura Mazda. It can be compared with the Egyptian Maat, the Vedic *rta* (both meaning "truth"), the Greek and later the Christian *logos*, the Buddhist *Dharma*, and so on.

According to Sri Aurobindo, the Vedic terms *Satyam* (Reality), *Ritam* (Truth), and *Brihat* (Vastness) (*Atharva Veda* 12.1.1), together constitute the formula of the Supramental consciousness that will bring about the transformation of the world. In a sense, Sri Aurobindo's Integral or Supramental Yoga is the continuation of the original Zoroastrian theology.

In addition, there is *Manah* (Purpose), *Khshatra* (Dominion), *Armaiti* (Devotion), *Haurvatat* (Wholeness and Health), and *Ameretat* (Immortality). Later, attributes like good and best were added. Hence Manah became *Vohu Manah*, the "Good Purpose."

Each of the seven has an antithetical counterpart associated with Angra-mainyu, for example. *Asha* (Truth) opposes *Druj*. The resulting cosmic conflict involves all of creation, mental/spiritual and material.

Druj, meaning falsehood and disorder, comes from Angra Mainyu, the destructive spirit or mentality. In later Zoroastrianism, Angra Mainyu was elevated to a higher position as the enemy (which implies in some way the equal) of Ahura Mazda, and is referred to as "Ahriman."

In the *Younger Avesta*, Spenta Mainyu has less prominence, and the main task of opposing Angra Mainyu now falls to Ahura Mazda. The Amesha Spenta and various other deities called Yazatas, meaning "worthy of worship," are venerated more prominently. In the still later Pahlavi sources, Zoroastrianism is an entirely dualistic religion [Emadinia, 2017, pp. 48-46]. Spenta Mainyu is now called Vohu Mainu, the Good Mind.

Man is created with free will; hence, one's choices define one's values and existence. Therefore, in accepting Zoroaster's message, one dedicates oneself to the principles of Good Thoughts, Good Words, and Good Deeds [Mark, 2019]. Interestingly, Tibetan Buddhism refers to taming and properly using the body, speech, and mind.

Each Amesha Spenta represents a good moral quality that mortals should strive to obtain. In this way, through good thoughts, words, and deeds, each individual should endeavor to assimilate the qualities of an Amesha Spenta into oneself.

As with Vedic India, the sacred words or *mantra* has soteriological powers. Like the biblical "let there be light," but more so, Ahura Mazda, or Ohrmazd (as he is called in Pahlavi), fashions his creations through a sacred recitation (*yasna*). His primordial recitation of the Ahuna Vairya formula (prayer, mantra, invocation) – which has talismanic virtues and healing power – as well as being a potent weapon against demons), means Ahriman's ultimate defeat.

In Zoroastrian eschatology, Ahura Mazda will ultimately prevail over Angra Mainyu, at which point reality will undergo a cosmic renovation called *Frashokereti*, and limited time will end. Then, all of creation, even the souls of the unredeemed dead, will be resurrected and united with Ahura Mazda in the *Kshatra Vairya* (meaning "best dominion").

10-iv. *The Duality of Light and Darkness*

Although the theme of a duality between good and evil can be found in ancient Egypt in the personalities of Osirus, later Horus, and Set, this was never formalized in a metaphysical or cosmological sense. Like the

Scandinavian Loki, Set remains a somewhat ambiguous figure, still part of the original undifferentiated mythic matrix of the collective unconscious, like the original Trickster theme.

The actual duality (or war) between good and evil only begins with later Zoroastrianism, with the two cosmic forces of Ahura Mazda (or Ohrmazd) and Angra Mainyu (or Ahriman). In Jungian terms, this was the differentiation of Self and Shadow, which would later appear in Christianity as the dichotomy of Christ and Satan, one all good, the other all evil.

For Jung, the duality of ego and shadow, or self and shadow, was very real, but only existed at the level of the psyche. As a Kantean, Jung considered metaphysics to be futile. But at an actual esoteric, metaphysical level, good and evil are real and define moral existence. Anyone who doubts this must consider man's inhumanity to man and other sentient species and the natural world as a whole. And, as well as that larger impersonal context, some people simply are evil, not in the sense of being traumatized or abused as children and hence internalizing the monster and repeating that, but for no other reason than that's what they are.

Dualistic cosmologies such as later Zoroastrianism, Apocalyptic Judaism and early Christianity, Gnosticism, Mandeanism, Manichaeism, Shi'ism (both Ismaili and Twelver), Lurianic Kabbalah, Theonist Cosmic Philosophy, and on a more superficial level popular horror fiction of the Omen and AntiChrist genre, variously describe the cosmic tension of the two moral opposite forces, which from a monistic point of view is part of the dialectic of cosmic pre-creation Fall and Restitution.

I relate this to the fundamental cosmic duality, which is both metaphysical (for example, the phrase metaphysical evil is sometimes used for the adverse powers) and transphysical (the spirit world or non-physical realities). Here the transphysical includes two very different realities, which can be referred to as Supernal (being above) and Infernal (being below), as with, for example, the mythology of Dante and Milton, medieval Zoroastrianism, and the spatial arrangement of Jain heavens and hells. Here above and below are states of consciousness and subtle being existence, referring to the degree of freedom or limitation of the soul, with regular physical existence between these two. For some doctrines, however, such as Gnosticism, Manichaeism, and Lurianic Kabbalah, the physical universe itself is the fallen state.

Hence the psychophysical ego and, for that matter, the physical Earth and physical universe is the field of battle between good and evil, Self and Shadow. Jung, noting the reality of this duality in the psyche, could conceive of no way out of this dichotomy, other than coming to terms with one's shadow. Hence the popularity in the human potential and similar personal development movements of "Shadow Work," bringing one's repressed Shadow contents to the light of consciousness and addressing, dealing with, and incorporating it. This is even valuable and necessary, but it is only on the personal, individual level, in keeping with the emergent physicalist worldview of modernity, which is the highest narrative of the secular Western world. This contrasts with the more cosmic scope of Zoroastrianism, Lurianic, Integral Yoga, and other themes of the conquest of evil and the eventual victory of the Divine.

10-v. From Gloomy Afterlife to Moral Eschatology

In early Persian beliefs, predating Zarathustra but continuing into Zoroastrianism, after death, the soul or spirit, called the *urvan*, remains for three days before departing for the subterranean kingdom of the dead. After that, a beautiful maiden appears to righteous souls, as the personification of the soul's good thoughts, words, and deeds. For the wicked person, an ugly old hag appears instead.

The Persian underworld resembles the Mesopotamian Realm of Ereshkigal, Queen of the Dead, where shades roam in eternal twilight. The Persian version is ruled by Yima, whose name is almost the same as Yama, the Indian God of the Dead. As mentioned earlier, Yima goes back to Indo-European or even the Proto-Indo-European creation story. The idea that the first king, and the first man to die, becomes the lord of the afterlife, is similar to the 19th century *Oahspe Book*, where there are no gods or spiritual hierarchies as such, only disincarnate human spirits which try to rule over the recently deceased. According to Egyptian legend, Osiris also began as an ancient Pharaoh.

As with Chinese ancestor worship, the Egyptians, and other ancient cultures, the spirits depend on rituals performed by their descendants living on Earth [Mark, 2019].

This original pessimistic afterlife was replaced in Zoroastrianism by what could be called "moral eschatology" [Emadinia, 2017, p.16], the idea that post-mortem existence depends on one's moral status and deeds during life. Here the magical spells, passwords, and invocations used by the soul in the Egyptian afterlife are replaced by one's actions and moral and spiritual state of consciousness.

This marks the distinction between an earlier mythic culture stage or religion, characterized by a pantheon of archetypes/gods, representing amoral cosmic forces, as in Jung's interpretation of the amoral Yahweh as a force of nature in which good and evil are undifferentiated, and one in which the cosmos as polarized into good and evil, as in Christ (the Light) and Satan (the Shadow). Whereas man is helpless in the face of capricious gods, the moral revolution of Zoroastrianism, and later, the faith revolution of Christianity, gives assurance of salvation in the case of individual morality.

These various Zoroastrian ideas, which began in the Achaemenid period and fully developed in the Sasanian period, such as free will, judgment after death, heaven and hell, angels and demons, the resurrection, and the restitution of the cosmos, developed in the later first millennium B.C.E., perhaps beginning with the Hebrews during their time under the Persians. From there, they spread to, or perhaps independently developed in Second Temple Judaism, the Essenes, Jerusalem, and Pauline Christianity, and later forms such as Coptic, Eastern Orthodox, and Catholic churches. Persian cosmology was influential in Manichaeism and later in Suhrawardi's school of Illuminism, mystical Shia'ism, and (from the latter) Babism and Bahá'ísm. Gnosticism also incorporates similar cosmological ideas, although these may have been acquired independently from Jewish polemic or via late Egyptian mysteries.

11. THE INDIAN METAPHYSICAL REVOLUTION

11-i. The Indus Valley Civilization

The Indus Valley, or Harappan, civilization, was a bronze age civilization that developed in the northwest region of South Asia and the Indian subcontinent during the period from around 3300 to 1300 B.C.E., although it was at its height from 2600 to 1900 B.C.E. Rivaling in extent the contemporary civilizations of Egypt and Mesopotamia, it is known from sites as far apart as northeast Afghanistan and northwestern India. The best known archeological sites however are at Mohenjo-daro (in Sindh in the east) and Harappa (in Punjab, in the west), both in modern-day Pakistan. Indus Valley developments included city planning, engineering, and crafts such as pottery and metalworking.

Of particular relevance to the current study is a striking soapstone impression seal (intended to leave an impression in clay or wax) (*fig.3*). Called the Pashupati seal, it was found at Mohenjo-daro. It shows a seated, possibly three-faced (similar to the later deity of Brahma), figure wearing a horned head-dress, sitting in what seems to be a yogic posture and surrounded by animals. Pashupati, or "Lord of the animals," is one of the names of Shiva. The seal is dated to around 2350 to 2000 B.C.E., or even as early as 2500 to 2400, being of the Mature Harappan Phase [Mapacademy, 2022], and has been interpreted as the earliest representation of the Tantric deity Shiva, the Lord of Yoga.

Fig. 3. The Pashupati seal, unearthed in 1928–29 at Mohenjo-daro, in the Indus Valley, in what is now Sindh province in southeastern Pakistan. It shows a horned, three-faced figure, seated in an apparent yogic pose, surrounded by animals. This figure has been considered an early representation of Shiva, the god of the yogis, although this interpretation has been challenged. The exact age is uncertain, but it is generally dated to the Intermediate I Period, around 2350–2000 B.C.E. National Museum, New Delhi. Nomu420, CC BY-SA 3.0, Wikimedia Commons.

Assuming this interpretation is correct, which is by no means certain, the yogic tradition of self-transformation of North India is equal in age to the oldest Egyptian funerary texts, the *Pyramid Texts* of the Fifth and Sixth Dynasties (c. 2400-2300 B.C.E.) and *Coffin Texts* of the First Intermediate period (c. 2130-1938 B.C.E.). This would mean that both ancient civilizations independently and simultaneously developed techniques for self transformation, the Egyptian tradition with spells or magic formulas regarding passage through the afterlife (this later developing into Gnosticism and Western occultism), and Yoga being the transcendence of bodily existence during life. Significantly, no such tradition developed in Mesopotamia, which instead emphasized divination and astrology.

A number of Indus Valley symbols have been found on stamp seals, tablets, ceramic pots, and other materials. Some 400 to 600 distinct symbols are known (some of which can be seen at the top of the Pashupati seal. Inscriptions are usually only around five characters in length. They have never been decoded, and it is not even certain that they constitute an actual language. If they do, they may be related to, or a form of, proto-Dravidian. The Dravidian language family today is limited mostly to southern India and northern and eastern Sri Lanka, although pockets are found elsewhere in India and Pakistan. This language is quite distinct from both the Afro-Asiatic or Hamito-Semitic language family (which includes Ancient Egyptian, Semitic (including Akkadian)), Sumerian (a distinct language isolate that cannot be classified into a larger language family), and Indo-European.

Philology, the study of language, goes back at least to the classical world. Modern philology began with scholars like the orientalist William Jones (1746-1794). One of the founders of modern Indology, Jones noted strong similarities between Sanskrit, Greek, and Latin. He was the first to propose the idea of an Indo-European language family, descended from a common, now lost, ancestral language.

Languages are based on, or derived from, ethnic groupings. Concerning the distinction between Indus Valley (Proto-Dravidian?) and Vedic (Indo-European) civilization, there developed the idea that the Indo-Aryans people migrated down into the Indian subcontinent from Central Asia and Iran beginning around 1500 B.C.E., supplanting the Harrapans and establishing the Vedic religion in India. If this interpretation is correct, the Pashupati seal implies that Tantra, which developed later around deities like Shiva and Kali, was actually a synthesis between indigenous aboriginal beliefs and those of the Aryan immigrants from the north.

Aryan in this context refers to a language and ethnic designation used by Indo-Iranians and Indo-Aryan speakers during the Vedic period. It was later used by "master race" philosophers such as the French writer Joseph Arthur de Gobineau (1816-1882) and the British-German anti-semitic philosophy Houston Stewart Chamberlain (1855-1927) becoming the basis of Nazi ideology, which also incidentally appropriated the swastika, an ancient Indo-European solar symbol.

In the late 1940s and mid 50s British archaeologist and army officer Robert Mortimer Wheeler (1890-1976) gave a new spin on this (perhaps influenced by the recent war against Nazi Germany), proposing and popularizing the idea that Aryan invaders from the north caused the extinction of the Indus Valley Civilization. He interpreted the presence of unburied corpses in the upper levels of Mohenjo-daro as the victims of massacres by the invading Aryans. However, his theory was refuted by later discoveries at Harappa.

Recent DNA studies go further by supporting the genetic identity of Harrappans and modern Indians, rejecting the theory of migration of Iranian or Central Asian peoples into India [Sharma, 2019].

Regardless of which interpretation is correct, the current view is that the Indus Valley Civilization was already in decline by the mid second millenium B.C.E., probably as a result of environmental factors such as climate change or even the alteration in the course of the Indus river.

11-ii. *The Vedas*

The oldest and most revered of the Indian sacred texts of the immigrants from the north are the Vedas (literally "knowledge" or "wisdom"). These developed from the same Indo-Aryan religion and mythology that gave rise to Zoroastrianism in Persia, and are dated in their oral form to around 1200 to 1500 B.C.E.

Apart from the earlier texts from Egypt and Mesopotamia, the province now of scholars, mythographers, and esotericists, these are the world's oldest religious scriptures still in practice. According to legend, they were said to be revealed to the Vedic Rishis or seers in meditation. Although in modern times, there are said to be four Vedas (*Rig, Sama, Yajur,* and *Atharva*), in the Upanishads, only three are listed (*Rig, Sama,* and *Yajur*). In fact, there is really only one Veda, the oldest, largest, and most important one, the *Rig Veda*. This is a collection of over 1,000 hymns, addressed to various gods, with many invoking Agni, the sacred fire. The *Sama Veda* is only a collection of *Rig Veda* hymns that are used for singing. The *Yajur Veda* is a small book that gives directions on one type of ritual. And the *Atharva Veda* is only a collection of theurgical mantras to be recited for the cure of various afflictions or to be recited over the herbs to be taken as medicine for those afflictions, but has since been incorporated into the modern alternative/holistic healing or Wellness movement. There are also commentaries, called the Brahmanas, which date to around 900 B.C.E. These texts were entirely oral, preserved by a priestly Brahmanic tradition.

As with Zoroastrianism, fire altars were central to ancient Vedic religious life and the place where many *yajnas* or rituals are still performed in the presence of the purifying fire. Similarly, in Vedism, the central element is the fire sacrifice, which is considered the source of time, space, and the universe. The building of the fire altar represents the symbolic reconstruction of the cosmos. The proper placement of sacrificial implements and correct chanting of mantras (sacred syllables) enables the turning of the year and the correct order of the three realms. While Agni, the fire god, is of central importance, the Vedas also speak of Father Sky (Dyaus, same etymological root as Zeus), Indra, the original King of the Gods (Deva), with myths and powers that are similar to other Indo-European sky deities, and Earth (Prithvi).

In the Vedas, the cosmos is divided into three *lokas* or worlds: *bhur* (earth), *bhuvah* (air), and *svah* (heaven), these being also the three worlds of Asiatic Shamanism (which may indeed be influenced by Indo-Aryan elements, rather than the reverse). These are not only spatial but also mental states. Loka can also mean the "freedom to exist unimpeded" or "expansiveness" as much as it can mean a physical location [Kloetzli & Patton, 1987/2005].

In one famous cosmological hymn (*Rig Veda* 10:90), the universe itself is presented as the cosmic person (*Purusha*), who is sacrificed in a primordial ritual. From the parts of his body emerge the various elements of the universe and the sacrifice, the most important of which are the four social categories or "colors" or *varna*, popularly but incorrectly interpreted as castes. These are the *brahmins* (priests), *kshatriyas* (kings, warriors), *vaishyas* (merchants and artisans), and *shudras* (craftsmen and servants).

The word "caste" is from the Portuguese word "*casta*," used by early traders to describe India's complex class structure of varnas, governing religious, social, and economic interactions, including hundreds of sub-castes called *jatis*, literally birth groups.

The reference to color would seem to refer to the lightly-skinned Aryan invaders from the North taking over from the indigenous and darker-skinned Dravidians, who are now relegated to the lowest social categories.

The story of the cosmic man whose body became the world or the universe is found in Babylonian (Kingu), Chinese (Pangu), and Norse (Ymir) creation myths. More esoteric variations are found in Gnosticism and Manichaeism with the spiritual Anthropos, and in Lurianic Kabbalah with the Adam Kadmon as the original archetypal form of the En Sof or Absolute.

Much of the Vedic material is mythological and symbolic, as with Egyptian, Mesopotamian, and other ancient teachings. Although defining them this way is still from the perspective of the rational intellect, the default instrument of Western modernity. From the Indian (Hindu) perspective, the Vedas only appear mythic because the keys to symbols and evocative figures are not easily understood by the modern mind [Aurobindo, 1995; Deshpande, 2018]. The lexicon of the Vedas requires a certain degree of spiritual preparation to grasp, besides a basic sense of ancient Sanskrit. Traditions are understood best through mystical awareness, especially regarding a mythic/premodern interpretation of nonduality. This is a different faculty to the middle mental. The same can also be said about the other esoteric-mythic traditions, such as Pharaonic Egypt, with its profound theogonies, sacred architecture, occult symbolism, and Pythagorean and Platonic arthimosophy.

11-iii. *The Upanishads*

The early to mid-first millennium B.C.E. is marked by a paradigm shift: from high mythic symbolism to contemplative mysticism and metaphysics, from Vedic ritual guaranteeing the cosmic order to personal liberation and spiritual enlightenment. This is part of a collective consciousness transition in the evolution of civilization worldwide, referred to in different ways by various visionary authors [Gebser, 1986; Jaynes, 1976]. However, as mentioned, one must be careful to avoid rationalistic reductionism. This transition appears most clearly in India in the Upanishads, a corpus of treatises from about the seventh or eighth century B.C.E. onward.

The word Upanishad means "to sit down near"; i.e., to sit at the feet of the Master. They take the form of dialogues between teacher and student and mark the transition from the fire altar of the Vedic literature to questions of the deeper, inner meanings of the ritual, especially as it gives insight into the origin, basis, and support of the universe. Here the emphasis has shifted to a new principle called Brahman, which means to expand or grow. This is distinct from the similar words for the original commentaries and the priestly caste [Eck, 1994; Kloetzli & Patton, 1987/2005]. The Upanishads are also called "Vedanta," meaning the end or culmination of the Vedas. The word Vedanta also refers to one of the six branches of Indian philosophy.

Brahman is referred to in hundreds of Vedic hymns with different meanings. Still, in the Upanishads, it comes to mean the principle or ultimate reality behind every being and every element in the universe, the Whole that transcends even the gods (*Brihadaranyaka Upanishad* 2:5). Specifically, there is, in the early Upanishads, the identity of the individual self or consciousness (*atman*) with the Absolute Reality, Brahman. It's as if the center of gravity of esoterism and gnosis was already shifting from Egypt – at this time in religious and political decline following the end of the New Kingdom in 1070 B.C.E. – to Northern India.

Here we have the Great Sayings (Mahavakya) such as "I am Brahman" (*Brihadaranyanka Upanishad*, I. 6.11-11), "This Self is verily Brahman" (*Brihadaranyanka Upanishad*, II.5.19; IV. 4.5), and "That art thou" (*Chandogya Upanishad*, VI.8.7) [Radhakrishnan, 1953].

One of the crucial figures here is the legendary philosopher and sage Yajnavalkya, who often appears in the *Brihadaranyaka Upanishad*, describing the ineffable nature of Brahman as *neti neti* ("not this, not this"), ideas that would later be developed in Madhyamika Buddhism, as well as independently appearing in the West in the late Neoplatonism of Damscius and Pseudo-Dionysius,

The realization that the "I" or self is ultimately synonymous with the Absolute or "God" – both the metaphysical god or First Principle of philosophy and the anthropomorphic god of religion – is one of the great insights of humanity. The unitive state is the basis of the Perennial Philosophy and the mystical experience [Huxley, 1970; Stace, 1961].

This universal self, in phenomenological terms the transcendental ego, replaces the old mythic, kathenotheistic, polytheistic, and monotheistic theology and cosmology, in which man as helpless before the capriciousness of god or the gods, who must be placated through worship and offerings. Instead, the focus of being shifts from the other, the outside reality (which in the case of god or the gods includes the collective unconscious) to the self or the immediate I-ness.

This is the transition from myth to metaphysics, from limitation (as a finite created being subject to the whim of the gods or of god) to identity with the All, from the collective unconscious that defines the premodern mythic world to limitless transcendent consciousness.

11-iv. Reincarnation and Liberation

Along with the insight of the transcendent, immortal "I', the concept of reincarnation, *karma*, and *samsara*, the endless cycle of birth and death, appeared in the Upanishads, as well as in the teachings of Mahavira (the founder of Jainism) and Guatama (the founder of Buddhism). However, there was, as yet, no concept of a subtle body or an intermediate state. Instead, upon departing one body, the soul is immediately born into another. As with the universal Self, this marked a radical departure from the previous Vedic, Indo-European mythic beliefs.

Reincarnation replaces the single afterlife of Pharaonic Egypt and the life of miserable shades in early Persian, Babylonian, and Greek beliefs, with an immortal soul that automatically transmigrates, suffering moral reward or punishment according to its deeds in former life. Here the judgment, rather than existing in an afterlife realm, becomes part of and determines ordinary embodied existence.

Here the emphasis on salvation involves not the attaining of heaven or afterlife or immortality, since all souls are considered immortal anyway, but rather that of *moksha*, nirvana, *kaivalya*, and similar terms and concepts, all of which refer in various ways to liberation from cyclic existence.

This shows how different this new North Indian way of thinking was, and still is, in the religions and mysticism of the Indian subcontinent, from the Mediterranean, Near and Middle Eastern, and the Western way of thinking. These cultures, mythologies, and religions are essentially materialistic, with bodily death meaning the end, apart from possible existence as an unhappy shade. The hope of immortality involves the materialistic magical wish-fulfillment theory of bodily resurrection since the concept of a soul apart from the body was alien to the levant and the Semites.

The cosmology of Ancient and Medieval India was equally pessimistic, but since it already comes with immortality, the emphasis shifts from how unhappy embodied existence is, as it is assumed most lifetimes are spent in unfortunate circumstances, with even fortunate lives are temporary, due to impermanence of existence. The only permanence and certain happiness are in total transcendence of embodied existence. This world-negating mindset, also found in Gnosticism, Christian mysticism, is the diametric opposite and inverse of the worldly hedonism and spiritual nihilism of modernity.

11-v. *Karma*

As with Zoroastrianism, a moral core forms the basis of all Indian religions. However, in this case, it is not that morality is part of the cosmological conflict of good and evil, but rather that the moral status of individual deeds becomes karma that determines one's future rebirth and drives the endless wheel of samsara or rebirth.

The whole theme of samsara and endless reincarnation is that we don't have control over our current existence, which is determined by past actions. And similarly, our present actions determine our future lives.

This idea would prove to be incredibly popular, essentially because of the concept of natural justice, which counters the apparent absurdism and injustice of the world. The idea of karma would be incorporated into Theosophy, and then into the New Age movement and, ultimately, popular culture.

The whole idea of karma, however, in Jainism, Buddhism, and Hinduism, is not to do good deeds to ensure a pleasant future life but rather to restrain oneself from desires to avoid creating the seeds of future bondage and rebirth, and instead generate the karmic factors for a life of spiritual renunciation. So while a pleasant life is obviously preferable to an unpleasant one, even this has to be superseded for the life of a monk, dedicated to the attainment of Liberation.

11-vi. Moral Purification

The movement away from Vedic ritualism and mythic enaction and towards Upanishadic and Yogic mysticism involved the renunciation of everyday life. This meant the adoption of an ascetic and celibate lifestyle. This may be because it is challenging to attain focus and transcendence when one is constantly pulled by everyday demands. While one often comes across Eastern teachings in the secular, materialistic West, these are usually so watered down as to be nothing short of farcical. Of course, there is certainly nothing wrong with incorporating spiritual insights into everyday existence, such as "lifestyle tantra"; indeed, this is what religion, cleared of guilt-tripping and puritanism ideally should be about. But the attainment of spiritual enlightenment and transcendence requires far more discipline.

Hence the fundamental element of most Indian spiritual traditions is *brahmacharya*, literally, the teaching about Brahman (the Absolute), but in this context, meaning the celibacy and self-control undertaken by a student of sacred knowledge. Other purification practices include ahimsa or non-harmfulness, a vegetarian lifestyle (an important ethical advance as it does not involve killing nonhuman animals for food), few or no possessions, spiritual contemplation, and a renunciation of family life. These values have been shared by mystics worldwide since at least the mid-first millennium B.C.E.

11-vii. Emanation and Ascent

Metaphysics and cosmology are still found in the Upanishads, representing the theistic or pantheistic worldview. But whereas the theologies and cosmologies of Egypt, Greece, and elsewhere posited genealogies of gods or creators, with the first gods emerging from original chaos or formlessness, representing the undifferentiated collective unconscious, Upanishads brought in the idea of emanation to explain the origin of the universe by tracing things logically back to their first principles, as described in the *Chandogya Upanishad*:

> From this Self (Atman), Space (*akasha*) arose; from Space air; from air fire; from fire water; from water the earth... [Radhakrishnan 1953, p.542].

Here there are five elements, the most subtle is Space or akasha (usually but wrongly translated as "ether," while the popular Theosophical conception of the "Akashic Record" has absolutely no foundation in Indian metaphysics), then Air, Fire, Water, and Earth. These became the five standard elements of Indian cosmology. They were later incorporated into Samkhya, Advaita Vedanta, Tantra, and the Puranas (syncretic devotional literature) along with emanation.

In the *Katha Upanishad*, which, as perhaps the oldest of the Middle Upanishads, dates to around the fourth century B.C.E. (contemporary with the *shramana* religions), there is a shift of emphasis from Monism to Theism, combining this with a Samkhyan series of tattvas to describe the ascent to the Absolute through a consideration of the various levels of being. The *Katha Upanishad* II 3. 10-11 reads:

> 10. Beyond [or "higher then"] the senses (*indriyas*) are the objects; beyond the objects is the mind (*manas*); beyond the mind is the intellect (*buddhi*); beyond the intellect is the great self (*mahan atman*).
>
> 11. Beyond the great self is the unmanifest (*avyakta*); beyond the unmanifest is the Person (*Purusha*). Beyond the Person is nothing. That is the end; that is the final goal" [Radhakrishnan 1953, p.625].

Here there is a shift of metaphysics; from cosmology to psychology and theology. Instead of the emanation of elements, we have a succession of higher and higher faculties of consciousness here. Rather than a process of emanation, we have a yogic ascent of consciousness. Withdrawing from the senses and the objects the senses experience – i.e., from the external world – one enters the subjective world of the mind. Beyond this is the principle of higher consciousness, or buddhi, then there is the "great self" or atman, which is not the same as the Atman of earlier Monism, because it does not represent the supreme principle. Then there is the shift to theology, to principles outside the self; first, the "unmanifest" and then, finally, the Godhead, conceived theistically in the form of the Supreme Person or Purusha. These two non-self principles are placed above the "self" or "Atman" principle for polemical reasons. Clearly, they represent a rival school to the Monistic emanationist school of the *Chandogya* and *Taittiriya Upanishads*.

These later Upanishads are composed in verse rather than the prose of the earlier ones, and develop the theme of brahman into a theistic rather than monistic conception. They also focus on the idea of liberation through meditation (or Yoga). Both are themes common in later Puranic cosmologies.

11-viii. The Five-fold Self

Along with the universal self and with emanation, there is the theme of degrees of self culminating in the highest Absolute. This appears very early. In the *Taittiriya Upanishad* (3.1-6), which is among the older Upanishads, the sage Varuna guides his son Bhrigu from the level of the physical body, the *anna-maya-atma* or the "self (atma) made of Food" (perhaps a reference to the web of life, all creatures feed on something else (except for primary producers like plants which photosynthesis) and are food for other beings, or perhaps this refers to temple offerings), to the level of *prana-maya-atma* or "the self-made of vital breath (prana)" which is associated with five pranas that would later become a central part of Hatha Yoga (and hence also of Tantra). This corresponds to what in modern esotericism is generally referred to as the subtle body (the Theosophists use the term "etheric body"). After the prana self comes the *mana-maya-atma* "the self-made of mind (*manas*)," which is associated with the Vedas or scriptures, perhaps referring to intellectual understanding. Then the *vijnana-maya-atma* or "the self-made of consciousness (*vijnana*)," which is related to spiritual virtues and attainments like faith, righteousness, truth, yoga, and mahat or "the great," a term elsewhere used in Samkhya to refer to the first evolute, buddhi. In other words, higher or cosmic consciousness. Finally there is the *ananda-maya-atma* or "the self-made of bliss (*ananda*)," where one attains to Brahman. In the quest for self- and god-realisation, the spiritual aspirant passes under the guidance of the Guru through each of the five selves, finally attaining the Absolute or Brahman, which is synonymous with the highest or bliss self.

With its degrees of physical, vital, mental, spiritual, and blissful selves, the *Taittiriya Upanishad* gives the first account of an ontologically graded reality, even if it is not yet formalized metaphysically or cosmologically.

Some thirteen hundred years later, Shankara and the Advaita Vedanta school would reduce the five pantheistic selves to five *koshas* or "sheaths" that veil the true Self (Atman). Another thirteen hundred years later, Sri Aurobindo would interpret them as five evolutionary stages, of which four – matter, life, and mind) have been actualized so far. The Advaitin interpretation, meanwhile, would become part of standard Yoga psychology and New Age holism. The Aurobindonian interpretation is quite different. For one thing, it is much more world-affirming. For another, it pertains to an evolutionary or "integral" worldview. The various degrees of Self are now evolutionary stages in the emergence of consciousness in and from matter (prana being life and manas mind; vijnana is then Supermind).

11-ix. *The Shramanas*

Alongside the original kathenotheistic Vedic religion (which evolved into medieval and modern Hinduism), several meditation-based atheistic schools developed around the 7th to 6th centuries B.C.E.

These rejected the religious and ceremonial trappings of Vedism and Hinduism, although still retaining the same basic philosophical and soteriological (concerned with spiritual liberation) orientation. Each of these schools was centered around a single charismatic founder, which shared common themes such as atheism, spiritual self-reliance, liberation through asceticism, and Yoga or meditation techniques. They came to be known as shramanas, from *shramana*, meaning one who performs acts of austerity (not to be confused with the phonetically vaguely similar but unrelated "shaman").

At least sixty-two shramana religious or yogic-ascetic groups developed and flourished in India during the 6th century B.C.E. [Bodhisattva, 2021].

11-x. Kapila and Samkhya

The central message of the early Upanishads was a sort of transcendent monistic idealism. But alongside this, around the early centuries B.C.E. to C.E., there developed a materialistic or realistic theory of being, and of the nature of phenomenal existence, as proto-science or natural philosophy, similar to Ionic Greek or early Chinese thought.

This realist position is best represented by Samkhya. One of the Six Schools of Hindu philosophy, Samkhya philosophy is also considered to be the oldest. As an atheist system, it fits in well with the contemporary shramana traditions such as Jainism, Buddhism, and Ajivika. All these systems of thought developed from the same contemplative-meditative tradition in Vedic and post-Vedic India during the Upanishadic period.

Kapila, the founder of Samkhya, was not technically one of the shramanas, as the system of metaphysics he established became one of the six main schools of Hindu philosophy. He is revered as one of the traditional ancient sages of India. He is traditionally dated to the 7th to 6th century B.C.E., although basically everything about him is mythologized to the extent that, like the Hebrew patriarchs and the historical Jesus, it is difficult to say anything for certain about him.

Kapila is credited with authoring the *Samkhya-Sutra* (also called *Kapila-Sutra*), which aphoristically presents the dualistic philosophy of Samkhya. However, the actual text of that name only dates to the medieval period. Elsewhere, he appears in many dialogues of Hindu texts, such as in explaining and defending the principle of *ahimsa* (non-violence) in the *Mahabharata*.

Samkhya came to be associated later with the practice of Yoga (meditation and austerities), if indeed these two were ever separate, and reached its classical form around the first century C.E. [Larson, 1979, p.134]. Sometimes these are referred to as a single system, i.e., Samkhya-Yoga.

The word Yoga is from the Sanskrit verb meaning "to yoke" or "to join" (which is similar to the Latin religio, to tie to). As with the various shramana traditions, it combines living a spiritual life, mastery of the body, focus, and absolute control of the mind.

Today Yoga is best known through the *Yoga Sutra of Patanjali*. The *Yoga Sutra* is a short aphoristic text that, as with the similarly terse *Tao Te*

Ching, has been translated numerous times into English and other Western languages. Contrary to popular belief, Patanjali's Yoga is simply one form of Yoga. For a long time, Yoga referred to similar but distinct practices, and Patanjali is as much a legendary or mythical figure as Kapila.

Central to Yoga (whether Samkhyan, Jain, Buddhist, Patanjali, or other) is the principle of controlling, focusing, and stilling the mind. When the field of agitated prakriti (matter, nature, phenomena) within the individual mind is stilled, the true person (purusha, self or soul) is experienced, and the false idea of the limited self disappears. One then realizes one's true nature and transcendent, blissful identity [Campbell, 1962, p.256].

11-xi. Mahavira and Jainism

One of the most extraordinary of all the Indian spiritual philosophies is Jainism. Nowadays, a minor religion even in its home country, almost unknown relative to its big brother Buddhism, Jainism is one of the most rigorous spiritual philosophies.

Mahavira (traditional date: 599 to 527 B.C.E, current scholarship has this as 540-468 [Dundas, 2002, p.24]), the founder of Jainism, was purportedly a prince who renounced his royal heritage at around age 30, becoming a wandering mendicant and ascetic in search of spiritual awakening. After many years of austerities and meditation, he attained *Kevala Jnana* (omniscience) and became the Tirthankara, meaning ford-maker or stream crosser, one who has conquered the cycle of death and rebirth, and laid out a path for others to follow.

Allowing for local doctrinal and theological differences, all the various terms, Tirthankara, Buddha, prophet, messenger, avatar, and so on, all refer to the same theme of a spiritually enlightened teacher who serves as a guide for others to attain salvation.

Mahavira's teachings are based on the three principles of ahimsa (non-harmfulness), *anekantavada* (relativism), and *aparigraha* (renunciation and asceticism).

According to legend, Mahavira wasn't even the founder of Jainism but rather the last in a long line of Tirthankaras. His parents had also been

Jains, following the teachings of the previous (twenty-third) Tirthankara, Parshvanath, whose symbolic animal was the serpent (representing wisdom), who is traditionally dated to c. 872-772 B.C.E (or alternatively, he was more recent, and died in 720 B.C.E., which makes him contemporary with, or slightly older than, the oldest Upanishads). Their biographies are described in the *Kalpa Sutra*, ascribed to the Jain sage Bhadrabahu (c. 367-c. 298 B.C.E.), but probably compiled in its present form around 500 C.E.

There is some controversy over whether Parshvanath was a real historical person. However, if he was, and was in turn preceded by earlier Tirthankaras as in Jain mythology, the line could be traced further back to the pre-Vedic Indus Valley civilization, as shown by the Pashupati seal [Campbell, 1962, pp.218-219]. Certainly, in Jain mythology, the dating of most of the Tirthankaras is mythical.

The first Tirthankara of this cosmic cycle was Rishabhanatha, also called Adinath, who was born some 8.4 million years ago [Pezarkar, 2017], which means we are looking at mythology rather than history.

Of all the Eastern philosophies, Jainism places the most significant emphasis on ahimsa or non-harmfulness towards all beings. This gentleness is extended to all things, even inanimate matter and objects, as these are considered to be souls trapped in these particular forms for a period of time.

Jain monks (*sadhu*) and nuns (*sadhvi*), called *munis* ("silent" holy ones, this title was applied to the Buddha, who was called Shakyamuni), traditionally move from village to village, accepting only what food someone offers them along the way (again, this is the case with Buddhist monks). They go by foot, for travel by vehicles is seen to be much more damaging to the multitude of tiny life forms. They carry a variety of brooms, taking care not to crush small insects as they sit or walk. Some wear a white cloth over their mouth to avoid accidentally inhaling microscopic organisms. They don't use scissors to cut hair, in case insects in the hair are injured or killed. Instead, hair is pulled out by the roots. During the four months of the monsoon season, they live in the villages so as not to harm the many organisms that emerge in the rain. During this time, they perform various services, such as teaching, for the lay community [Eck, 1994].

While some of these practices are undoubtedly extreme when taken literally, the basic principles of compassion for all sentient beings (a common Shramana theme also found in Buddhism) represents a profound advance on the humanistic and anthropocentric moral philosophy of the Semites and the Greeks (apart from the Pythagoreans). The West's Animal Liberation and Vegan movements are the modern-day successors of the Jain principle of compassion and non-harmfulness (ahimsa), and walking lightly on the Earth.

The primary division of Jains is between the Shvetambara or "white clad" as they wear two pieces of white cloth, and purist Digambara or "sky-clad" (in those days, the yogi-ascetics were naked, representing total renunciation, as a few still are in India today, and women were not permitted to become ascetics). Incidentally, the term "sky-clad" was incorporated into Wicca (Neopaganism) in the West, for whom both sexes practice nudity during pagan ceremonies. Gerald Gardner (1884-1964), the father of modern Wicca, was a noted folklorist with an interest in Far Eastern culture who spent several years in Ceylon, so it is not unlikely that he would have been familiar with the term.

The origin of the two monastic groups began in the third or fourth century B.C.E. when according to the Digambara version, Acharya Bhadrabahu, considered the last Shruta Kevalin (complete knowledge of the Jain scriptures), predicted a twelve-year-long famine and moved from Magadha (a region of North-East India) to Karnataka in South India with his disciples. One of his pupils, Sthulabhadra, was in the group that stayed in Magadha. When Acharya Bhadrabahu's followers returned, they were appalled to discover that those who had remained at Magadha had started wearing white clothes (or at least loincloths).

The Shvetambaras introduced other pragmatic changes as well, including performing *puja* (worship) before the *murtis* (images) of the Jinas or Tirthankaras, in the manner of standard Indian religious practice. Even though they acknowledged that such rituals have no supernatural value, as the Tirthankaras have already totally transcended embodied existence and have the ability to influence worldly circumstances, this gives psychological comfort to the lay practitioner.

The best-known recent example of Jainism in practice was the religious leader and social revolutionary Mohandas Gandhi (1869-1948), who came to be known as Mahatma, or "Great Soul." Close contact with the Jain community in his native Gujarat (western India) influenced Mahatma Gandhi's views of non-violence. He studied law in London and then spent twenty years helping the Indian community in South Africa before returning to India, applying the principle of ahimsa, which he called *satyagraha* or "truth force," in his and his followers' rebellion against British rule. His ashrams included people of all religions and castes, including untouchables, for whom he had special sympathy. Gandhi's message inspired nonviolent social reform worldwide, such as Martin Luther King, the 14th Dali Lama, and much of the modern social activist movement.

11-xii. Jain Philosophy

Metaphysically, Jainism is a pluralistic realism in which the objects we perceive are real, as are various abstractions such as space, time, movement, etc. The universe is traced to two eternal, uncreated, independent categories of *jiva* (the sentient life monad or reincarnating soul) and *ajiva* (everything else). Even karma is a material substance, and liberated jivas float to the highest levels of the cosmos.

As with the gnostic and yogic teachings in general, in Jainism, liberation is achieved through one's efforts, rather than through the help of an external deity or savior. Hence the liberated soul is called a victor (*jina*) and a hero (*vira*) as they have overcome all obstacles independently. This also relates to Buddhist, Sufi, and similar ideas regarding self-mastery.

As with the unrelated Western dualistic esoteric systems of Gnosticism, Manichaeism, and Lurianic Kabbalah, bondage is due to the soul's (or the divine spark's) association with matter. Only through extricating the soul from the taint of matter is it possible to achieve spiritual liberation. Likewise, ignorance in the soul is due to its being associated with matter.

A unique teaching in Jainism is its interpretation of karma. Karma is not the cosmic law of action and reaction, as in Hinduism, Buddhism, Theosophy, and the whole New Age movement, but a type of matter (*pudgala* – a word that means "person" in other contexts). It consists of tiny particles imperceptible to the senses and pervading the entire universe. This subtle form of matter covers and taints the soul and physically weighs it down.

Every living being is covered in this karmic matter and has been since beginningless time. Karmic matter that keeps the soul away from realizing its true nature. Instead, due to karma, the soul only has limited knowledge, has a body (which may be elemental, plant, animal, human, hell-being, or god), duration of life, and undergoes birth, death, pain, and pleasure. The entirety of Jain philosophy is about this theory of karma and how the soul can free itself from these pesky karmic particles.

So whereas Jainism, like Samkhya-Yoga, refers to a plurality of souls, it differs in that the soul is conceived to be physically contaminated by matter, whereas in Samkhya (and Yoga), there is no actual contact.

As with Buddhism and Samkhya-Yoga, removing ignorance and karma begins with intellectual study and following a particular practice. This involves studying the teachings and scriptures of *Tirthankaras*. Right knowledge, right faith, and right conduct are called the three jewels (*Triratna*). An almost identical system is found in Buddhism, which also has three jewels (of the Buddha, the Dharma (teachings), and the Sangha or community of monks). Unfortunately, as time passed, the whole system seems to have become more and more formulaic. The final aim is to liberate the soul so that it can return to its essential state of infinite knowledge, vision, power, and bliss.

And in keeping with scholasticism and metaphysics in general, there is a massive emphasis on categorization, which takes the place of both science and phenomenology. So there are, for example, nine tattvas or principles (the word also appears in a different context Samkhya): soul, matter, *Asrava* (influx of karma), *Bandha* (bondage of karma), *Punya* (virtue), *Papa* (sin), *Samvara* (Stoppage the influx of karma), *Nirjara* (exhaustion of accumulated karma), and *Moksha* (liberation from embodied existence).

Asrava is the cause or influx of good and evil karma. This includes further subcategories such as mithyatva or delusion/ ignorance (equivalent to avidya or metaphysical ignorance), *avirati* or lack of self-restraint (equivalent to the epithymia or lower psyche), pramada or unawareness of unmindfulness (this would be the same as the state of "sleep" in Gurdjieffian Fourth Way teachings), *kasaya* or passions like anger, conceit, deceit, and lust (in part the kleshas of Yoga and Buddhism and in part with the Greek epithymia), and Yoga, which here refers to activities of mind, speech, and body [JAINA org, n.d.].

Bandha is when the karmic particles (*karma pudgala*) infiltrate the soul and combine with it, just as water unites with milk or fire unites with a red-hot iron ball. Here passions or disposition (*bhava*) is the primary cause, and material bondage (*dravya*) is the effect [Doley, 2015].

The different types of karma (called *prakriti bandha*) obscure different powers and attributes of the transcendent soul. Here *Ghati karma* obscures the inner nature of consciousness or the soul (such as gnosis, charity, etc.), and *Aghati karma* obscures the soul by means of causing it to identify with a physical body. This is very similar to the five *kanchukas* and three *malas* of Kashmir Shaivism [Singh, 1980, p.138], which are the aspects of maya that veil the universal, omniscient, and omnipotent self, reducing it to limited knower and doer. In keeping with the Perennialist insight, these various teachings use different concepts and terminology to say the same thing.

Removing ghati karma results in *kevala jnana* (absolute knowledge or supreme spiritual enlightenment), and one then becomes an Arihant (equivalent to the Vedantic *jivanmukti* – liberated while alive). However, complete liberation only occurs after the death of the body and associated aghati karmas [JAINA org, n.d.].

This liberation (moksha) is attained through the discrimination between, and the complete dissociation of, the soul from matter. This involves two stages, samvara (i.e., the stoppage of influx of karmic particles) and the second nirjara (i.e., exhaustion or wearing out of karma in the soul) [Doley, 2015].

Samvara is the reverse of asrava. It is accomplished by living a spiritual life, such as correct belief, observance of vows, awareness, passionlessness, and so on. Nirjara goes further by involving austerities and penance. Again, in keeping with the overall mind-body dualism, there are two groups; external and internal.

External nirjara include various austerities such as fasting, reducing food in general, not having anything that tastes good, traveling barefoot even in extreme heat and cold, and so on.

One can only wonder at the obsession with asceticism and negative attitudes to the body. Indeed, these seem to be representative of world-negating mysticism everywhere. At the very least, weakening the body would make it harder for the mind to focus, making it more difficult to practice the more important internal nirjara.

The internal nirjaras are considered the true austerities because they purify the soul and exhaust the attached karma. They are repentance for breach of vows, politeness towards teachers and elders, selfless service to the suffering and deserving, studying (or listening to the recitation of, as presumably few could read and there were few books) scriptures, and meditation (*dhyana*), Yoga posture (*kayotsarga*), and ascetic indifference (*vyutsarga*) [JAINA org, n.d.].

As in Buddhism, all of these categories and sub-categories are based on pragmatic psychology. The whole thing is a sort of fastidious, almost obsessive, very much autistic systemizing, a rational-mental system of categorizing. The entire point of Jainism, as with Buddhism, Yoga, and other soteriologies, is not a metaphysical explanation of the universe, as in, say, Neoplatonism (although medieval Jainism certainly did develop an incredibly detailed cosmography or map of the (premodern) universe), or the psychological dynamics of consciousness, as with Freud or Jung, but rather a practical and very one-pointed system of liberation from embodied existence.

Much as I have the highest appreciation for the Jains and their rigorous path of non-violence to all sentient beings, I can't help but feel something is limiting about this extreme religio-mystical view of life. You don't get to know the whole or become an all-rounded being because your entire focus is on denying embodied existence and rejecting the world. This is the distinction between the classic world-negating mysticism and more modernist approaches such as Theosophy and Integral Yoga.

Indeed, within these systems are explorations in cosmology, theosophy, metaphysics, mythohistory, and so on. But these are ultimately just distractions and divergences from the central purpose of these respective traditions.

11-xiii. Siddhartha and Buddhism

Siddhartha, a younger contemporary of Mahavira, was another prince who renounced the world to seek liberation. However, the exact dates are dubious as different chronologies give different dates; the modern chronology is 563-c. 483 B.C.E. [Mark, 2020b].

According to the foundational legend, Siddhartha's father was a king named Suddhodana, and his mother was Queen Maya. In response to a prophecy that the child would become either a great king or spiritual leader, his father ensured his son did not witness any form of suffering, so as not to feel any need to embrace the renunciate life. But one day at age 29, he was out riding in his coach or chariot when he saw an old man, a sick man, a dead body, and an ascetic. Having never seen anything like this, he asked his driver, who explained what they were. This so took him aback so that night he left his wife, Princess Yashodhara, his baby son, and the palace, for the life of an ascetic.

Not only does Siddhartha appear to be a deadbeat dad, walking out on his young family without a word, but the whole story is so absurd (he never stubbed a toe or was sick a day in his life?) it is clearly fictional.

Modern scholars such as the British Indologist Richard Gombrich have argued that the Shakya community was not a monarchy but governed by a small oligarchy or republic-like council [Gombrich, 1988]. However, there is no doubt that, as with the life of Mahavira in Jainism, this was a teaching tool invented and interpolated at a later time. The symbolism is pretty obvious; he was even born of maya. But, as is often the case, it was taken literally by people who came later and failed to understand the original meaning.

After years of austerity and meditation, Siddhartha attained spiritual enlightenment, becoming the Buddha (the Awakened One). He was given the title Shakyamuni (mendicant-sage of the Shakya clan).

His central teaching is the Four Noble Truths: suffering, its cause, its cessation, and the way to achieve cessation (or transcendence).

Whereas materialism and modernity emphasize hedonism, running after pleasures, and spiritual shallowness, Buddhism, like all the shramanas, and indeed like all mystical teachings in general, takes the opposite orientation and denies there is any good in worldly existence.

The Buddha's teachings begin with the statement that all existence is unsatisfactory (*dukkha*, usually translated as suffering) because of attachment and impermanence. We get attached to things and to beings, but, like everything in existence, these are impermanent. Hence there is a constant craving (*tanha*) and running after these states and things, which keeps us caught in samsara, the endless cycle of repeated rebirth, dukkha, and dying again.

Liberation from this state of samsara (karma and rebirth) is via the Eightfold Path, which consists of eight moral and meditative practices: Right Understanding, Right Intention, Right Speech, Right Action, Right Livelihood, Right Effort, Right Mindfulness (a potent technique, presented in Vipassana retreats today), and Right Samadhi. This results in Nirvana, the cessation of individual existence.

The whole Buddhist theory and practice system is summed up in a fantastic diagram called the Wheel of Becoming (*Bhavacakra*). However, its present form only dates to the late 1st millennium C.E. Nevertheless, these diagrams are very popular in Tibetan Buddhism where, as with the mythologized biography of the Buddha himself, they serve as a teaching device for the common folk.

There are so many similarities between Buddha and Mahavira that it seems as if they shared the same biography (or hagiography). Both were Kshatriyas, in contrast to the Brahmin priesthood of the Vedic religion. Both were natives of the lower Ganges country below Benares, the classic land of the forest sages. Both, after marriage, left the world at age 29 or 30 for spiritual enlightenment. Having achieved enlightenment after strenuous effort, each became a teacher for a company of ascetic disciples.

In short, this seems to be a common North Indian trope and is quite likely a later interpolated myth, like the Mediterranean myth of the dying and resurrected God, or the Hellenistic/Roman theme of a peripatetic miracle worker and spiritual teacher (Jesus of Nazareth, Apollonius of Tyana). Doubtless, there was some cross-fertilization between Buddhism, Jainism, and Samkhya. Perhaps not surprisingly, according to the myth, the Buddha's father ruled the city where Kapila had taught.

All three were atheistic but efficient systems of applied spiritual psychology that involved rejecting desire (*kama*, not to be confused with action or karma) through a system of cumulative vows regarding thoughts, speech, and action. For all three, the end result is the elimination of karma and rebirth and hence liberation (moksha, nirvana) from embodied existence. In contrast to the other Shramanas and the Upanishads, the Buddha even denied the existence of a persisting soul, as this would indicate something permanent.

As with Mahavira, who was the twenty-fourth Tirthankara, the Buddha was not considered the founder of the Buddhist teachings, but merely the restorer, and the most recent of a line of Buddhas stretching back into beginningless time.

Buddha's teachings, however, may have been more moderate than Mahavira's. Hence he referred to the Middle Way between the two extremes of asceticism and indulgence. But if Gautama was indeed originally a moderate, his later successors became more ascetic in approach, especially the purist Theravada or southern school.

Vedanta, beginning with the early Upanishads, and most fully in the developed Advaita school, emphasizes the transcendent "I" and changeless consciousness or awareness as the only Reality. All forms of Buddhism emphasize observing the objects of consciousness arising and passing away, without becoming caught up in them. The Mahayana branch was especially concerned with abiding in this state of pure observing consciousness, where even the sense of an ego or identity drops away. In fact, they are using different language and philosophical methodologies – Buddhism being phenomenological and psychological and the Vedantins being metaphysical – to say the same thing.

11-xiv. *The Swastika, a Solar Symbol*

Joseph Campbell points out the solar mythology of the Buddha. He is called the Lion of the Shakya Clan, who sits upon the Lion Throne, and the symbol of his teaching is the Sun Wheel [Campbell, 1962, p.255], hence the turning of the wheel of Dharma. But, of course, as mentioned, all this only came some centuries later, as the Buddha's life is primarily fictional, very much like the life of Jesus.

The wheel symbolism is also found in Jainism and Hinduism, as is the swastika (or *svastika* to give a more correct transliteration), a solar symbol that dates to at least 500 B.C.E. and is associated with auspiciousness. Like a number of other esoteric symbols, it was appropriated by Nazi Germany. However, the belief that the Nazis switched it from clockwise to anticlockwise spinning (assuming the bent edges of each arm are the trailing edges) is incorrect, as both versions of swastikas are known from traditional representations (according to references cited in Wikipedia, the anticlockwise (left-facing) swastika is a sacred symbol in the Bon (Tibetan Shamanism) and Mahayana Buddhist traditions, while the clockwise spinning (right-facing) swastika is found in Hinduism, Jainism, and Sri Lankan Buddhism.

It is likely, therefore, that the Nazis, who represented an extreme or unbalanced solar or masculinist cult (fascism being defined psychologically by the "System A" polarity of Stan Gooch [Gooch, 1972]), stole the iconography from Tibetan Buddhism.

11-xv. Some Other Early Schools

Samkhya, Jainism, and Buddhism are only the best-known of what was once a diverse assemblage of Shramana schools and teachings.

The Ajivikas

Makkhali Gosala was a contemporary of Mahavira and Buddha, and the founder of the Ajivika, a monastic, deterministic, atheistic school of Indian philosophy, that, for a while, rivaled early Buddhism and Jainism. But unfortunately, no original writings remain, only derogatory accounts by Jains and Buddhists [Bodhisattva, 2021].

As with the Jains, the Ajivikas practiced extreme asceticism. Gosala also taught the existence of the soul (atma) but rejected free will and karma. Reincarnation and even the attainment of liberation are predetermined. In keeping with most of the shramana schools, existence is explained by the aggregation of several fundamental principles called *kaya* (Sanskrit: assemblage, collection, elemental categories). These are earth, water, fire, air, joy (*sukha*), sorrow or suffering (*dukkha*), and (life) *jiva*. In contrast to the Jains, the soul is considered to have a material form [Basham, 1951].

As with the Epicureans and Stoics of ancient Greece, a good or spiritual life was not a means to Liberation, but a way of living for its own sake. Ajivika philosophy reached its height during the Mauryan Empire (322-185 B.C.E.). The religion survived until the 14th century C.E. in south India.

The Materialists

Ajita Kesakambali systematized materialist philosophy, called *Lokayata* (literally "aiming at the world" or "worldly") or *Charvaka*, by setting it down in the form of aphorisms. As with the other extinct shramana schools, no original writings from its followers have survived, but the teachings can be reconstructed from secondary sources.

The Charvakas denied any afterlife, reincarnation or karma, emphasizing rational thought and skepticism instead. Until the 12th century, Charvaka remained a respectable school of Indian philosophy and retained its reputation to the extent that 20th century Indian Marxists considered themselves its modern-day representatives. At the same time, the Charvaka Ashram, founded by Boddu Ramakrishna in 1973, still promotes the cause of Indian rationalism, opposing Hindu chauvinism and debunking claims of the irrational [Teja, 2019].

The Atomists

Pakudha Kaccayana was the founder of the atomist school. He taught that everything is made of the rearrangement of seven basic building blocks: earth, water, fire, air, happiness, pain, and soul. This is the same basic theme of realism or materialism found in Samkhya, Jainism, Buddhism, and Ajivika. In Buddhist Abhidhamma metaphysics, for example, everything and all experience consists of Dharmas or atoms of experience (which include the five elements)

Atomism, whether in its Indian or Greek variants, is the opposite of Emanationism. Emanationism also refers to the physical elements and consciousness, but arranges these in a series in which the first principle gives rise to the next, and so on, whereas Atomism asserts a radical pluralism.

The Sceptics

Sanjaya Belatthiputta was the founder of the Ajnana, or radical agnostic school. He denied any knowledge was possible regarding concepts such as the afterlife, karma, God, the soul, and so on. Ajnana philosophy may have influenced Pyrrho of Elis, who traveled with Alexander's army to India and met the Gymnosophists or "naked philosophers," either Jains or Ajnanins. Pyrrho's students established Agnostic thought in the West. However, most of what is known as Pyrrhonism comes from the physician Sextus Empiricus of the mid-late 2nd century C.E. Agnosticism would later independently appear in the skeptical empiricism of David Hume and rejection of metaphysics by Immanuel Kant, both of whom were seminal in the establishment of the limited worldview of rationalist modernity.

11-xvi. Schopenhauer - a 19th Century Shramanist

A modern representative of the Shramana atheistic ascetic Yoga-philosophy tradition was the German philosopher Arthur Schopenhauer (1788-1860), one of the first Western thinkers to affirm Indian philosophy, specifically Buddhism (and even there of the more traditional and ascetic Theravada tradition). However, his philosophical pessimism could equally apply to Jainism, Samkhya-Yoga, or Ajivika.

Schopenhauer, in his classic 1818 work *The World as Will and Representation*, developed an atheistic, metaphysical, and ethical system that built on the transcendental idealism of Immanuel Kant, considering the phenomenal world as the product of a blind noumenal will.

Schopenhauer's philosophy centered on a psychological impulse that he observed took precedence over reason, which he called the Will to Life (*Wille zum Leben*). It is a constant force, blind, dumb, and insistent, which causes us to cling to existence and always look to our own advantage. This is the same as what in Buddhism is called craving, the principle of attachment that causes rebirth.

Schopenhauer observed the way the Will to Life focuses on sex. He was very aware of the disruption caused by sexual and romantic infatuations, but he did not believe these were trifling or accidental. Instead, it is an inherent drive within human beings and all creatures, to reproduce, ensuring the species' survival. These thoughts on sexuality foreshadowed and combined Darwin's theory of evolution and Freud's concept of the unconscious mind and psychic energy as libido.

A minimal number of people, such as sages living alone away from the distraction of city life and Buddhist monks, are able by a great effort to override the demands of the Will to Life towards selfishness, sex, and vanity. But a more straightforward method than ascetic renunciation was to focus on higher pursuits such as art and philosophy.

In his later years, he lived a quiet life in an apartment in Frankfurt with his dog, a white poodle whom he named Atman, after the universal self of the Upanishads, but whom the neighboring children less respectfully called Mrs. Schopenhauer [School of Life, 2015].

12. THE I CHING AND TAOISM

12-i. Early Chinese History

Although premodern Chinese history (or traditional historiography) refers to the Xia dynasty as the first Chinese rulers, who are said to have ruled from around 2100 B.C.E. to 1600 B.C.E., there are no contemporaneous historical records of the Xia. For example, they are not mentioned in the oldest Chinese texts, such as the earliest oracle bone inscriptions dating from the late Shang period (13th century B.C.E.).

The earliest Dynasty of which we can be historically certain therefore is the Shang Dynasty (1600 B.C.E. to 1046 B.C.E.), which was centered in the Yellow River Valley and is known for its advances in bronze metallurgy, writing, and agriculture.

The Yellow River valley is commonly considered the cradle of Chinese civilization, although Neolithic cultures originated along the Yellow River and Yangtze River.

The Shang Dynasty was eventually overthrown by the Zhou Dynasty (1046 B.C.E. to 256 B.C.E.), characterized by its feudalism system and the development of the Mandate of Heaven, a philosophical concept that held that the right to rule was granted by divine approval.

After the collapse of the Zhou Dynasty, China was divided into many smaller states, known as the Warring States period (475 B.C.E. to 221 B.C.E.). This period saw significant advances in philosophy, military technology, and governance as different states competed for power and influence.

In 221 B.C.E., the state of Qin emerged victorious from the Warring States period, and its ruler, Qin Shi Huang, became the first emperor of a unified China. The Qin Dynasty (221 B.C.E. to 206 B.C.E.) was characterized by its authoritarian rule, centralization of power, and its construction of the Great Wall of China and the Terracotta Army.

After the Qin Dynasty came the Han (206 B.C.E. to 220 C.E.), considered a golden age of Chinese civilization.

12-ii. Folk Mythology

Chinese cosmology is derived from folklore and folk religion. It features the earth, the universe, mythological places, beings, and the four cardinal points, each with their associated color, animal, element, and so on (these correspondences would later be of great importance in Taoism, design (Feng Shui) and holistic/traditional medicine), and even an entire supernatural world parallel to that of earth, with a heaven and later (through Buddhist influence) a hell, complete with their own hierarchical government with an emperor, bureaucracy, judges, clerks, secretaries, guards, and servants, reflecting the structure of earthly society.

This latter is still very much represented in pop culture today. For example, in Japanese manga artist Akira Toriyama's successful *Dragonball* series, there is even a celestial martial arts academy where the hero, Goku, and others can train when he has left his body. In the West today, equivalent versions of celestial bureaucracies are found in TV shows such as Michael Schur's American fantasy-comedy-philosophy series *The Good Place*.

12-iii. The I Ching

Coming from the same culture but more interesting is a remarkably sophisticated premodern science, the Yin-Yang system, based on polarity and derived from the I Ching. Among the oldest Chinese texts, the I Ching, or "Classic of Changes," began as a divination manual in the Western Zhou period (1000-750 B.C.E.). It is based on a binary system, like the 1s and 0s of a computer, except that Yin and Yang, or negative and positive, are used instead here. The combination of six lines, which could be either broken (Yin) or unbroken (Yang), gives the sixty-four *kua* or hexagrams, comprising the totality of archetypal principles.

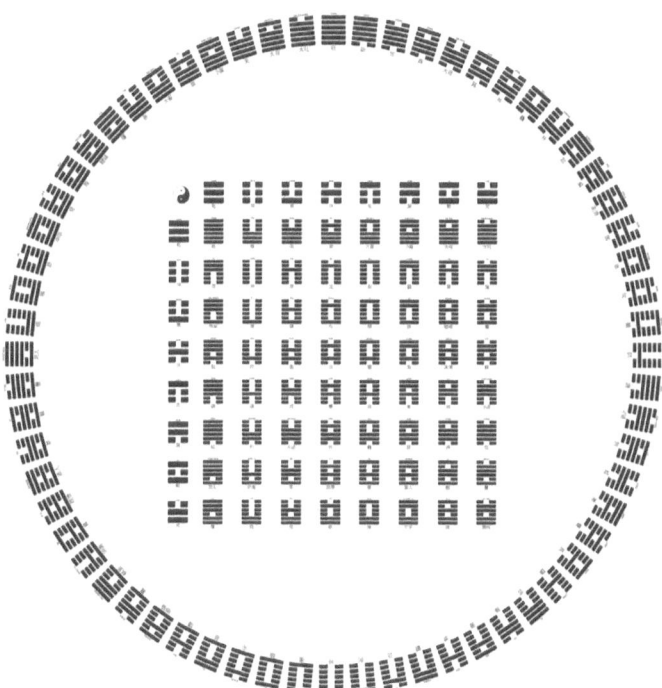

Fig. 4. The sixty-four hexagrams of the I Ching are shown in both a circular arrangement and doubled trigrams. Although Chinese tradition asserts the trigrams came first. They were then assembled into hexagrams by a legendary cultural hero, such as the purely mythical Fu Hsi (who, among other things, gave humanity music, hunting, fishing, domestication, cooking, and writing) or King Wen of the late Shang dynasty. The modern scholarly consensus is that hexagrams came first, and the trigrams were extrapolated later. The circular arrangement shows the binary nature of the hexagrams, as with a modern digital computer, where each bit of processor instruction can only be either 1 or 0. Each position or line likewise has only two options, Yang or Yin.

This polarity of Yang and Yin, or heaven and earth, aligns with the common archetypal theme such as the Proto-Indo-European pairing of Dyeus and Dheghom, as well as the general psychological and psycho-cultural polarity [Gooch, 1972].

The difference is that the Chinese took it further, making this polarity the basis of a cosmic computer powered by synchronicity.

So from the basic binary unit of reality comes the four (2 x 2), which takes us to the Jungian mandala and the Pythagorean tetraktys. Times two again, and we have the eight trigrams, an important element in Chinese cosmology. Modern scholarship indicates that they were only formulated after the hexagrams. 4 x 4 x 4, however (or 2 to the power of 6), gives 64, the number of hexagram symbols that make up the I Ching oracle, and the number of possible DNA codons. The way DNA, which is a sort of organic computer (there is even talk of building nano-computers using the DNA molecule), transmits information is through combining any of the four fundamental nucleotide bases (four again) in sets of three, hence 64 possible amino acid sequences [Schonberger, 1992].

Although the original idea of the dichotomy of Yin and Yang dates to the I Ching or Book of Changes, it is only in the developed philosophy of the later strata of the I Ching that the complete Yin-Yang philosophy was developed.

Later it became one of the five classics of Confucianism, traditionally used for divination and as a moral, philosophical, and cosmological text concerning the balance of opposites and acceptance of the inevitability of change.

The characteristics of Yin and Yang described in the mature layers of the I Ching are very similar to other pairings, such as the later Pythagorean sets of opposites.

Yin	*Yang*
"Shady side of mountain"	"Sunlit side of mountain"
Broken line	Unbroken line
Earth	Heaven, spirit
Dark	Light
Yielding	Hard
Negative	Positive
Feminine	Masculine
Warm	Cold
Square	Round
Common person	Sage

Table 1. The Chinese system of Yin and Yang; here, some of the basic attributes are considered. In the Japanese philosophy of Macrobiotics, there is the same polarity, only "Yang" refers to what is here Yin, and vice versa. Thus terms like Yang and Yin and some of their superficial attributes are relative and culture-dependent, even if the essential reality is universal.

The same polarity defined here as Yin and Yang can be found in other forms of esotericism, such as Pythagoreanism, Tantra, Kabbalah, and Jungian psychology. But this is not the same as the duality of Zoroastrianism and Gnosticism. While Yin and Yang are described as light and dark, this is not equivalent to good and evil. They are complementary, not contradictory. Both are necessary for the creation and existence of all things.

It would only later appear as the famous "Tao" glyph and become the basis for Taoist cosmology, Neo-Confucian philosophy, and traditional Chinese medicine.

12-iv. The Three Sages

Chinese religion and spirituality have been divided, by both Chinese and foreign scholars alike, into three great streams: Confucianism, Buddhism, and Taoism. In the spirit of Asiatic syncretism, these three teachings were often considered complementary rather than contradictory, Confucianism being concerned with how one should act in the human world, and Buddhism and Taoism with the spiritual and world-transcending path. Chinese writers frequently spoke of these "three sages": Confucius, Lao-tzu, and Buddha. A similar approach was taken in India regarding the reconciliation of the six classical systems of philosophy – the "six *darshanas*" – which were codified around the time of Christ. But quite apart from the arbitrary nature of such a conciliation, we are faced with the fact that Confucianism and Buddhism could each be considered self-contained religions. Taoism was little more than a "catch-all" category with which to include anything that did not fit within the other two religions: from the sublime philosophical-spiritual teachings of Lao-tzu and Chuang-tzu to the magical-occult folk beliefs of the village shaman.

Some Western scholars tried to make sense of Taoism by distinguishing between "philosophical" Taoism (by which is meant the tradition of Lao-tzu and Chuang-tzu) and "religious" Taoism. However, such terms are rather inappropriate. Lao-tzu and Chuang-tzu's Taoism is hardly "philosophical" but rather "spiritual" in the sense that sophisticated – as opposed to "popular" or "village" – Buddhism and "Hinduism" are. And "religious" Taoism can be divided into many categories, such as Village/

Shamanic on the one hand and Yogic/alchemical/self-transformative (see Nei-Tan) on the other.

While Taoist teachings vary, they generally emphasize "naturalness," simplicity, spontaneity, and the Three Treasures: compassion, frugality, and humility, along with the attainment of *wu wei* or action through non-action.

12-v. *Lao-tzu*

Quietist Taoism (pronounced Dau-ism, not Tay-oh-ism), more usually spelled Daoism now with the shift from Wade-Gilles to PinYin transliteration), is a mystical-philosophical Chinese system that emphasizes living in harmony with the Tao, literally: "the Way," or "The Path."

The central text is the *Tao Te Ching*, a brief, aphoristic mystical text, roughly translated as *The Classic of the Way and its Virtue*, traditionally written 600 B.C.E. but more likely about the 4th century B.C.E. by the Taoist sage Lao-tzu, the "Old Master." It influenced not only many classical and post-classical East Asian philosophies, including Quietist Taoism, Neotaoism (Confucian and Taoist synthesis), and Chinese Buddhism, but also 20th century Western thinkers such as Carl Jung, the physicist Niels Bohr, the philosopher Martin Heidegger, and the spiritual philosopher Alan Watts. In addition, its slim size and poetic quietist aphorisms made it very popular as a New Age text during the 1970s and 80s. There are a large number of English translations.

The author, Lao-tzu, is a legendary or even partly mythological figure, or maybe a compilation of several historical personalities or legends. He is traditionally considered a contemporary of Confucius (c. 551-c. 479), who lived during the Spring and Autumn period (about 770 to 476 B.C.E., the first half of the Eastern Zhou period). The name is from the Spring and Autumn Annals, a chronicle of the state of Lu, which tradition associates with Confucius. Unlike Lao-tzu, Confucious can be reliably considered an actual historical figure. In later centuries, the two were contrasted, especially by the Taoists, with Confucius as representing filial piety, good government, civic duty, and human moral virtues, and Lao-tzu the renunciation of civilization and proper manners, and the return to the state of innocence and spontaneity of the child.

According to one story, Lao-tzu grew weary of the moral decay of life in Chengzhou (now LuoYang, a city at the confluence of the Luo and Yellow Rivers in the west of Henan province) and decided to leave civilization and live as a hermit. At the city's western gate (or alternatively at the western pass out of the Luo–Yi valley), he was recognized by a guard called Yin-hsi, who refused to let him pass unless he wrote down his teachings. The result was the *Tao Te Ching* or *Daodejing*, literally *"The Scripture of the Way and its Power,"* a work of poetic utterances and aphorisms that present the theme of aligning human life with the natural rhythms of nature and of the universe, that is, with the Way (the Tao). Literally meaning road, channel, or path, this is the natural order of the universe, the mysterious creative process which gives birth to heaven, earth, and myriad things. Though imperceivable and ineffable, it is not separate from the world's sights, sounds, and objects.

The Tao, then, is equivalent to the Brahman of Vedanta and the Shunyata of Mahayana Buddhism. However, the emphasis here is on the spontaneous flow of phenomena rather than the transcendent Paramatman of Vedanta or the One of Neoplatonism.

Modern historians now consider Lao-tzu, assuming he was an actual figure, to have lived somewhat later, during the Warring States period of the 4th century B.C.E., which would put him (or the *Tao Te Ching*), contemporary with Chuang-tzu. But the text includes material from different periods.

The border guard Yin-hsi meanwhile, would go on to become a legendary figure of Zhou Dynasty China.

12-vi. *Chuang-tzu*

Chuang-tzu (c.369-286 B.C.E.) (or Zhuangzi as his name is more usually transliterated now), second only to Lao-tzu in importance regarding Taoism. Unlike Lao-tzu, we are more confident regarding his status as a historical figure. He lived during the Warring States period, when various feudal empires contended for power in the vacuum left by the decline of the Zhou dynasty. Seven main kingdoms were involved, the Yan, Zhao, Han, Wei, Qi, Chu, and Qin.

This period of political uncertainty was a period of bureaucratic and military reforms, development, and diversity in Chinese philosophy, with the so-called Hundred Schools of Thought. These included Confucianism, Legalism, Taoism, Mohism, the Yin-Yang or Naturalist school, and the Logicians.

Although Chuang-tzu was a contemporary of the equally esteemed Confucian thinker Mencius, the two philosophers wrote in isolation from each other. His eponymous work, the *Chuang-tzu*, became, along with the *Tao Te Ching*, became one of the two foundational texts of Taoism (although, as with the *Tao te Ching*, it appears that the work is a compilation produced by several authors). It is renowned for its wordplay, poetic and humorous style, and use of parables to convey messages. It offers a simple life far removed from everyday Confucian society's intellectual and political disputes. Due to Chuang-tzu's influence, Buddhism in China developed into Ch'an, better known by its Japanese name, Zen.

But he is best known for his parable of the butterfly [Wu, 1990], one of the best-known anecdotes in the philosophical literature:

> Once upon a time, I dreamt I was a butterfly, fluttering hither and thither, to all intents and purposes a butterfly. I was conscious only of my happiness as a butterfly, unaware that I was myself. Soon I awaked, and there I was, veritably myself again. Now I do not know whether I was then a man dreaming I was a butterfly, or whether I am now a butterfly, dreaming I am a man.

The question this raises is how do we know that what we experience is real? Chuang-tzu uses the example of a dream, as when we are dreaming, unless it is a lucid dream, we consider it as our normal waking existence. In a sense, this is the oriental equivalent to Descartes' *Meditations on Method*, in which he also refers to dreaming and waking. Descartes goes further and asks how can we be sure that anything we experience is reliable, and not placed in our minds but an evil genius. Through this proto-phenomenological method of radical doubt, in which he questioned everything, Descartes concluded that the only thing he could not doubt was his own consciousness ("I think (i.e., I am conscious) therefore I am") [Descartes, 1968]. This is the foundation of phenomenology, and the insight by Western philosophers like Kant, Husserl, and Sartre of the transcendental ego, the observing "I" consciousness.

The transcendental ego is basically the same as the Indian concept of the universal Self or Atman of Vedanta, individual soul or atma of Ajivaka, individual transcendent consciousness or purusha of Samkhya and Yoga, and the life-monad or jiva of Jainism.

13. ABRAHAMIC MONOTHEISM

13-i. Monotheism, Polytheism, and Animism

Although 19th century Western positivist and Christian ideas assumed a progressive spiritual and theological evolution from animism to polytheism to monotheism (specifically Judeo-Christian), and from there to the rationality of atheism, an ethnocentric idea first proposed by Edward Tylor. This misleading nature of this narrative is shown by the fact that many supposed "primitive" people have a monistic, pantheistic, or monotheistic belief system, as with the Plains Indian's concept of *Wakan Tanka*, Lakota for "Great Sacred" or "Great Mystery," but usually translated "Great Spirit." It can be understood as the Divine conceived as both impersonal Essence and personal Creator.

The standard religious forms seem to be kathenotheism, as in Pharaonic Egypt and Vedic India – worshiping a particular god while not denying the existence of others, specifically as forms of the deity one is worshiping. From there, one could go to polytheism on the one hand, such as Greek and Roman pantheons, and monaltry and monotheism on the other. Even with polytheistic pantheons, a single deity tends to be considered the primary one, reflecting human family and social structure, such as in Mesopotamia, Greece, and Scandinavia. I remember one orthodox Jewish rabbi speaking approvingly of Greek religion, considering Zeus a monotheistic deity.

Hence myth and religion have many layers. At the most basic, it is the projection of the personal unconscious, the internalized parents that have become all-powerful supernatural figures. These then serve as the basis for Jungian archetypes. And these archetypes, in turn, are the individual experiences or reflections of supra-physical gods and spiritual hierarchies, and at a much more antagonistic level, the anti-divine powers.

And not only that, but there are also local cultural and environmental differences. Whereas, say, the North European polytheist religion and mythology was, at its most superficial, a personification of the forces of nature as a way of making sense of the universe (such as Thor, the god of thunder and so on), in the equally harsh desert world of the Middle East, mythology was based instead on the stern father. The whole idea of loving and fearing God to avoid his wrath shows how the Old Testament religion of the Hebrews was, in certain ways, the externalization of the toxic parent [TheraminTrees, 2015].

All these aspects and layers need to be unraveled and separately recognized to understand the nature of individual and cosmic reality, and the various forces and powers involved.

13-ii. The Origin of the Hebrews

Initially, the Hebrews were a social, not an ethnic, group [Sledge, 2023, 7:13]. They would raid the Egyptians, resulting in the need for the Pharaoh to lead an army or war party out against them.

Taking the linguistically most archaic strata of the Hebrew Bible, it appears that Yahweh's original heartland was the north-west Arabian peninsula just East of the Dead Sea. Yahweh, whose name means "the one that exists," was originally a warrior and storm god whose central manifestation was the catastrophic thunderstorms resulting in deadly flash flooding that still plague the region today.

The Canaanite god Ba'al seems to be similar, another lightning-wielding warrior-storm god. Baal, or Ba'al, was a title and honorific meaning "owner" or "lord" in the Northwest Semitic languages of the time. It then came to be applied to gods. Although scholars previously associated the name with solar cults and various patron deities, inscriptions have shown that the name Ba'al was particularly associated with the storm and fertility god Hadad [Wikipedia - Baal].

During the late Bronze or early Iron Age, the Yahweh cult made its way to the Judean Highlands (represented by the Biblical period of the book of

Judges). From Egyptian proclamations, it seems that southern Levantine raiders and nomads were associated with Yahweh, and that by the 9th century B.C.E. the Israelite house of Omri (one of the early kings) seems to have had Yahweh as an essential and possibly national God [Sledge, 2023, 8:41].

13-iii. The Bronze Age Collapse

The Bronze Age collapse was a period of widespread societal collapse in the eastern Mediterranean region during the late 12th century B.C.E. This affected all the major civilizations of the region, such as the Hittites, Mycenaeans, and Egyptians. The situation was one of almost post-apocalyptic chaos, which may have been a factor that allowed a raiders' warrior god to have such appeal at the time. As esoteric scholar Justin Sledge puts it, imagine what sort of religion would have developed in the world of *Mad Max*. In this context, it is easy to understand the cultural background between the particularly abhorrent passages in the Old Testament.

The causes of the Bronze Age Collapse are still debated. One of the most popular theories is that it was the result of invasions and migrations by the so-called "Sea Peoples," a confederation of maritime raiders from the Aegean and eastern Mediterranean regions, earlier equivalents of Vikings perhaps. More likely there was a whole convergence of factors, including economic instability, environmental disaster, and political and social unrest, with the Sea Peoples as simply one more factor.

Among the cultures that emerged in the wake of the collapse, the Phoenicians and the Israelites, would significantly impact the course of history in the region and beyond.

13-iv. The Storm God

The storm god myth seems particularly appropriate to the post-apocalyptic chaos of the Bronze Age Collapse, and gods like Yahweh and Baal began as classic storm gods. However, like the sky god, the storm god is a common theme in many cultures around the world, and indeed there is an apparent connection between the two, especially for premodern peoples, trying to make sense of the terrifying and apparently capricious power of nature which they were at the mercy of.

Hence, early myths often have the storm god as a central figure responsible for creating and maintaining the natural world. In the ancient Sumerian religion, the god Enlil was associated with wind, storms, and agriculture, and was considered one of the most powerful gods. In the Maya civilization, Chaac was the god of rain and agriculture, depicted with a reptilian head and sometimes carrying a lightning axe.

One of the best-known examples of the storm god, at least today due to TV series like Vikings, and the Marvel Cinematic Universe, is Thor in Norse mythology, who wields his mighty hammer Mjolnir. In Greek mythology, Zeus was the king of the gods and the god of thunder and lightning, often depicted with a lightning bolt in his hand. Similarly, in Hindu mythology, Indra, another sky god, was also the god of thunder and rain, riding on a white elephant and wielding a thunderbolt.

13-v. From Monolatry and Monotheism

Canaan was a Semitic-speaking culture, civilization, and region in the Ancient Near East during the late 2nd millennium B.C.E. Canaanite religion was polytheistic and, in some cases, monolatristic (that is, having a belief in many gods, but only worshiping one, a term coined by 19th/early 20th century German biblical scholar and orientalist Julius Wellhausen). Around the start of the first millennium B.C.E., after the Bronze Age collapse, the Israelite religion developed through the monolatristic worship of Yahweh, one of the Canaanite gods. Yahweh would later fuse with El (literally god), the head of the Canaanite pantheon.

13-vi. The Babylonian and Hebrew Genesis

Although the Hebrew Bible would only be codified much later, its cosmological elements can be found in the general Mesopotamian and

Levantine mythologies, hence the various parallels between the Hebrew and Babylonian creation accounts.

One uses a "divine word" or "divine speech" to bring about creation. For example, in the *Enuma Elish*, Marduk uses his words to bring order to the chaotic universe, while in Genesis, God creates through his words: "And God said, 'Let there be light,' and there was light" (Genesis 1:3). This emphasis on the power of language or speech to create reflects a common ancient Near Eastern belief in the potency of words and incantations.

Another similarity is the concept of humans being created in the image of the divine. In the *Enuma Elish*, humans are created to be servants of the gods, while in Genesis, humans are created to have dominion over the earth. However, both accounts suggest that humans have a special relationship with the divine and are somehow connected to the divine nature.

Finally, both the *Enuma Elish* and Genesis include a sense of cyclical time. In the *Enuma Elish*, the creation of the universe is seen as a repeat of a previous cycle of creation and destruction, while in Genesis, the seventh day of rest marks a weekly cycle of work and rest. This cyclical understanding of time reflects the ancient Near Eastern belief in the recurring patterns of the cosmos.

13-vii. The Babylonian Exile and the Development of Judaism

The Jewish–Babylonian Wars (601–586 B.C.E.) were attempts by the Kingdom of Judah to escape dominance by the Neo-Babylonian Empire. This resulted in a Babylonian victory and the destruction of the Kingdom of Judah, including Solomon's Temple in Jerusalem. A large number of Judeans were taken into captivity, this period being known as the Babylonian captivity or Babylonian exile.

The Babylonian captivity was a crisis of faith for the Jews, as they believed their prayers could not be answered in a foreign land. In response, certain groups of Judahites developed pre-existing ideas about Yahweh-centric monolatrism, election, divine law, Covenant, and pre-existing Babylonian elements such as the Genesis account of creation.

The so-called Deuteronomistic theology, which includes the "school" that produced the Book of Deuteronomy and other books (such as Joshua, Judges, Samuel, Kings, and the Book of Jeremiah), is based on the idea of a covenant or treaty between the Israelites and Yahweh, who he has chosen as his people. Hence Israel is to be a theocracy under Yahweh, the Lord, with religious law over all worldly sources of authority. The law given through Moses is the complete revelation of the will of god, and nothing further is needed (Eleven hundred years later, this idea of a comprehensive and final revelation was to be repeated with Islam).

Central to this religion are absolutist exhortations such as Deuteronomy 6:5: "You shall love the Lord your God with all your heart and with all your soul and with all your might," which recall those strange modern-day North Korean political slogans [Beschizza, 2016] that declare enthusiastic obedience to the Party. Conspicuously absent is "and all your mind," reflecting the primary sense, secondarily feeling, ego-orientation of the ancient Hebrews (in contrast to the strong emphasis on thinking in Indian, Greek, and Confucian philosophy).

The covenant theory explains Israel's successes (faithfulness to Yahweh) and failures (disobedience, not fully following the Commandments), such as the destruction of the Kingdom of Israel by the Assyrians (721 B.C.E.) and the Kingdom of Judah by the Babylonians (586 B.C.E.). So rather than humans dependent on the capricious whim of supernatural powers, there is a reason why things happen, and hence a way to improve the collective circumstances (through faithfully following Yahweh's law). Previously, this could only be done through making offerings, animal or human sacrifices to the gods, or through magical rituals (for example, success in the Egyptian afterlife, or mantras and yantras in Indian village tantra). Although this earlier way of thinking still persisted, for example, with animal sacrifices and temple offerings, it was now subsumed under theistic religion.

Given the way that identity politics work, with one's own ingroup as the ethnocentric, narcissistic summit, it was inevitable that monaltry, the worship of Yahweh to the exclusion of other, equal gods, would become monotheism, the denial of the very existence of all other gods, whether Canaanite or foreign. Traces of the original monaltry remain in, for example, the prohibition on making graven images due to Yahweh being "a jealous god." As the Judeo-Christian Gnostics would some centuries later point out, the fact that Yahweh is jealous shows that there must be other gods, because who else would he be jealous of?

In contrast to the individual moral responsibility or early Zoroastrian, classical Greek, or Confucian thought, or for that matter, the Secular Enlightenment and modern-day humanism, agnosticism, and atheism, there is the emphasis on the group or the collective, especially in terms of the destiny of the nation of Israel as a whole. Everything, morality, social responsibility, and personal meaning, is based on this Deuteronomistic worldview and the idea of a special relationship with this archon or celestial ruler (to use the Gnostic interpretation).

During this time, Zoroastrian influences on late Judaism were pervasive and profound. While the Jews seem to have independently developed monotheism, what they picked up from the Persians was the belief that one god rules universally and will save not only the Jews but all those who turn to him. This universalism only appears in Second Isaiah, written during and after the Babylonian exile. Ideas of heaven and hell also seem to come from Zoroastrianism, replacing the Hebrew concept of either no afterlife or a shadowy existence in Sheol [Gier, 1994].

With the conquest of Babylon by the Persians under Cyrus the Great in 539 B.C.E., the Jews returned to Jerusalem, where they began work on the Second Temple. From then on, a strict monotheism would dominate the former Kingdom of Judah, and, starting some eight centuries later with the Christianization of the Roman Empire, most of the known world.

13-viii. *The Abrahamic Religions*

The Catholic scholar of Islam Louis Massignon (1883-1962) coined the phrase "Abrahamic religion" to refer to the religions that worship the God of the Hebrew patriarch and prophet, Abraham. He adopted the term from the plural form of a Quranic reference to *din Ibrahim*, the "religion of Ibrahim (Abraham)," which includes Judaism, Christianity, and Islam, as the faithful of these religions are considered the "people of the book," to use the Quranic term.

All the Abrahamic religions share a common belief that a supreme being imbued meaning into the universe, that this knowledge is available to us via one or more texts revealed through prophets or saviors, and that it is our responsibility to learn about it.

Abraham is traditionally thought to have lived sometime around 2000-1700 B.C.E. He is the father of Isaac by Sarah (Genesis 12.25), and Ishmael by Hagar (Quran 37.83-113), the former being a Jewish patriarch and the latter a Muslim prophet. Hence Judaism and Islam are considered sibling religions. However, archaeologists now understand that it is impossible to recover archaeological evidence for the existence of purported 2nd millennium B.C.E. figures like Abraham, Isaac, Ishmael, or Jacob (the son of Isaac). And even if they had existed, they would not have been monotheists in the conventional sense, as Jewish monotheism only dates back to the 6th century B.C.E.

Of course, this is an example of the difference between myth (totally imaginary characters, such as the Greek gods or biblical figures like Noah), legend (characters who may have existed but whose lives and stories have been greatly exaggerated, such as King David and Solomon), and history (characters who existed, such as Julius Caesar) [Baker, 2020], the Jewish patriarchs being either myth or legend, depending on one's interpretation. The same threefold categorization could be made with other ancient religions and belief systems; for example, in Taoism, Lao-tzu was a legendary character, while Chuang-tzu is historical.

The contradiction between outer (exoteric) literalism and inner and transcendent mysticism means that each of the three Abrahamic religions have developed their own often incredibly profound esoteric or inner, mystical traditions. As a result, esotericism has almost always been rooted in religious belief of one form or another (this also goes for the Eastern religions, where there is less distinction between exoteric and esoteric). This extends even to their respective esoteric traditions; e.g., Traditional Kabbalah only references the Jewish people. Sufism requires one to accept Islam, and so on.

According to Deuteronomistic Judaism, God only made a covenant with the people of Israel. The Pentateuch, the Five Books of Moses, are supposed to be God's infallible law and contain not only advice to the nation of Israel, but also all the secrets of creation.

Post-Jerusalem Church Christianity shifts the emphasis from the collective to the individual, with its claim of a new revelation and the only possible way to salvation being through personal acceptance of Christ. However, it includes the Law of Moses as the backstory.

Islam, in turn, puts forward its claim to be the only true faith, with that Muhammad is the seal of the prophets, who includes the message of all the others, and that there will never be another prophet or revelation from God. To rational modernity, this is pretty surreal; imagine humanity continuing for millions of years into the future, perhaps space-faring, but without ever having any further guidance from the supposed Supreme Being. But it should be remembered that premodern mythic thinking, which is linear rather than cyclic, sees the lifetime of the entire universe as only around seven or nine thousand years. The tendency by YouTuber Islamic apologetics now is to refer to the Koran as the "third testament," after the Old (Judaism) and New (Christianity) Testaments. Jewish and Islamic theology tends more to a similar absolutist monotheism, misinterpreting the Christian Trinity as another form of polytheism.

Finally, Baha'is, who represent a reformist and modernist movement coming out of Islam, consider that Muhammad was the seal of the prophets of the old cycle, and that their prophet, Baha'u'llah (1817–1892), initiated a new cycle of revelation. Not surprisingly, this didn't go down well among the Islamic theocrats of Iran and elsewhere, with a history of persecution and imprisonment that continues to the present day.

All this is not to mention the countless messianic figures within each of those religions. For example, the 17th century Sabbateans believed the Sephardi (Hispanic) rabbi Sabbatai Zevi (1626-676) was the long-awaited Jewish Messiah. According to the Ahmadiyya, the Indian religious figure Mirza Ghulam Ahmad (1835-1908) is the Mahdi expected by Muslims to appear at the end of history. The Unification Church believes that the Korean conservative Christian Sun Myung Moon (1920-2012) is the second coming of Christ (or "Lord of the Second Advent). And so on with every prophet and avatar claimant. Wikipedia pages such as "List of messiah claimants" and "List of people claimed to be Jesus" include everyone from religious founders to cult leaders to YouTube personalities, some of whose claims are more serious and others more farcical.

All this refers to one of the primary characteristics of the Abrahamic religion, according to which, as in the movie Highlander, there can only be one. This is in contrast to polytheistic, henotheistic, kathenotheistic, and monistic religions and belief systems, all of which are more universalist in approach. The rigidity and exclusiveness of monotheism as a whole with its sole supernatural deity make it easy to rationally refute [Woodford, 2021], and that's not even considering the way each religion claims to be the only true one. It can be argued that polytheism stands up better to criticism in this regard, as it rejects the premise of a single anthropomorphic supreme being [Ocean Keltoi, 2022].

One way around this is the esotericist Traditionalist movement of Rene Guenon and Fritjof Schuon, influenced by Sufism and Advaita Vedanta, according to which all traditional extant religions (not just the Abrahamic ones) share a common, esoteric revelation behind the external difference [Schuon, 1975]. Hence they are all, in a sense, true, although this implies esoteric monotheism, or even just monism. The limitation here is the claim that gnosis and liberation can only be had through traditional religion.

13-ix. Monotheism, Monism, and Duality

Monotheism traces the cause of existence back to a single first principle, as with most mythical, religious, and metaphysical systems. But whereas in polytheism and kathenotheism, the first principle might be an original principle of chaos, formlessness, or night, representing the depths of the unconscious (or of the Inconscient, to use Sri Aurobindo's somewhat equivalent term), from which God or the gods emerge, in monotheism this original cause is the personal God himself.

The problem is that in making God separate from the soul and creation, Monotheism reduces reality to an ultimate duality. Many mystics and philosophers such as Ramanuja, al-Ghazali, Maimonides, and St. Thomas Aquinas followed this interpretation, to ensure their theology conformed to the duality of their religion. As with the Buddhist prohibition on metaphysics, they either had to work around and conform to the dead weight of intellectual or religious dogma, or, assuming an authentic experience of Soul and God, they had to deny the ultimate unity of the two and instead emphasize the duality, and so orientate away from the source and to duality.

Various alternatives to monotheistic duality include immanent pantheism (e.g., Stoicism, Taoism), transcendental acosmism (e.g., Advaita Vedanta), or cosmological emanationist monism (e.g., Neoplatonism), in which all creation and all existence are traced back to a single principle, an impersonal ultimate reality or Absolute.

Some mystics, like Utpaladeva (Kashmir Shaivism), Ibn Arabi (Sufism), Meister Eckhardt (Christianity), Sri Aurobindo (Integral Yoga/Hinduism), and Meher Baba (Sufi-Vedanta synthesis), have been able to reconcile both one and many, devotion (bhakti) and nonduality (jnana), in a single panentheistic theology and metaphysical cosmology.

14. GREEK PHILOSOPHY

14-i. Periods of Greek History

The Greeks were one of the most striking of the classic civilizations of the ancient world. They were not a single empire but several city-states. Without rich natural resources, and constantly at war with each other, they nevertheless spread their civilization across the known world [Roberts, 2009/2019].

The history of Ancient Greece is traditionally divided into many periods, these being into the Bronze Age (c. 3000-1100 B.C.E.), the Iron Age (c. 1100-750 B.C.E.), the Archaic Age (c. 750-479 B.C.E.), the Classical Age (479-323 B.C.E.), and the Hellenistic Age (323-30 B.C.E.). Here the first two represent the Mythic period, the Archaic and Classical, the Axial Age, and the Hellenistic period the further development of Axial insights, continuing with later civilization during the Roman and Medieval eras.

The Greeks laid the foundation for Western civilization with the Hebrews, another culture that had an enormous influence disproportionate to its size. One contributing reason, and the other faith, represented the polarity of the Axial Age. The third element, gnosis, only comes later, with the Hellenistic Age synthesis epitomized by the city of Alexandria.

14-ii. The Bronze Age

The Bronze Age began with Minoan civilization and culture, centered on the island of Crete, which was the oldest in Europe. It is not clear what the Minoans called themselves, since the name "Minoan" was coined by British archaeologist Sir Arthur Evans (1851-1941) in reference to the mythical King Minos, as Evans identified the site at Knossos with the labyrinth of the Minotaur of Greek mythology. Nevertheless, the Minoans established a trade network around much of the Mediterranean, built elaborate palaces up to four stories high, complete with plumbing systems and decorated with frescoes, and developed a distinct script, called Linear A, which has yet to be deciphered.

In contrast with most religions of the time, and for that matter of today, with their strong patriarchal element, Minoan religion seems to have been centered on a primary goddess figure, which would have had various aspects. The snake goddess figurines, such as those excavated in 1903 at Knossos, dating to around 1600 B.C.E., are perhaps the most striking. Minoan religion ties in with Erich Neumann's thesis of the Great Mother archetypes. Arthur Evans also referred to the mythological continuity of the Great Goddess, from the ancient Near East to Minoan Crete, and thence to Classical Greece, a thesis supported by Joseph Campbell, especially concerning the underworld and the myth of the dead and resurrected god. The Minoans, it seems, also had a tree of eternal life, similar to the Scandinavian Yggdrasil or world-tree, and representing the afterlife [Campbell, 1964/2017 pp.83-5]

Minoan civilization began declining from c. 1450 B.C.E., possibly the result of volcanic eruptions on the nearby island of Thera (which is one of the candidates for the original basis of Plato's Atlantis myth, although scientific dating of the main eruption to around 1600 B.C.E. predates the decline of Minoan civilization), finally ended around 1100 BC, as part of the wider Bronze Age collapse.

Around the 18th century B.C.E., Minoan contact with mainland Greece may have led to the development of the late Bronze Age Mycenaean civilization. They developed architecture, military organization, art, and a writing system distinct from the Minoans, called Linear B. However, as with the Minoans, they were the victims of the apocalyptic 11th century Bronze Age collapse. This ushered in the Greek Dark Ages, represented by the Iron Age, a technological development most likely caused by the warlike nature of the time.

14-iii. The Archaic Period

Following the Greek Dark Ages, the Archaic Age of Greek history and society saw the beginning of Greek civilization in the more classical sense. It extended from the 8th century B.C.E. to the early 5th century B.C.E., and was part of Karl Jaspers' theory of an Axial Age transformation of culture, philosophy, and religion.

This period was characterized by a growing population, trade and commerce, the development of writing and the arts (especially in pottery and sculpture), and most importantly the *polis* (plural *poleis*) or city-state. These were self-governing entities that controlled their own territory and had their own government, culture, and traditions. Among the most important were Athens, Sparta, Corinth, and Thebes (this last being a city in Boeotia, Central Greece, not to be confused with the ancient Egyptian city of the same name).

One institution that was established during the start of the Archaic period was the Olympic Games. These were held every four years in Olympia, beginning in 776 B.C.E., and brought together athletes from different city-states. In contrast to their revival as the modern, secular, Olympic games established in 1896, these ceremonies were steeped in religion; athletes were male only and would compete naked. In these and other games in ancient and classical Greece, they trained in the Gymnasium, a public institution for physical training, education, and socializing. The word itself is from *gymnos*, "naked," physical training encouraging aesthetic appreciation of the male body. The Greeks considered the well-developed naked body as pleasing to the gods, in contrast to the Abrahamic shame of the body (as, for example, Genesis 9:20-27 where Ham was cursed for seeing his father Noah naked) that would later develop through the Christian takeover of the classical world.

Sporting events go back further to the Bronze Age Mycenaeans and Minoans of the second millennium B.C.E. Here, the Minoans gave far more empowerment to women than in Greece and Rome. They also practiced the extraordinary and, one might assume, quite dangerous, sport of bull leaping, in which it seems that perhaps not only men but also women took part [Milner, 2023].

Dating from the start of the Archaic period are the epic works of Homer, the *Iliad* (concerning the Trojan War) and the *Odyssey*, representing Western literature's foundation. An epic is a lengthy narrative poem that describes the deeds of extraordinary characters who, in dealings with gods or other superhuman forces, shape the mortal universe for their descendants [Meyer, 2005, cited in Wikipedia – Epic Poetry]. Other examples include the Neo-Sumerian *Epic of Gilgamesh*, the Indian *Mahabharata* and *Ramayana*, the Old English *Beowulf*, Dante's *Divine Comedy*, and Milton's *Paradise Lost*. A 20th century example is Sri Aurobindo's *Savitri*, which is based on an earlier Hindu story, rewritten to describe the coming Supramental transformation. Epics can be prose narrative as well, J.R.R. Tolkien's *Lord of the Rings*, the foundational text of the modern Fantasy genre, is a revisioning of Nordic mythology and cosmology in terms of a Christian mindset, in which the fate of the world turns on a humble hobbit rather than a Wagnerian hero. Science fiction examples may be secular and based on history, such as Asimov's Foundation series (inspired by 18th century English essayist, politician, and historian Edward Gibbon's six-volume *Decline and Fall of the Roman Empire* (1776 to 1788), itself an epic of a non-fictional sort), Frank Herbert's *Dune*, or even, to give a pop culture example, George Lucas' *Star Wars*. Such epics, whether poetry, prose, or even cinematic, represents the ultimate instance of mythopoesis (myth-making) and story-telling.

Slightly younger than Homer's works are the poems of Hesiod, of which the *Theogony* (c. 730–700 B.C.E.) is of particular interest. As with the Egyptian theologies of one or two millennia earlier, this gives the family history or creation sequence of the gods. Such accounts are both mythology and also the beginning of metaphysical and even scientific cosmology, as the gods are often the personifications of natural forces or cosmic entities like Earth and Sky.

Bridging the gap between mythology and philosophy was Pherecydes of Syros (fl. 6th century B.C.E.), the author of a book on cosmogony, known as either the *Pentemychos* or *Heptamychos*. Only a few fragments, mostly quotations in later works, survive. His cosmogony was based on three divine principles: Life, Earth, and Time. He seems to have been one of the first thinkers to introduce the doctrine of the transmigration of souls to the West, assuming this wasn't solely the contribution of Pythagoras. Such teachings, along with various legends and stories of miracles, tie him to the development of Pythagoreanism or Orphism [Wikipedia – Pherecydes of Syros].

Finally, there are the Presocratic philosophers, beginning with Thales and his Milesian school in the 6th century B.C.E., representing the foundation of the Western philosophical and scientific tradition, which is described in the following sections.

The demarcation point for the end of the Archaic Age is the second Persian invasion of 480–479 B.C.E. After the defeat of the first Persian invasion by Darius a decade earlier, his son Xerxes built up an enormous army and navy. Despite his great numerical superiority, he was still defeated by an alliance led by the traditional rivals of Athens and Sparta. The Greeks chose to defend strategic geographical bottle-necks, where the Persians couldn't bring their full forces to bear. Had the Persians won, European history may have turned out very differently. History is full of decisive battles like this, which sci-fi and alternative history writers find a rich source of inspiration (for example, Philip K Dick's *The Man in the High Castle* is based on the premise that the Axis powers won World War II).

14-iv. The Presocratics

The world of the Greek philosopher marked the emergence and dominance of the thinking type, in contrast to the Chinese intuitives (Taoism) and the Indian yogi-ascetic's emphasis on pure consciousness (the transcendent ego and beyond).

This begins with the Presocratic Greek philosophers of the Archaic period. They sought to understand the natural world and the universe through rational inquiry. They were interested in questions related to the nature of reality, the origins of the cosmos, and the relationship between matter and mind. Their ideas laid the foundation for the development of Greek philosophy in the Classical period, which would go on to have a profound influence on Western thought.

Earliest are the Milesians, named after the city of Miletus in Ionia (the central part of the western coast of Anatolia, today part of Turkey), at the time among the greatest and wealthiest of the Greek cities. They are represented by Thales (624/623-c. 548/545 B.C.E.), his student Anaximander (c. 610-c. 546 B.C.E), and his student Anaximenes (c. 586-c. 526 B.C.E.). These were the first rational philosophers as they sought to explain the origin (*arche*, beginning, substance) of the cosmos in a single principle, this being, respectively, water, *apeiron* (the unlimited), and air (or nous, mind or intelligence).

Some Presocratic philosophers were also mystics, especially another Ionian, Pythagoras of Samos (582-496 B.C.E.), from whose followers we get the word "esoteric." Pythagoras may have been a student of Anaximander, and after that, may have been acquainted with the yogi-ascetics and the Egyptian mysteries, before founding his own mystery school in Southern Italy. From Pythagoras and his school, which stands at the origin of Western Esotericism, the Western mystical tradition would be continued and further developed by Plato, from Plato Neoplatonists, and from them the Neoplatonists, Islamic philosophy, and Renaissance Hermeticism.

Then as now, not everyone could appreciate esoteric insights. One of Pythagoras' critics was the poet and philosopher Xenophanes of Colophon (c. 570-c. 478 B.C.E.), who fled to Ionia at the age of 25 when the Persians invaded. Xenophanes was the first known skeptic who denied that truth could be known. Xenophanes ridiculed the anthropomorphic representations of deities in various religions and cultures, famously stating

> But if cattle and horses and lions had hands
> or could paint with their hands and create works such as men do,
> horses like horses and cattle like cattle
> also would depict the gods' shapes and make their bodies
> of such a sort as the form they themselves have.
>
> ...
>
> Ethiopians say that their gods are snub–nosed and black
> Thracians that they are pale and red-haired

But he wasn't an atheist in the modern sense (as in YouTube debates between theist literalists and materialists). Instead, he posited an ineffable, unchanging, unitary God, absolute mind, capable of comprehending all things in Itself. The God of Xenophanes (and of some of the other Presocratics such as Parmenides) is not unlike the Absolute or Atman Brahman of the Upanishads, except that it isn't identified with the individual Self.

Another Ionian, Heraclitus (c. 535-c. 475 B.C.E.), was from the city of Ephesus, which was then part of the Persian Empire. A melancholy individual, he emphasized the impermanence of all things with the sayings "No man ever steps in the same river twice" and to *panta rhei* ("everything flows").

Existence as constant change is also described, in different ways, by the I Ching (Book of Changes), Gautama Buddha (impermanence, denial of a persisting self), and 20th century philosopher Alfred North Whitehead (Process Philosophy). Although he attributed fire to the arche of the world, this seems to have been a metaphor for change. In this context, he also referred to the logos as a single universal law uniting the cosmos, although the few surviving fragments don't say much about it. The Stoics later adopted the doctrine of the logos.

The Eleatic school was centered around the ancient Greek colony of Elea in present-day Campania in southern Italy. Parmenides (late sixth/early fifth century B.C.E.) is known only from fragments from a single poem, where he refers to two views of reality. Reality itself is one, changeless, and timeless, in contrast to the world of appearances. This position, which can be called "acosmism," would also be propounded a millennium later in India, by Shankara, who called his own branch of metaphysics Advaita Vedanta. Parmenides students included Zeno of Elea (c. 495-c. 430 B.C.E.) and Melissus of Samos. The former presented several logical paradoxes, such as Achilles and the tortoise, the dichotomy argument, and the paradox of the arrow, supported Parmenides and denied anything can move, all the evidence of the senses notwithstanding.

These two contemporaries from opposite ends of the Greek world, Parmenides, who denied change, and Heraclitus, who denied constancy, both influenced Plato and, through him, all of Western philosophy.

14-v. Life and Teachings of Pythagoras

Pythagoras is one of those first millennium B.C.E. figures, like Lao-tzu, Gautama Buddha, Mahavira, Zarathustra, and the pre-exilic Hebrew prophets, who even to this day define the modern spiritual landscape, but about whom very little is known for sure. His followers, therefore, similarly created an idealized biography, based on various myths and legends circulating at the time. His homeland may have been the island of Samos, where he was born sometime around 580 to 569 B.C.E., if he wasn't born in Syria where according to his much later biographers Iamblichus and Porphyry, his father Mnesarchus, a Phoenician, was trading [Godwin, 2016, p.13].

He is said to have studied with the Ionian philosophers Thales, Anaximander, and Pherecydes of Syros (who was intermediate between Hesiod and Ionian philosophy, who taught the origin of the universe and the immortality of the soul) who traveled to the Phoenician settlements in Syria, where he was initiated into mystery religions. As both Phoenician trade routes and Persian conquests led to the transmission of ideas between the Near East and Greece via the merchants, artisans, mercenaries, philosophers, and physicians [McEvilley, 2002], this may have been how Pythagoras encountered Indic teachings. The Athenian rhetorician Isocrates (436-338 B.C.E.) was the first to describe Pythagoras as having visited Egypt.

After traveling widely, he settled in Croton in southern Italy around 530 B.C.E. He founded a school where initiates were sworn to secrecy and lived a communal, ascetic lifestyle. From here, we later get the word "esoteric" for the inner circle of initiates. As the introduction mentioned, Pythagoras was the father of Western Esotericism.

Unusually for its time, the school was coeducational. The students lived a monastic spiritual life, abstaining from meat, alcohol, and sex and renouncing fame and wealth [Godwin, 2016, p.17]. Unfortunately, around 500 B.C.E., the school was destroyed, although it is unclear if Pythagoras survived.

The earliest reliable source on Pythagoras is a satirical poem probably written after his death by his contemporary Xenophanes, who describes him interceding on behalf of a dog that is being beaten, professing to hear in its cries the voice of a departed friend. What Xenophanes, in his ignorance and ridicule, fails to understand is the principle of sentientism, that the lives of all sentient beings, not just humans, have value.

Today we associate Pythagoras with basic geometry, specifically his famous theorem that bears his name. This describes the way to find the area of a right-angle triangle, which is: the square of the hypotenuse (the diagonal side, opposite the right angle) is equal to the sum of the areas of the squares on the other two sides. Taught to every schoolchild, this is probably the most well-known mathematical theorem ever written. Of course, this sort of thing was essential for the Greeks, for whom mathematics was a sacred science, and included only arithmetic and geometry.

But some of Pythagoras' teachings had nothing to do with the foundation of mathematics and respectable knowledge of rational modernity. One of these is metempsychosis, or the "transmigration of souls," which holds that every soul is immortal and, upon death, enters into a new body. This was the first Western conception of the immortal soul, replacing the earlier pessimistic idea of afterlife existence as a miserable shade.

In keeping with the belief in reincarnation, Pythagoras was also the first Westerner to espouse sentientism, or ahimsa (non-harmfulness), which he also seems to have acquired from India. The historian Herodotus (c. 484-c. 420 B.C.E.) states that Pythagoras taught his followers how to attain immortality, which may also be tied in with the Indian idea of Liberation.

Pythagoras is credited with the discovery of musical ratios, the five regular solids (which are also known from Neolithic Britain), the sphericity of the Earth (but not heliocentrism), and the identity of the morning and evening stars as the planet Venus.

Also traditionally attributed to him is the doctrine of *musica universalis*, which holds that the planets move according to mathematical equations and thus resonate to produce an inaudible symphony of music. That the universe has a unitive order that is both mathematical and numinous became a central insight not only of the Pythagoreans but also of Plato and Platonism, along with Hermeticism, Middle and Neoplatonism, and Renaissance esotericism. Some scholars believe that these teachings were developed by his later followers, particularly Philolaus of Croton (c. 470-c. 385 B.C.E), but this is only because he was the first to write on Pythagorean doctrine.

That the whole cosmos, with its various planets and stars, seen as a harmonious musical or entity, is a theme that would remain a constant element in the Platonic and Neopythagorean traditions, Medieval Christianity, Islam, and Judaism, the Renaissance, astronomers and esotericists of the Baroque period, scientists and philosophers of the 18th and 19th century secular enlightenment and romanticism periods, and esotericists and musicologists of the twentieth century and to the present day [Godwin, 1992].

Finally, the Golden Verses are a collection of spiritual aphorisms written in poetic rhyme, extolling the Pythagorean life and principles. As usual, these religious and mystical teachings are ascribed to the founder of the movement, in this case, Pythagoras. They seem to go back at least to the third century B.C.E. They were highly popular and widely distributed during the late classical period. The Neoplatonists used the Golden Verses as part of their program of moral instruction. The current version dates back to the translation and commentary by the fifth century C.E. Neoplatonist Hierocles of Alexandria. During the Renaissance, they were translated into Latin by the Byzantine grammarian Constantine Lascaris (1434-1501) as part of the printer and humanist Aldus Manutius' edition of his *Grammatica* of 1494-1495 [Wikipedia - Golden Verses].

14-vi. The Tetraktys

Whereas the Chinese I Ching is based on a binary computational representation, the Pythagoreans use arithmetic ratios. The harmonic intervals Pythagoras is credited with discovering involve the simple numerical ratio of the first four natural numbers derived from the relations of string length. These represent musical ratios of stringed instruments: the Octave (1/2), the Musical Fifth (2/3), and the Musical Fourth (3/4). The sum of these numbers (1 + 2 + 3 + 4) is ten, which was, therefore, for the Pythagoreans, the perfect number.

Like the Hebrews and other ancient peoples, the Greeks did not have an abstract system of numbers and used the letters of their alphabet instead (hence words can have numerological value; this is where Jewish Gematria and Cheiro's 20th century pop Pythagorean numerology comes from). They also used pebbles to learn arithmetic, placing small stones on calculating boards. From this, we get the word calculation, from the Latin calculus, "pebble." This resulted in a very visual style of arithmetic, represented, for example, by the Tetractys, a mystical symbol involving ten points arranged in four rows, as follows:

```
   o
  o o
 o o o
o o o o
```

This represents the stages of creation as well as the attributes of the Cosmos [Guthrie, 1987].

The Monad or Unity is associated with the first principle; for example, Plotinus refers to the absolute reality as The One.

The Dyad or duality represents Limit (*peras*, considered positive) and Unlimited (*apeiron*, negative).

The Triad is referred to as Harmony.

The Tetrad is identified with the Kosmos, and the Tetractys as a whole.

Geometrically, the number 1 is a point, 2 is a line (one dimension, connecting two points), 3 is a two dimensional shape like a triangle (three points), and four the three dimensional world, represented by a tetrahedron defined by four points.

It seems strange that the Dyad should be associated with Power, as two, the first even number, would be expected to be yin or passive, as in, for example, the Chinese system. In Shaivite and Shakta Tantra, however, the original polarization of the Supreme Shiva results in Shiva (representing Consciousness) and Shakti (power, creation).

The Triad is the first actual number, the Monad and Dyad being roots or principles, not numbers. It is also the first to signify totality because it comprises a beginning, middle, and end. And finally, the four sums up and repeats the whole pattern.

The symbolism of the number four had a vast influence on later esotericism, especially relating it to the ten sefirot of Christian Kabbalah (Cabala) in Renaissance Hermeticism, as well as the Tetrad or four letters of the Kabbalistic divine name and other symbolism such as the four worlds and four elements. For Jung also, the Tetrad symbolizes wholeness and integration, represented by the mandala and the four ego functions.

This symbolism and much more was explored in great detail in terms of Jungian psychology by Marie-Louise von Franz in her book *Numbers and Time*, a dense but essential work on numerology and archetypal symbolism [MacLennan, 2019; von Franz, 1975].

Beyond four (or five as the return to the center), number mysticism can be extended indefinitely, each number with its archetypal characteristics. Usually, however, at least in Western esotericism and occultism, the focus is on the first nine numbers (with ten as the return to one).

Pythagorean ideas on mathematical perfection influenced Plato, whose dialogues, especially his *Timaeus*, exhibit Pythagorean teachings. His teachings underwent a major revival in the first century B.C.E. with both the Middle Platonists and the Neopythagoreans. Through Iamblichus, these ideas were incorporated into Neoplatonism, and Western esotericism. In addition, they influenced early scientists such as Nicolaus Copernicus, Johannes Kepler, and Isaac Newton, the latter being the last great thinker to include science and esotericism in a single holistic worldview.

The unique quality of Pythagorean arithmosophy and the science of ratio and musical tones is that it represents a rare example of esotericism that transcends the human subjective dimension to become truly universal and objective, just as science later would. It represents an outward and empirical movement that balances religion and mythology's inner, phenomenological, and Jungian emphasis.

Modern science is grounded in mathematics that is far more complex than the immediately intuitive Pythagorean arithmosophy. Yet this describes the attributes of the physical universe to such a degree that the physicist Eugene Wigner would refer to it as "the unreasonable effectiveness of mathematics in the natural sciences" in a paper of the same name [Wigner, 1960]. Which supports the Pythagorean dictum that "all is a number."

14-vii. Post-Pythagorean Duality

A list of 10 pairs of contrary qualities is attributed to the Pythagoreans but has nothing to do with Pythagoras or his followers. The oldest reference is Aristotle, who said that it was in use among some contemporary Pythagoreans, although the original author seems to be Plato's nephew Speusippus. In any case, it appears to have also been in use among Aristotle's contemporaries.

The list is as follows.

- Unlimited – Limited
- Even – Odd
- Plurality – Unity
- Left – Right
- Female – Male
- In Motion – At Rest
- Curved – Straight
- Darkness – Light
- Evil – Good
- Oblong – Square

As with the Chinese Yin and Yang, the female principle is attributed to the negative pole, and the male principle to the positive polarity. One finds the same thing in Gnosticism and in Lurianic Kabbalah as well. Time and again, we will find chauvinistic and speciesist references in esoteric teachings and perennial philosophy. These show us the need not to be caught up in thought forms that date back to ignorant feudal cultures. On the other hand, it would be equally mistaken to just throw everything out in an appeal to superficial materialism and secular modernity bereft of cosmic meaning.

This general symbolism (although varying in details) gained greater significance among later occultists and esotericists, such as the Neoplatonists, and again more recently 19th and 20th century numerology.

14-viii. *Empedocles*

Empedocles (c. 494-c. 434 B.C.E.), from Akragas, a Greek city in Sicily, combined ideas from his predecessors such as the Ionians, the Pythagoreans, and the Eleatics. He is best known for originating the cosmogonic theory of the four classical elements. These are indestructible and unchangeable, and like the atoms of the atomists, combine in different ways to make all things. This can be compared to the five elements and five states of change and Indian and Chinese thought respectively. The difference being that the Indian (Upanishadic and Samkhyan) system is based on emanation, and the Chinese explanation is on the change of one element into another. Empedocles' four elements would remain the standard theory of natural philosophy in both the West and the Muslim world until the rise of empirical science in the 17th and 18th century.

In all these cases – Western, Indian, and Chinese – the four or five elements are not so much bumbling attempts at proto-science as phenomenological intuitions of the pattern of gross and subtle physical reality.

In Empedocles' cosmology, the four elements are subject to the two divine powers, Love and Strife (Philotes and Neikos). Love is responsible for the attraction and mixing of different forms, and Strife is the repulsive force that causes their separation.

Like the Pythagoreans, Empedocles believed in the transmigration of souls, and rejected animal sacrifice and killing animals for food.

14-ix. The Atomists

If one aspect of Greek philosophy, represented by Pythagoreanism and following him, Platonism, tends towards mysticism and esotericism, the other, represented by the Atomists and later Aristotle, tends more to natural philosophy and physicalism. Indeed, Atomism, as much as Aristotleanism and Nominalism, constitutes the foundation of the materialistic worldview of modernity.

The idea here is that the universe can be reduced to a plurality of fundamental principles or units, called atoms ("indivisibles"). This is similar but not the same as the *tattvas* (essences) or Dharmas of the shramana yogi-ascetics of Indian philosophy, as it is based on materialism and proto-science rather than phenomenology or pragmatic spiritual psychology

Atomism goes back to the little-known pre-Greek philosopher Leucippus (fl. 5th century B.C.E.), who apparently founded a school in Abdera, in Thrace, but was overshadowed by his famous student Democritus (c. 460-c. 370 B.C.E.), the father of Atomism.

The Atomists rejected the Eleatic school's denial of change and motion, and argued instead that the only thing that exists are atoms interacting deterministically with each other. Everything, even consciousness, comes about through the movement and combination of various types of atoms. As such, Atomism was the classical world's version of positivism and eliminative materialism.

The most influential of the Atomists was Epicurus (341-270 B.C.E.), who followed Democritus in believing the world was composed of atoms and the void, operating according to natural laws. Contrary to popular belief, Epicurus and his followers did not propose fine food and drink and a life of luxury and indulgence, but rather living simply as a way of maximizing happiness. Epicurus applied Democritus' theories to helping people take responsibility for their own well-being, and emphasized happiness, fulfillment, and dignity. The gods, if they exist at all, at best exemplify moral ideals, and do not bestow supernatural aid. Epicurus, in many ways, was the original humanist.

His ideas reappeared in the works of the Roman poet and philosopher Lucretius (c. 99 BC-c. 55 BC), who wrote *On the Nature of Things*, according to which the universe and consciousness are the results of atoms moving and colliding according to chance.

Atomism and materialism fell out of favor during the Christian era, reappearing in the 16th, 17th, and 18th centuries with the development of early modern mechanical philosophy and scientific and empirical thinking. This sometimes took the form of Corpuscularianism, which differs from Atomism in that corpuscles have their own property and are further divisible. Prominent philosophers and scientists here include the Hermeticist and cosmologist Giordano Bruno (1548-1600), Galileo Galilei (1564-1642), the father of modern science, who proposed that phenomena are produced by "matter in motion"), Isaac Beeckman (1588-1637), and Dutch atomist philosopher and scientist, Rene Descartes (1596-1650). Beeckman's student, whose corpuscularian theory that everything physical in the universe was made of tiny vortices of matter, would later reappear in the "permanent atoms" of the Theosophist C.W. Leadbeater, Pierre Gassendi (1592-1655), a Catholic priest and natural philosopher who Beeckman had inspired to adopt the philosophy of Epicurus, but sought to purge Atomism of its heretical and atheistic aspects, and Robert Boyle (1627-1692), whose 1661 work *The Sceptical Chymist* marked the transition between alchemy and chemistry.

French nobleman Antoine Lavoisier (1743-1794) played a crucial role during the chemical revolution of the 18th century, discovered oxygen's role in combustion and respiration, while the English meteorologist and physicist John Dalton (1766-1844) established atomic theory and the modern science of chemistry, completing the transition from natural philosophy to empirical science as regards atoms.

The first decades of the twentieth century saw this mechanistic, deterministic model replaced by quantum physics, emphasizing the observer principle, the wave function, and electrons as probability clouds rather than miniature planets whizzing around the atomic nucleus. This inspired parallels with Eastern philosophy in the mid to late 1970s [Capra, 1975; Zukav, 1984]. In the 1970s and 1980s, the Holistic, Human Potential, Transpersonal Psychology movement [Ferguson, 1980] referred to itself as the "New Paradigm" [Capra, 1982], in contrast to the old "Cartesian-Newtonian" atomistic and mechanistic worldview. The New Paradigm was similar but more intellectual than the intuitive-feeling of the New Age, although both share values like a holistic and pantheistic worldview, creativity, environmental sustainability, implications of quantum physics (and also New Age pop quantum mysticism), the Gaia hypothesis (both of the empirical and the pantheistic and new age sort), and the empowering of the individual.

Today (early 21st century), both the "thesis" of Atomistic, reductionistic, positivistic paradigm, and the "antithesis" of New Paradigm/New Consciousness holistic thinking, holistic thinking, are being replaced in the "synthesis" of non-reductionist theories of complexity, emergent evolution, and panpsychism [Institute of Art and Ideas. 2019].

14-x. Classical Greece

The 5th century B.C.E. marked the beginning of the Classical Age. This was the Golden Age of Ancient Greece, a high point for art and architecture, mainly its pottery, sculpture, and monumental buildings such as the Parthenon, a temple dedicated to the goddess Athena. Construction started in 447 B.C.E. when the Delian League – the association of Greek city-states under the leadership of Athens, fighting the Persians – was at the peak of its power. It was completed in 438; work on the decoration continued until 432.

The term democracy appeared in the 5th century B.C.E. in Greek city-states, notably Classical Athens, to mean rule by the people, in contrast to aristocracy, which meant rule by the elite. Yet Athenian democracy was very different from the democracy of today. Citizenship excluded women, slaves, foreigners, and youths below the age of military service. This meant that only about 1 in 4 residents in Athens actually qualified as citizens.

Whereas Athens was known for its democratic government, emphasis on education and the arts, and military and naval power, Sparta was characterized by its strict social hierarchy, military prowess, and emphasis on physical training and discipline.

This was also a time of significant intellectual development, particularly in philosophy. Some of the most prominent philosophers of this time included Athenians like Socrates, Plato, and Aristotle. They explored questions concerning the nature of reality, the role of the individual in society, and the relationship between the human and the divine.

14-xi. *The Sophists*

The Greek word *sophos*, wise man, is related to *sophia*, wisdom. In the Homeric period, this referred to an expert at a particular profession or craft, but later came to refer to politics and ethics, and philosophy, with figures such as the statesman Solon and the natural philosopher (or proto-scientist) Thales, and it was the meaning that appears in the histories of Herodotus. By the fifth and fourth centuries B.C.E., the Sophists had become itinerant public intellectuals who challenged traditional morality and religion, or speculated about the nature of language and culture, using rhetoric to persuade or convince others.

The sophists taught rhetoric and how to address issues from multiple viewpoints. In Athens, they included professional debaters like Protagoras, Gorgias, Hippias, Thrasymachus, Prodicus, Callicles, Antiphon, and Critias. Sometimes they specialized in specific topics such as philosophy, rhetoric, music, athletics, and mathematics, teaching *arete* – "virtue" or "excellence" – to young statesmen and nobility.

As with the Ajivika of India, most of what we know of the Sophists comes through the writings of their opponents, in this case primarily Plato (who named some of his dialogues after them) and Aristotle.

From Protagoras, we get the famous quote, "man is the measure of all things," which might refer to the rejection of the mythical and cosmic in favor of the pragmatic and humanistic, or it could refer to replacing metaphysics with a phenomenological understanding. He also was the original agnostic concerning the nature and existence of the gods.

Gorgias, in his *On Nature* criticized the Eleatics' concept of being and non-being, although there is disagreement as to whether or not he was a serious thinker, a skeptic, or merely a charlatan.

Since the sophists and their pupils were persuasive speakers in court or in public, they were accused of moral and epistemological relativism, which some sophists did appear to advocate. Plato disliked the Sophists, as he felt philosophy should be reserved for those who could understand it, whereas the Sophists would teach anyone who would pay for tuition.

14-xii. Plato and Philosophical Idealism

Born into an important Athenian family, Plato (429-348 B.C.E.) was expected to enter politics but chose philosophy instead. However, when his teacher, Socrates, was executed by the State, Plato was so appalled that he left Athens. He only returned later to establish his Academy.

A lot of Plato's thought was influenced by his rejection of skepticism, represented by the Sophists. However, in rejecting skepticism, Plato's understanding was in many ways the opposite of that of the modern world, whether that be the empiricism of science, the cultural relativity of postmodernism, or the disinformation of political propaganda and vested interest in think tanks.

For Plato, truth is objective and can be accessed through pure reason, such as philosophy and mathematics. Plato argued that transcendental Forms or archetypes are eternal, unchanging, and perfect. These are the blueprints of the senses. For example, any triangle that we can draw, will only be an imitation of the ideal triangle. We think the former is real and the latter an abstraction and hence unreal. For Plato though, the abstraction is the perfectly real, and the concrete is the lesser expression of that.

In the famous analogy of the prisoners in the cave (*The Republic*, 514a-517a), shackled prisoners see shadows cast on the wall ahead of them, and mistake these shadows for the real people who are behind them.

Actual knowledge and understanding come from extrapolating from particulars, the things in the sense world, the shadows on the wall of the cave, to universals, the immutable Forms or archetypes. Souls experienced the world of Forms before they were born into physical bodies, and all education and learning is simply remembering what we originally knew.

The world of Forms of Plato is not a systematic esoteric cosmology, or a mythological one, but rather rational philosophy as mysticism. The premise of an immutable spiritual reality superior to the senses can perhaps be compared to concepts such as Indic spiritual enlightenment (in Buddhism *sambodhi* – "complete awakening"), but it is not yet as radical. There are still spiritual forms in Platonism, whereas in the state of mystic unity, such as the Atman-Brahman of Vedanta, there is only identity with the absolute. This contradiction would only be reconciled later, in Neoplatonism.

Plato is referring to the metaphysical premise that the world of the senses is not so much an illusion as a poor copy of reality. This hypothesis, further developed in Neoplatonism, and later Kabbalah (the four worlds) and more recently Theosophy, is that the original source generates a reality which, although sublime, is not of the same excellence of its origin, and this created reality or the world itself makes or emanates another reality and so on.

Plato's take on politics was quite different from that of today. For him, democracy, that contribution of Classical Athens that was to be revived with the ideals of 17th and 18th century political philosophy (such as the social contract theories of Thomas Hobbes and John Locke), was the second-lowest form of government, preferable only to pure anarchy (chaos, lawlessness, not Anarchy in the modern political definition).

It was Athenian Democracy, after all, that ordered the execution of his teacher Socrates. And today, in the early 21st century, following the brief and glorious flowering of Western secular humanistic values, represented most of all by representative democracy, such as the parliamentary monarchy like Britain and the Commonwealth, or a republic like France or America, we see the loss of center, fragmentation of society between an increasingly polarized left and right, and the rise of the appeal of the charismatic strongman [Nai & Martínezi Coma, 2019], a particular characteristic of a civilization that has lost its sense of values.

14-xiii. The Soul

Plato, following Pythagoras, strongly rejected the Homeric (and general Mythic) idea of the dead as a mere shade. The soul (*psuche*) is no longer a image or double (*eidolon*) of the body, but an eternal principle that constitutes one's real being. This insight, beginning with Pythagoras and fully developed by Plato, marked a radical paradigm shift in understanding, equivalent to the equally radical but unrelated insights of the Brahmanic transcendent Self (Atman) and the Zoroastrian morality-based afterlife. Today's popular concept of the soul goes back to Plato, just as the popular concept of heaven and morality (rather than religious fundamentalism) derives from Zoroastrianism.

In the *Phaedo*, one of his earlier middle-period works, which marks the transition from the Socratic dialogues based on the ideas of his teacher to his own original ideas as a philosopher [Kraut, 2004/2022], Plato describes how the soul resides in the body as though in a prison, and is liberated from it at death (*Phaedo* 63-69, 81a); a similar idea is also found in the slightly later *Phaedrus*. This is in keeping with the world-negating position of a lot of mysticism, especially Gnosticism and Vedanta.

Going beyond the simple spiritualist idea of a uniform soul and simple body-mind duality, Plato also describes the soul as having several faculties. For example, in the *Phaedrus*, he uses the analogy of a chariot pulled by two winged horses, one of which seeks to ascend, while the other tries to pull the chariot down (*Phaedrus* 246a–247b).

> First the charioteer of the human soul drives a pair, and secondly one of the horses is noble and of noble breed, but the other quite the opposite in breed and character. Therefore in our case the driving is necessarily difficult and troublesome.

In this allegory, the charioteer represents intellect or reason (*logos*), the part of the soul which is in touch with transcendental Ideas. One horse represents the moral impulse or higher passionate nature (*thumos*, righteous indignation), and the other represents the soul's irrational passions, and lower appetites (*epithumia*).

The theme of an irrational or lower nature that pulls the soul down and is an obstacle to spiritual enlightenment would become the standard in Western Mysticism. In Sufism and Kabbalah especially, great effort is devoted to overcoming the tendencies of this lower Self.

A similar allegory is found in the Indian *Katha Upanishad* (5th century B.C.E.), which presents a monistic version of Samkhya metaphysics.

> Know that the Atman is the rider in the chariot,
> and the body is the chariot,
> Know that the Buddhi is the charioteer,
> and Manas is the reins.
>
> The senses are called the horses,
> the objects of the senses are their paths,
> Formed out of the union of the Atman, the senses and the mind,
> him they call the "enjoyer."
>
> — *Katha Upanishad*, 1.3.3-1.3.4

Here, instead of the duality between the higher and lower parts of the soul, there is the contrast between the Atman, the transcendent Self, and the senses and ordinary consciousness. As the intelligence or rational faculty, the buddhi is the direct equivalent of Plato's logos. The manas, in contrast, is simply the field of consciousness which unites the thoughts and senses. The Upanishads don't have an equivalent to thumos or epithumia. However, this would be developed in Yoga and Buddhist psychology, especially the idea of kleshas, which can be compared to the irrational soul or the Christian concept of sins.

In *The Republic*, Plato's utopian idea of an ideal state, which was probably written just before the *Phaedrus*, the three faculties of the soul correspond to the three classes of society, viz. the rulers, the military, and the common people. Desire or the appetites (*eros, epithumia*), corresponds to the stomach and the common people; spiritedness or righteous anger (*thumos*) corresponds to the chest and the soldier or warrior class; and mind and reason (*logos*), which corresponds to the head and the philosopher class. This is very similar to the four basic human types which arise from the body of the primordial cosmic man (Purusha) in the *Rig Veda*.

The word thumos itself is derived from Indo-European words meaning "smoke," which we find even in modern words, e.g., "fumigate" from the Latin *fumus*, smoke. This relates to the original Mediterranean idea of the soul as insubstantial and several terms in Greek that associate psychological activity with air and breath, e.g., psuche. In the Homeric epics, thymos is one of a family of terms associated with the process of thought, emotion, volition, and motivation. This reappears in Plato's model of the tripartite soul [Cairns, 2019].

Plato's psychology is for the purpose of illustrating mysticism rather than as a general theory of psychology akin to the work of Aristotle, Brentano, Freud, or Jung. Logos or reason here would be the rational mind orientation to higher truths (metaphysical gnosis or spiritual enlightenment), rather than the type of rational thinking preferred by modernity. In Jungian-inspired Myer-Briggs typology, these could be interpreted as Intuition Thinking and Sensation Thinking, respectively.

Interestingly also, these correspond to the three *gunas* or qualities of the contemporary Indian Samkhya, *sattva* (clarity, calmness, revealing the transcendent), *rajas* (activity, energy, passion, desire, restlessness), and *tamas* (inertia, obscurity, heaviness).

Plato's three degrees of the soul also feature in Sri Aurobindo's Integral Yoga psychology. The relation between the mental and vital being is most relevant here. As with Plato's chariot allegory, the lower principle often predominates over the higher. As Sri Aurobindo explains, the thinking mind does not have the most influence. It is the vital propensities and the vital mind that predominate. Their function is not to think and reason but to plan and imagine for the future, imagining stories, adventures, and great doings with oneself as the hero [Aurobindo, 2012, pp.178-180]. In this case, the vital mental and its superior principle central vital would be equivalent to the thumos (the vital mind is still distinct from the irrational soul or vital proper). Whereas the epithumia, driven by physical desires, represents the small vital or physical vital [Aurobindo, 2012, pp.195-196], but also perhaps the lower vital mind, the commanding soul in Sufism, which has to be purified as part of spiritual enlightenment.

Plato's *Republic* was never intended as anything other than a thought experiment. Apart from there being many more human types than the three he mentions, his *Republic* would be immediately undermined by psychological dark triad-type charismatic despots, who would use their silver tongues to convince the masses that they are selfless philosophers. Ultimately, this ideal system wouldn't work because it doesn't address the problem of evil.

For Plato and his successors, such as Aristotle, Plotinus, and Aquinas, evil is simply the absence of good. That is, it is a lack of something rather than an active antagonistic force, as in Zoroastrianism, Gnosticism, and Manichaeism. Like those dualistic religions, Jung was fully aware of the reality of human evil, which he explained with his concept of the Shadow. Much of his disagreement with the Catholic priest Victor White was because of this central disagreement [Carl Jung Depth Psychology, 2020].

14-xiv. The Story of Er

In keeping with this concept of the soul, Plato presents in *The Republic* 614b-621d what is perhaps the earliest known Near Death Experience, albeit one that has been overlaid with his own cosmology. This is the story – usually called the "Myth of Er" as mythos in this context simply means story – of a certain Er, the Pamphylian (Pamphylia was part of what today is Southern Anatolia in Turkey), a soldier who died in battle. When the bodies of those who died in the battle were collected, his body remained undecomposed. Two days later, he awakened on his funeral pyre and told others what he saw in the next world. As the account is quite similar to current out-of-body accounts and near-death experiences, it seems that behind the mythic embellishment was an actual experience.

Er's account, in brief, is as follows. With many other souls as his companions, he came to a mysterious place with four openings, two leading to or from the sky and two to or from the ground. Between these, judges ordered the souls which path to follow: the good guided into the sky, the immoral under the ground.

Other souls arrived from these two realms, those from below being haggard and weeping as they recounted their hellish experiences, where each was required to pay tenfold for each wicked deed. In contrast, clean and bright souls floated down from the sky; those from above described heavenly delights and visions of inconceivable beauty.

Everyone encamped, and those who knew one another embraced and conversed while the souls from the underworld enquired about things above, and the souls from heaven about the things beneath.

The only ones from below who weren't allowed to return were the very worst and most immoral tyrants and criminals, who, on trying to leave the mouth of the cave, were seized and dragged off by savage wild men to be further tortured, a remarkable convergence with the popular Medieval and modern conception of Hell, not present in original Christianity, Judaism, or even Homeric and other Mediterranean accounts.

After seven days, the souls and Er were required to travel farther. After four days, they saw a column of brilliant rainbow light, which took another day's travel to reach. This was the Spindle of Fate (or Necessity), which spun the heavens and the various planets, and where Sirens sang on the planetary rings (*Republic* 617 b-c). This is the first literary evidence of the Harmony of the Spheres. Plato later added his own cosmology to what would have been the original account. In Neopythagorean and Neoplatonic doctrine, the soul hears this music as it passes through the planetary spheres on its way down to Earth and back again [Godwin, 2016, p.16].

The souls, except for Er, were required to come forward to choose the lottery tokens that represented their next life. There were more lives (tokens) than souls present, including every animal and man in every condition.

Those who had come from the heaven realm often chose a wicked life, whereas those who had been punished were reluctant to choose but often chose a better life. Each soul was assigned a guardian spirit to help them through their life.

All the souls, having now chosen their lives, marched through the scorching heat. Towards evening they camped by the River of Forgetfulness (River Lethe). As they drank, each soul forgot, the degree of forgetting depending on how much they had drunk. As they lay down that night to sleep, each was lifted up into the night in various directions for rebirth, completing their journey. Because Er didn't drink the waters of Lethe, he was able to recall his journey through the afterlife [Gill, 2021].

Er describes a moral afterlife (as with, but independent of, Zoroastrianism) where the just are rewarded and the wicked are punished. Souls are then reborn into a new body and a new life, and the new life they choose will reflect how they have lived in their previous life and the state of their soul at death (as in the Indian concept of karma). Such ideas of post-mortem judgment, followed by reward and punishment, were deeply embedded in Hellenic and Hellenistic culture. For example, the Theban poet Pindar (c. 518-c. 438 B.C.E.)'s Second Olympian Ode, 58-68, and the Athenian playwright Aristophanes' (c.446-386 B.C.E.) *Frogs* 452-477 may reflect Orphic influence [BeDuhn, 2020].

14-xvi. *The Demiurge*

Here, Plato introduces the concept of the Demiurge. The *Timaeus* is his most influential of the dialogues of Plato's mature period, especially for its elaboration of the Pythagorean philosophy and gnosis. Here, Plato is more positive about the material world, which he says has been carefully built by the Demiurge (creator) in imitation of a prototype in his own spirit (*Timaeus* 29-30) [Van Den Doel & Hanegraaff, 2006, p.608].

The Demiurge is an elevated but not supreme being. This artisan-like figure fashions the cosmos according to the rational pattern expressed in mathematical principles and Pythagorean ratios, such as the motions of the seven planets.

It is distinct from the traditional supreme being of theism in that it is neither the first principle nor a personal religious deity to whom prayers and supplications are addressed. Instead, it is a cosmological entity that fashions the cosmos according to eternal transcendent forms.

Whereas both Zoroastrian and Hebrew theists identify the creator of the cosmos with the source of morality and of being, these roles are distinct for Plato. Morality derives from the Idea of the Good, which is the highest of the Platonic forms. The creator is a more intermediary being.

This is an example of the rational-intuitive Greek attitude to metaphysics and first principles, in contrast to the very feeling-orientated, absolutist, and totalitarian Semitic deity. In any case, the Demiurge wasn't a major element in Plato's philosophy in the way that god was and is in theistic religion.

In Middle Platonic and Neoplatonic thought, the Demiurge had greater importance and was sometimes even replaced by the idea of a series of demiurges or gods, while the Gnostics made the Demiurge a demonic entity, presumably because it fashioned the visible cosmos.

14-xvi. The Lambda

However, Plato is more concerned with the arithmological details of these principles than theology or metaphysics.

He provides an example, in an arrangement that later came to be called the "Lambda," after the Greek letter shaped like an upside-down V. As with the Tetraktys, the top number is the monad, while the left diagonal arm has the square and cube series goes 2, 4, 8, and the right 3, 9, 27. These refer not only to the seven planetary spheres, but also to the arithmetic, geometric, and harmonic or musical representations, which the Demiurge or Creator uses to form the cosmos.

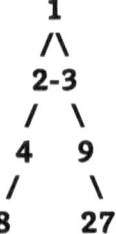

If these numbers are arranged hierarchically, the geometrical is the most metaphysical or heavenward, representing the intelligible (noetic) realm, the harmonic the mediating or central (representing the soul (psychic)), and the arithmetic the most earthly, physical, or sense domain.

The Platonic Lambda can also be converted to a Tetraktys by adding the three missing places, as follows.

As shown in this diagram, the musical fifth ratio would be the horizontal series reading right to left (3:2); the musical fourth goes one up and one to the right (4:3), and the octave is the right diagonal (2:1). There is also the tone interval of 9:8 [Critchlow, 1988, pp.12ff].

In this way, the Pythagorean-Platonic philosophy creates a single grand theory of everything based on the harmony and relation between numbers, shapes, music, and the celestial spheres (astronomy/astrology).

This vision of a harmonious cosmos was the guiding orientation of the Platonic and Neoplatonic worldview until the fall of the classical world. It was rediscovered during the Renaissance, when it became central to hermetic esotericism. Even after Copernicus had overturned the Aristotlean-Ptolemaic geocentric universe, the German astronomer, astrologer, and mathematician Johannes Kepler, whose planetary laws of motion are still valid today, attempted to explain the ratios and distances between the planets in terms of the five Platonic solids.

The Pythagorean-Platonic harmonial gnosis is distinct from both the nonduality gnosis (spiritual enlightenment) of the Indian Jnana Yoga traditions, and the cosmological gnosis of the Hermetic, Kabbalistic, and Ishraqi-Ismaili cosmologies. Instead, it represents what could be described as the plane or universe of pure mental-spiritual forms.

This understanding of an ordered cosmos ties in with the idea of "star music," which can be found throughout the history of musical theory in the West, from Pythagoras and Plato through to the Middle Ages, the Renaissance, the Romantic era, the twentieth century, and even up to contemporary New Age music [Heyning, 2017].

According to Aristotle, the main differences between Plato's philosophy and "the Italians" (the Pythagoreans) were that Plato regarded numbers not as ultimate realities, but as intermediate between the sensible world and the forms and that Plato's primary opposites were not the Limited and the Unlimited (see the Pythagorean pairs of opposites), but the One and the Dyad, with the latter generating all numbers [Magee, 2016].

The Pythagorean and Platonic revelation describes the pattern of organization and harmony behind physical reality. These principles of number, ratio, and music may or may not be the same as spiritual hierarchies or personalities described by Iamblichus, Dionysius, and Rudolf Steiner. It may also be that modern physicists and mathematicians tap into something similar with their mathematical theories, although these are more complex and abstract than the original Pythagorean-Platonic versions. Hence, if Atomism represents the forerunner of positivism and empiricism, Pythagorean and Platonic arithmosophy constitutes the esoteric foundation of quantum physics and cosmology, in which even the orbits of electrons take on precise geometric arrangements, called Orbitals.

14-xvii. Aristotle and Immanent Forms

Plato's student Aristotle (384–322 B.C.E.) was a polymath during the Classical period in Ancient Greece. The founder of the Lyceum, the Peripatetic school of philosophy, his writings cover every possible topic, from physics to ethics, to poetry to philosophy, theatre, psychology, linguistics, politics, the natural world, and more.

Whereas Plato represents the transcendental, dualistic approach, which was further developed by the Middle and Neoplatonists and their successors, Aristotle's naturalism constituted the basis of the modern secular worldview.

Aristotle rejected the objective idealism (transcendent spiritual forms) and Pythagorean arithmology of his teacher in favor of immanent forms that give shape to material things, but do not exist apart from them. Although he was not a scientist in the strict sense, as he did not use the empirical or experimental method that would only be developed in the 16th and 17th centuries later by philosopher and statesman Francis Bacon (1561-1626) in England and his contemporary Galileo in Italy, Aristotle's mindset was very much compatible with that of the modern world, based as it is on nominalism and physicalism.

Subsequent philosophy, especially in the medieval Islamic and Christian civilizations, would be determined by this contrast between Plato's idealism and Aristotle's immanentism, the latter leading to the Nominalism of William of Occam. In a sense, Western metaphysics can be traced back to the mysticism of Plato, whereas science and secular modernity can be traced back to the this-worldly orientation of Aristotle.

14-xviii. Aristotle's Psychology

For Aristotle, the soul is the imminent form of a living being, not a distinct spiritual reality. It is what endows living beings with those characteristics specific to them. His treatise *De Anima, On the Soul*, belongs to his mature period, and reflects his interest in biological taxonomy in relation to physical and metaphysical theory [Shields, 2000/2020].

Instead of one soul with a three-fold nature, he posited three kinds of soul, each based on a particular function. These are the nutritive (or vegetative) soul, the sensitive soul, and the rational soul. The plant only has a vegetative soul; hence it is capable of growth and nourishment; but lacks sentience. The animal adds a sensitive soul, possessing sensations and movement but lacking reason. Here, the faculty of desire (*orektikon*) is what initiates motion. Finally, man adds to these two a rational soul, which provides intellect (nous) and reason (logos).

This general theory of natural psychology is quite distinct from Plato's more mystical approach. The contrast between nous (mind) and orektikon (desire and volition) was for a while popular in late 19th and early 20th century psychology, but it never really caught on. Its most crucial proponent was outside academia and exoteric knowledge, in Rudolf Steiner's threefold theosophy and psychology with his thinking, feeling, and willing. A closer convergence was developed independently, with Sri Aurobindo's contrast between the mental and the vital.

Aristotle's three categories of the soul were later combined with another of his ideas, that of three kingdoms – animal, vegetable, and mineral. In his work *Historia Animalium and Parts of Animals*, Aristotle classified living organisms into two groups, animals and plants, based on their ability to move and perceive the world around them. The concept of a third kingdom, mineral or inanimate objects, is also attributed to Aristotle, but it is unclear whether he used the term "kingdom" to describe it.

Later, in the 18th century, the Swedish botanist Carl Linnaeus expanded on Aristotle's classification system and introduced the system of taxonomy that is still used today. In his classification system, Linnaeus also recognized three kingdoms of nature: *Animalia, Plantae,* and *Mineralia* (later changed to *Regnum Lapideum*).

So while the idea of three kingdoms of nature can be traced back to Aristotle, it was Carl Linnaeus who popularized and formalized this concept in his classification system.

As an early representative of modern science, Linnaeus understood, a century before Darwin, that man was a member of the animal kingdom. This was even though he only had a static, non-evolutionary worldview, in keeping with the Biblically-informed science of the time.

Steiner's anthroposophical theory of evolution, however, rejects the animal status of man. In his system, minerals have only a physical body, plants an etheric body as well, animals an astral in addition, and only man with an immortal Ego as well as the other three elements. Adding the human kingdom gives four divisions: matter, plant, animal, and human, as a premodern Traditionalist explanation [Schumacher, 1977].

All of this perpetuates the anthropocentric fallacy that only man can reason. This is like the Abrahamic belief that only man has a divine soul and is made in the image of God.

The opposite position is that of the Indian (Hindu, Jain, Buddhist, etc.) and Pythagorean premise of a transmigrating soul, according to which there is only one type of soul. Plato's story of Er also allows transmigration between human and animal. The Theosophical (Blavatsky, Post-Blavatsky, and New Age) model of evolutionary reincarnation is somewhere between the two; although animals don't yet have a developed higher mental body, they will eventually acquire one through evolving into human souls. Similar ideas are found in Aurobindo and the Mother's Integral Yoga and Meher Baba's Vedanta-Sufi synthesis.

Today, ethnology (animal behavior and psychology) is slowly overturning the Aristotlean-Christian dogma with the discovery of intelligence, problem-solving, and self-consciousness (such as the mirror test) in higher animals.

Ultimately, much of premodern thinking is as much based on speciesism as it is on sexism (the female principle is always assigned to the negative polarity – e.g., the Indian concept of maya and prakriti, and the Kabbalistic polarity of *gevurah* or severity) and ethnocentrism. This is why a new perspective, a "third way" is required, taking the best of both traditional metaphysics and modernity, but avoiding the limitations of both.

14-ix. Orexis or Desire

Plato's definition of thumos is, in turn, a point of reference for Aristotle's interpretation of thumos as a type of desire, or *orexis* [Cairns, 2019]. However, he retains Plato's threefold classification of the soul. In *De Anima* (*On the Soul*), Aristotle says that desire (*orexis*) comprises appetite (*epithumia*), passion (*thumos*), and wishing (*boulesis*) [Feldblyum, 2016].

Phenomenologically, orexis means that consciousness, in terms of intentionality, is not directed at the (spiritual or material) object itself, but at the desire for that object. This could be categorized as follows:

- Boulesis – desire for the good (spirituality) – noetic/rational
- Thumos – desire for the imagination (*phantasia*)
- Epithumia – lower appetites, desire for sensual things (lower irrational)

In Buddhism, the equivalent term would be *tanha*, craving. Of course, at least in its literal meaning or translation, this is too strong a word. Still, it reflects the difference between the ascetic-yogic inspired North Indian philosophy of Liberation/Transcendence, and the humanistic classical Western philosophy concerned with this world.

For Sri Aurobindo, desire represents the vital being, which he divides into four, the mental vital, emotional, central vital, and physical vital, of which the central vital is similar to thumos, and the small or physical vital identical to epithumia. This lowest, most physical, sensual, and demanding of the irrational soul attributes or layers is the most obvious one, and hence most clearly described by the various esoteric philosophies and mystical and even religious teachings.

14-xx. Stoicism

In addition to Platonism and Aristotleanism, there was a third major school of Hellenistic philosophy, founded by Zeno of Citium (335-263 B.C.E.). Around the turn of the 3rd century B.C.E., Zeno gathered his pupils in the *stoa poikile*, a colonnaded hall in Athens. This building gave its name to Stoicism, which would become one of the most influential philosophies of the ancient world.

The early Stoics developed a highly moral ethical system. This is based on *eudaemonia*, a word that means both virtue and happiness, and living in accordance with nature. At the heart of Stoic doctrine is the distinction between what is in our power and what is not, such as opinions, desires, likes and dislikes, which are subject to our control, and what is not. The Stoic life consists in distinguishing one from the other and adapting oneself to the laws of those things outside our control. Stoic ethics would, in later centuries, find approval in Rome with the writings of Seneca, Epictetus, and the philosopher-emperor Marcus Aurelius.

Zeno's ideas were developed by his student Cleanthes (331-232 B.C.E.) and especially by Chrysippus (c. 280-207 B.C.E.), under whom Stoic psychology reached its most developed form. According to this, a refined form of the elements is called *pneuma* (Spirit, but originally breath, air, wind). Compare it to the Hatha Yoga prana and Tibetan or Tantric Buddhist *vayu*), an organizing principle that pervades the cosmos. The greater degree of pneumatic activity, the greater the scale of development. At a basic level, there is inanimate matter. Beyond that is *phusis* or organic nature, which has the power of growth and reproduction but not cognitive power. The next tier of pneumatic activity is soul (psuche), characterized by impulse and perception. Finally, there is reason (logos), the highest degree of pneumatic activity, possessed by man, the gods, and the Cosmos or God as a whole [Rubarth, 2002].

And just as the Upanishads described a universal self or Atman as far back as the eighth century B.C.E. [Radhakrishnan, 1953], so the Stoics had the idea of a world soul, or of matter and the universe being conscious (panpsychism).

The Universe, therefore, is both active and passive. The passive substance is matter, and the active substance, is an intelligent aether or primordial fire, which acts on the passive matter.

The Stoics, like most premoderns, rejected the idea of chance events. Instead, they understood everything in terms of overall unity, which they called *heimarmene*, literally "fate" or predeterminism, but here referring to the cosmos as a vast organic being regulated by seminal reason (*logos spermatikos*), the generative principle of the universe which creates and takes back all things.

This also relates to the concept of sympathy (*sympatheia*), central to the magical worldview, specifically to Western esotericism from the classical period to the late Renaissance, and even astrology today. Philosophers and esotericists like Philo of Alexandria, Plotinus, and the Gnostics combined Stoic, Platonic, Hermetic, and astral-mystical themes, interpreting heimarmene both as a principle of fate but also providing a means of redemption [von Stuckrad 2005, pp.16-17].

GLOSSARY

Abrahamic Religion: Judaism, Christianity, Islam, Baha'i, and other religions which share a common monotheistic, prophetic, and messianic worldview and trace their origins back to the historical semi-mythological figure of Abraham. Each religion is based around a single religious text, considered to be a once and only Divine revelation, which can be variously interpreted in a literal (exoteric religion), academic (literary/biblical/historical criticism), symbolic/allegorical, or inner/mystical (esoteric) manner.

The Absolute: The ultimate reality, described rationally, as an abstract first principle, e.g. Brahman, The One, Tao, etc. As Reality in itself is inconceivable, all accounts of the Absolute are ultimately just "the finger pointing at the moon", rather than the moon (the object) itself.

Afterlife: The state or states of consciousness following death of the gross physical body. A subject of speculation since time immemorial. The most sophisticated mythic age concepts on the after-life were those of the ancient Egyptians, who believed that the souls of the deceased could live on in the next world if they were properly prepared for death. This was reflected in their elaborate burial practices, which included the construction of elaborate tombs and the burial of the deceased with a wealth of grave goods.

Ancestor Worship: Not so much worship as offerings to deceased ancestor.

Animism: Belief that there are spirits in all things in nature. See also Magic, Panpsychism, Shamanism.

Akh: In ancient Egypt, the immortal soul, higher self, or radiant shining one; alternatively, the unified Ba and Ka, which goes to the afterlife. Represented in hieroglyphics by an ibis or phoenix. Also called Akhu or Khu.

Archetype: A pre-existing, universal, psychological, or spiritual prototype, a god or God, a mythic, cultural, or even architectural theme. In Platonism, an ideal spiritual form, of which the phenomenal world is a mere imitation or copy. In Jungian psychology, a primordial symbol of transformation within the Collective Unconscious appears spontaneously in the myths and legends of all cultures and spontaneously in individual dreams and visions.

Arithmosophy: Understanding numbers from the perspective of esotericism, symbolism, and gnosis. Often used in reference to Pythagorean philosophy.

Astral Plane: Nothing to do with astrology or Astral Mysticism. This is the Theosophical and New Age term for the Imaginal World, the intermediate Reality between the Gross and Subtle Physical and the higher spiritual ("noetic," "celestial," "divine," etc.) regions. The state of existence upon leaving one's gross and subtle physical body.

Astral Mysticism: Religion or mysticism based on the celestial bodies as visible gods; i.e., as the external object of psychological projection of archetypes. The foundation for astrology.

Atma: Sanskrit, "self." Originally meaning "breath," this word for self or soul has many different meanings, depending on the school of thought. In the early Upanishads and Vedanta it is the Transcendent self or "I" which is synonymous with the Absolute; in the *Taittiriya Upanishad* it refers to any of the five levels of embodied self (physical, vital, mental, consciousness, and bliss); in Buddhism the impermanent relative self (Psychophysical Ego); and for the Ajivika it is the transmigrating soul.

Atheism: The denial of a supernatural supreme being. Modern atheism is the product of modernity-based Humanism and materialism, denying any non-material or supra-physical realities. It can be traced back to Greek atomism and to Cartesian dualism. In contrast, the ancient Indian atheism of the Shramanas held to a renunciation or yogic asceticism, the metaphysical Reality of consciousness, and the attainment of salvation (liberation) is through self-effort alone. They did not deny the existence of gods, but considered the gods just to be very long-lived but still mortal sentient beings, who would eventually reincarnate in other forms. The opposite of Theism.

Axial Age: Term coined by the German philosopher and psychologist Karl Jaspers to refers to the period from the 8th to 2nd centuries B.C.E., when various civilizations in Europe and Asia simultaneously emerged discussing the intellectual, philosophical, ethical, and religious systems that would subsequently shape human society and culture. Axial thinking did not change until the development of science and rationality with the modern world (17th and 18th century).

Arithmosophy: Understanding numbers from the perspective of esotericism, symbolism, and gnosis. Often used in reference to Pythagorean philosophy.

Ba: In ancient Egypt, the soul, represented by a human-headed bird. It is associated with the Ka or double.

Bhakti (Marga or Yoga): Realization of the Absolute through devotion and surrender to God. The way of theistic mysticism.

Bronze Age Collapse: Widespread social and civilizational collapse during the 12th century B.C.E., affecting a large area of the Eastern Mediterranean and the Near East.

Big History: A scientific, historical, and educational approach that situates human history in the wider fields of cosmology and natural history, taking a broad interdisciplinary approach that encompasses the natural sciences, social sciences, and the humanities. It integrates various scales of time, from the Big Bang to the present day, and across different fields of study, including astronomy, geology, biology, archaeology, and history. The modern-day equivalent of the premodern creation or origins story.

Chalcolithic: Archaeological period and technological stage characterized by the use of copper, but prior to the discovery of bronze alloys. Associated in Anatolia (in modern day Turkey) with the Late Neolithic and the agricultural revolution, and transitional between the Neolithic proper and the Bronze Age.

Chaoskampf: German for "struggle against chaos". A common Near and Middle East mythic theme involving a pre-creation battle between a creator God or a culture hero and a primordial monster.

Clairvoyance: Experiencing physical or nonphysical reality independent of the senses. Clairvoyant experiences are often unreliable as they have to go through the distorting medium of the individual psyche.

Collective Unconscious: As described by Jung, the deeper layers of the psyche that are not limited to the individual, but include cultures and races as a whole. The repository of primordial images or archetypes. Psychologically overlaps with and is in part synonymous with the imaginal world.

Cosmic Egg: Mythological theme found in many creation myths, whereby either the universe or a primordial being comes into existence by hatching from the egg. Some examples include:
- *The Orphic Egg.* According to Orphic Cosmogony, from the cosmic egg hatches the primordial hermaphroditic deity called Phanes or Protogonus, who in turn creates the other gods.
- *Hiraṇyagarbha* (Sanskrit "Golden Womb"). In the *Rig Veda*, this is associated with the creator deity Prajapati, while according to the Upanishads the two halves become Heaven and Earth.
- In the Egyptian Hermopolitan theology, within the Ogdoad or

precreation formlessness is the Cosmic Egg, from which all things are born, beginning with the sun god Ra.

Cosmogony: Theory, myth, or explanation regarding the origin of the universe.

Cosmological Gnosis: Gnosis orientated to cosmology and theosophy rather than to mystical transcendence and spiritual enlightenment.

Cosmic Evolution: The process of, or the field of study about, developmental and generational changes and increase in complexity of the composition of radiation, matter, and life throughout the history of the Universe. Apart from the stronger scientific basis, it largely overlaps with Big History.

Contrarian: Going against the mainstream consensus of science and academia, generally involves fringe science, conspiracy theory, and so on.

Creation: Premodern or mythic account of the origin of the cosmos; a poetic synonym for Cosmogony. Does not pretend to be science and hence not the same as Creationism.

Creationism: The modern fundamentalist religious and traditionalist esoteric rejection of physical ascent, emergence, and evolution, in favor of either a supernatural deity or a physically literalist interpretation of emanation. The term "design" or "intelligent design" is a synonym. A pseudo-science rather than a cosmogony.

Dualism: The belief in, or philosophical doctrine stating that, there are two fundamental principles.
- Soul-Body, Spirit-Matter, or Mind-Body dualism adopts the metaphysical position of an immortal mind, soul, spirit, or consciousness, which survives the death of the body and either becomes an ancestor, goes to the afterlife, reincarnates, or attains liberation. Examples include Shamanism, Platonism, the various Indian Yogic traditions, Cartesian dualism, and Spiritualism.

- Light-Dark or Moral dualism asserts that there are two cosmological principles, one representing good and the other evil, battling for the fate of the world, with hope for the victory of the Light principle. Examples include Zoroastrianism, the Apocalyptic genre, Gnosticism (the religion), Manichaeism, and some interpretations of Christianity.

Earth Energies: Winding paths of subtle Earth energy, which can be traced by water dowsers. In most cases there is no actual subterranean water, the subtle energy being of the nature of ch'i or prana (intermediate between physical and imaginal). Equivalent to Sensitive Chaos. In the New Age the term is used in a mostly unrelated context of the healing power of the Earth, although some places with greater healing power may be a focus of subtle energy flows.

Ego: The persisting individual consciousness or awareness. A distinction can be made between Psychophysical Ego and Transcendent "I."

Egregore: A built-up astral thoughtform that takes on a life of its own. A magical egregore is created deliberately through ritual magic. A religious egregore develops spontaneously out of thoughtforms created through theistic belief. They include a number of types, such as good gods (superhuman beings who take on the appearance and thoughtforms created by believers, and are helpful and answer prayers), negative parasites (feeding on the energy of worshipers), and demons (who pretend to be the supreme god, but are thoughtforms inhabited by an anti-divine entity, often appear as narcissistic, and inspire worshipers to evil).

Entheogen: Psychedelics used in Shamanic rituals. Recently these have become popular as part of the Western materialistic search for higher Reality without putting in the effort of self transformation.

Epithumia: From Greek, appetite. In Plato's tripartite psychology, part of the soul, pertaining to desires and appetites, and located in the belly. Its function is to produce and seek pleasure. Also referred to as Eros. Equivalent to the Irrational soul.

Eschatology: Pertaining to the last days, a common mythic theme in apocalyptic and messianic beliefs. These myths date back no further than the Axial Age, beginning with Zoroastrianism, and later, independently, with the Hindu theory of cycles or yugas. Persian and later Abrahamic versions feature the Day of Judgment, the Resurrection of the Dead, and so on.

Esoteric: Religion, philosophy, or spirituality that pertains to the inner, intuitive, subtle, transpersonal, or transcendent Reality or realities.

Esotericism: The body of esoteric knowledge and practice that has built up around experiences of gnosis. Includes mysticism, theosophy, and occultism.

Evolution: The tendency of the cosmos and of consciousness towards greater complexity and sentience. Here one might speak of four progressively more universal perspectives:
- *Biological:* Field of biology established by Charles Darwin and since expanded to include many more developments including biogeography, comparative anatomy, embryology, evolutionary development ("evo-devo"), genetics, molecular phylogeny, palaeontology, population dynamics, and much more. Religious, Traditionalist, and other criticisms are basically "straw man" attacks using already falsified Creationist arguments that are easily answered by actual science.
- *Cosmic:* The general process by which the physical universe tends towards increasing complexification and self-organization [Chaisson, 2001; Jantsch, 1980]. Biological evolution (above) is a subset of this.
- *Emergent:* The universal self-emergence and self-awakening of consciousness and being from matter through the stages of life, mind, and beyond [Aurobindo, 2005; Teilhard de Chardin, 1965].
- *Esoteric:* Collective and individual evolution of the soul to spiritual enlightenment and beyond over many lifetimes [Aurobindo, 2005; Meher Baba, 1973; Sinnett, 1883].
- The conception of a dynamic, creative universe is one of the main insights of modernity. 19th and 20th century esotericism (Theosophy, Integral Yoga, etc.) develops this in a larger metaphysical context,

applying it to individual spiritual evolution as growth through successive lifetimes.

Evolutionary Pantheism: The universe is God in the process of becoming.

Exoteric: Pertaining only to the external form of a religion, such as the literal text, or institutional and culturally accepted worship.

Faith: One of three modes of knowing (along with reason and gnosis), the essential feeling quality of religion.

Feeling: The evaluating, socializing, or empathic function of consciousness, centered in the heart chakra. Tends more to religion or faith than thinking does. For Jung one of the four ego-functions and the counterpole to Thinking; for Steiner one of three aspects of consciousness (along with thinking and willing).

Field of Reeds: In Egyptian, Sekhet-Aaru. The afterlife paradise, the final destination for souls who had been granted rebirth in the afterlife. Ruled over by Osiris, the god of the afterlife and of resurrection, it is described as the Ka (spiritual double) of the Nile Delta. Equivalent mythic concepts in other cultures are the Elysian Fields in Classical Greece, Valhalla and Fólkvangr in Norse mythology, Vaikuntha in Vaishnavism (Vishnu Hinduism), and Summerlands in the spiritualism of Andrew Jackson Davis.

God: (Note: few words are more confusing, or have been more mis-used. The following is a preliminary and imperfect attempt at clarification.)
- *Religion* – an attempt to define the Absolute in personal terms, using "faith", "feeling", or bhakti. Unfortunately exoteric religions, when they speak of or worship "God", tend to refer not to the Absolute or even an intermediate spiritual hierarchy, but to an egregore of the Lower Astral.
- *Psychology* – as in the preceding, but in the context of Jung's archetype of the Self, the center of the psyche and the individual representation

of the Divine. It may take a form such as Jesus, Buddha, etc.
- *Esotericism* – a personification or emanation of the Absolute; a cosmic power; an archetype or spiritual hierarchy.

There are countless, perhaps infinite, Gods or gods, any one of which, when experienced by the small ego, is so overwhelming as to appear subjectively without doubt as the ultimate or Absolute Reality.

Gnosis: Higher knowledge, insight, intuition, one of three modes of knowing. Transcends and supplements both faith and reason.

Gross Physical: Dimension of existence pertaining to empirical physical Reality. Hence "gross physical world", "gross physical body", etc. More "external" or "objective" than the Subtle Physical. The distinction between gross, subtle, causal, and transcendent (turiya, "fourth") was codified in the late short *Mandukya Upanishad,* which became the foundation for the Advaita Vedanta or Nonduality school, which in turn exerted a strong influence on Yoga Psychology, Theosophy, the New Age, and Integral Philosophy.

Holocene: The modern geological epoch, which follows the Pleistocene. It began c. 9700 B.C.E. The beginning of the Holocene marks the start of the current interglacial, and is associated with the Neolithic revolution in the Near and Middle East (see also Younger Dryas) and the extinction of the Ice Age megafauna.

Idea: In Platonism, an ideal spiritual form, of which the phenomenal world is a mere imitation or copy.

Imaginal World: The inner or spiritual, transpersonal reality revealed through imagination, intuition, and cosmological gnosis.

Inner Reality, Inner World, or Inner Being: Refers to the world of the psyche, imagination, myth, and meaning, the collective unconscious, or the imaginal world, as opposed to the outer or empirical world of science.

Integral Philosophy: Broad term, coined by Ken Wilber, for a number of evolutionary-developmental explanations of consciousness, culture, and cosmos, and integrating different subfields into a single big picture. There is generally also a reference to a further stage of evolution of consciousness, a common theme in Theosophy and the New Age.

Integral Yoga: Term coined by Sri Aurobindo to refer to a modern and individual approach to Yoga that has the goal of transforming the entire being; refers to the physical, vital, and mental; rejects otherworldly mysticism in favor of the transformation of this world.

Intuition: The orientating of consciousness to the inner or imaginal world; for Jung one of the four ego-functions and the counterpole to Sensation. An aspect of cosmological gnosis.

Irrational Soul: In esotericism and mysticism generally, the lowest aspect of the psyche, concerned with lower desires, additions, and urges.

Jnana (Marga or Yoga): Realization of the Absolute as nonduality through higher gnosis. Includes both the Upanishadic and later Vedantic realisation of the Supreme Self (paramatman) and the paradoxically correspondingly equivalent Mahayana Buddhist realisation of No Self (shunyata).

Judgment: The belief that the soul undergoes a post-mortem judgment, which determines reward and punishment (or even annihilation for the wicked). It is found in New Kingdom Egypt, Ancient and Classical Greece, Medieval Zoroastrianism, and Tibetan Buddhism.

Ka: In ancient Egypt, the double, which remains in the tomb and is sustained by offerings. It is represented in hieroglyphics by a pair of arms raised in worship. It is associated with the Ba or soul. In some interpretations, both the Ba and Ka are required for afterlife survival as an Akh or immortal soul.

Kali Yuga: In the cosmology of the Medieval Hindu texts called the

Puranas, this is the lowest and most limited and spiritually debased age of the four cosmic ages or yugas. 20th century esoteric writers, especially of the Traditionalist School, identify it with the materialism and secularism of Modernity, but this is a modern interpretation that has little to do with the original texts.

Kathenotheism: The worship of one god as the supreme being, while not rejecting the existence of others. Originally used by philologist Max Muller in reference to Vedic India, but has a wider application.

Kundalini: From Sanskrit, "coiled." In Tantra the latent energy or coiled shakti at the base of the spine (in the Muladhara chakra), which is activated through breathing and meditation techniques and ascends to the crown of the head, conferring spiritual enlightenment. Tantric religious tradition aside, Kundalini itself is an actual physiological phenomenon, which pertains to the subtle body.

Liberation: In Eastern (especially Indian) spirituality, the state of permanent freedom and abiding in Absolute Reality. Variously referred to by a number of Sanskrit terms: mukti, moksha, kaivalya, nirvana, bodhi, etc. While for most of these teachings this implies permanent transcendence of embodied existence, in Mahayana Buddhism, some forms of Tantra and the Siddha traditions, and in Integral Yoga, Liberation is not the opposite if embodied existence, and indeed the latter is often necessary for the full work of salvation of all beings.

Logos: Greek, discursive reason. In Plato's tripartite psychology, the rational principle, which according to the Greeks partook of the Divine. Located in the head region (equivalent to the Ajna chakra). The Rational Soul.

Lower Astral: New Age term for the negative psychic zone that is adjacent to the gross physical Reality. Its substance is of the Nature of coarse desires and lower appetites. It represents the cosmic equivalent to the Irrational Soul. In Theosophy and the New Age it is considered the lowest subzone of the Astral Plane.

Magic or Magical: As consciousness or thinking, refers to intuitive orientation to the forces and flows of the imaginal world, which follow principles of sympathy, correspondence, etc. As a practical technique, working with such forces or entities. As a culture stage, refers to the hunter-gatherer state of society, associated with animism and shamanism, and which involves magic as a psychic or imaginal technique.

Metaphysical: Refers to axial and post-axial age rational and spiritual philosophies and esoteric systems, concerned with first principles and understanding The Absolute.

Modernity: Pertaining to the society, culture, and way of thinking that developed from the 15th and 16th century Renaissance (including the printing press, the protestant revolution, the scientific revolution, and the rise of the merchant class) the 17th century Age of Reason and 18th century Age of Enlightenment, and the 19th century scientific and industrial revolution. Characterized by an emphasis on rationalism, empiricism, science, and history, over myth and symbolism.

Monaltry: The worship of one god to the exclusion of other, equal gods. Originally used in the context of the ancient Hebrews, representing the precursor to monotheism.

Monism: The philosophical or mystical assertion that there is only one Reality, which includes all things.

Monotheism: The religious belief that the personal god of one's own faith is the Absolute Reality, and that no other gods exist. A central premise of Abrahamic religion.

Mysticism: Spiritual techniques for attaining higher consciousness, where duality and the sense of a separate ego are transcended in a state of spiritual enlightenment. There are a number of different types, such as bhakti (devotion), jnana (gnosis), theurgy, and so on, each of which leads to different states of consciousness. In general though, mystical traditions reject existence in the world in favor of this higher state of unity and realization of the Absolute.

Myth: Premodern or traditional story, typically involving supernatural beings or events, which confer meaning makes sense of the world. Carl Jung showed that myths have a universal quality, which he explained in terms of the archetypes of the collective unconscious. Myths represent and are the carriers of archetypal symbols.

Mythical: A cultural stage. The period of early or pre-scientific civilizations or worldviews. As used here, refers to the period before the development of distinct metaphysical, esoteric, or theistic religious belief systems and worldviews with the Axial Age.

Neolithic: The New Stone Age, which followed the Palaeolithic, and dates to the early to middle Holocene (from around ten thousand B.C.E. to the start of the historical era). The term Mesolithic is occasionally used for a short intermediate period between the two. The Neolithic developing independently in Europe, across Asia and in Africa, it includes the introduction of farming, domestication of animals, permanent settlements, the beginning of pottery and metal working (Chalcolithic), and the transition from the "magical" or animistic hunter-gatherer Palaeolithic to the mythic era with its civilization, God-Kings, and alienation from Nature.

Nirvana: Sanskrit, "blowing out (of the flame)"; the Buddhist term for spiritual liberation, the extinguishing of craving and desire, freedom from rebirth (samsara).

Nominalism: Medieval philosophy developed in its current form by William of Occam (c.1287-1347) which rejects the Reality of "Universals' (Platonic Ideas), claiming that these are mere names without any corresponding objective reality. A precursor to the scientific revolution and its rejection of metaphysics.

Nonduality: Monistic gnosis and mysticism; the realization of all existence as beyond dualities and categories. Although elements can be found in the Upanishads, Taoism, the Eleatic philosophers like Xenophanes and Parmenides, and the apophatic or negative theology of Pseudo-Dionysius and Damscius, Nonduality was developed to its highest degree in the post-Axial Age Mahayana Buddhism and subsequent (Medieval) Advaita Vedanta. A central insight of Jnana Yoga.

Occultism: From Latin *occultus*, hidden or concealed), generally taken to mean understanding and accessing hidden realities behind the physical, in contrast to Mysticism which has a more religious and world-negating. Traditionally, in the Western medieval and renaissance world, occultism has been divided into astrology, alchemy, and magic In the 19th and early 20th century, occultism and esotericism were used synonymously.

Outer Reality or Outer World: Refers to the objective, material world of science and empirical observation, as opposed to the inner world of the psyche, imagination, myth, and meaning.

Out-of-Body Travel: Projecting the spirit body out of the physical, so it can travel around and experience remote physical locations and also non-physical dimensions. Also called Astral Projection and Traveling Clairvoyance. There is a large body of literature on this subject, all of which contradicts the physicalist worldview. See for example the work of Robert Bruce, Robert Monroe, Jurgen Ziewe, and many others.

Orphism/Orphic: Name given to Ancient Greek religious beliefs and practices ascribed to the mythical poet Orpheus, who, like Dionysus, descended into the underworld and returned. They developed a cosmogony and theogony involving a Cosmic Egg. Orphism may have been influenced by Pythagoreanism, alternatively both the Orphics and Pythagoras may stem from an earlier Mystery tradition.

Paleolithic: The Old Stone Age, the earliest period of human history, characterized by tools made of chipped flint, and also bone, ivory, etc. A very long period, lasting from about 2.5 million years ago to about 10,000 years ago. Sometimes divided into Lower (Early), Middle, and Upper (Later) Paleolithic.

Panentheism: The philosophical position that God is the same as the universe but also transcends the universe.

Panpsychism: Modern philosophical theory that all things (even what we consider inanimate objects) have a mind or mind-like quality.

Pantheism: The philosophical position that God (whether personal or impersonal) and the universe are the same.

Perennialism: The premise that there is a common, universal insight or set of timeless truths beyond history. The body of knowledge and practice based on this is called the Perennial Philosophy. There are various interpretations of Perennial Philosophy. Aldous Huxley for example [Huxley, 1970] presents a more easily accessible, secular mystical approach inspired by Vivekananda, whereas Guenon and the Traditionalist school are more technical, esotericist, and religious. While the roots of Perennialism go back to Vedic India and to the Hellenistic West, it only became a central theme with the Florentine Renaissance.

Philosophy: From Greek. Literally "love of wisdom", refers to intellectual and spiritual inquiry as to the nature of reality (metaphysics or ontology), morality, logic, and knowledge, which goes back to the Axial Age.

Physicalism: The materialistic and positivist claim, popular in modern science and philosophy, that consciousness does not have any existence apart from the physical body or physical matter.

Planes: In the context of metaphysics, "vertical" zones of consciousness or existence. The Gross Physical is considered simply one (usually the lowest) of the series. According to Theosophy, each plane has its own corresponding Subtle Body. So the etheric body represents the individualized etheric plane, the astral body the individualized astral plane, and so on. Whereas modern science and philosophy recognizes only the Gross Physical Reality of matter and energy, a "vertical" or stratified cosmology is central to both Evolutionary and Traditional Esotericism. Instead of planes, one could say spheres, worlds, hypostases, lokas, etc. This esoteric insight dates back to the syncretic esotericism of the (post-Axial Age) Hellenistic West, and independently to Medieval Puranic, Jain, and Buddhist India.

Pleistocene: Geological epoch which began around 2.6 million years ago and ended 11,700 years ago. The period of time characterized by repeated glacial and interglacial cycles, and human evolution.

Polytheism: Belief in many gods. True polytheism was probably quite rare, most mythic age societies were actually Kathenotheistic. Even in classic polytheistic religions like Mesopotamia or Greece, there is the tendency for a single deity (Marduk, Zeus, etc.) to take on a supreme role, or later (e.g. Hinduism, Neoplatonism, Neopaganism) the various gods to be different representations of the same ultimate Reality.

Positivism: Pertaining to rationalism, empirical science, and the secular enlightenment.

Post-Axial (Age): As defined here, the period of cultural syncretism represented by the Hellenistic civilization (from the empire of Alexander the Great to the Christianization of the Roman Empire) in the West, and by equivalent time periods in India and China. It represented further development of Axial Age insights, and especially the establishment of classical esotericism in the West and Middle East, and the non-duality and Yoga traditions in South and East Asia. It was followed by the Medieval period.

Premodern: Pertaining to traditional or prescientific thinking, based on cultural traditions, myths, religions, and exoteric and esoteric worldviews. Generally refers to anything prior to the renaissance and the scientific revolution, but can also refer to the survival of such modes of thinking and belief into the modern world, e.g. orthodox religion, traditional Sufism and Kabbalah, and Rudolf Steiner's Anthroposophy, are examples of premodern thinking, whereas Christian and Islamic creationism and other forms of religious literalism based on pseudoscientific claims are actually forms of modernity, despite their supernaturalism, because they are based on a literalist and rationalist approach to the Bible or Koran which masquerades as scientific empiricism.

Psuche: Greek, soul. As with equivalent terms like atma, pneuma, ruach, this originally meant "breath." The idea of an immortal, reincarnating soul apart from the body first appears in the West with Pythagoras. It was taken up by the Orphics, but only really popularized by Plato, who divided the soul into three faculties: reason, spiritedness, and appetites. His student Aristotle rejected the idea of a spiritual soul, but developed the first consistent psychology.

Psychophysical Ego: The center of personal identity within the psyche, which develops around the Transcendent Ego's subjective focus of consciousness attention. In psychology it is simply called the ego. It mediates between the inner (imaginal, phenomenological, unconscious) and outer (objective, empirical, quantitative) worlds, as well as, according to Freud, the instinctual self (Id) and the moral standards of society (superego). The personal as opposed to the transpersonal. Those psychic contents the Ego cannot acknowledge it represses and denies; these become, according to Jung, the Shadow.

Purusha: Sanskrit, "person." Originally (in the *Rig Veda*) God as the Supreme Person who includes and transcends the cosmos. Later (in Samkhya and Yoga) the individual Transcendent Ego which is untouched by phenomena.

Raja Yoga: "Royal Yoga," Swami Vivekananda's term for the yoga sutras of Patanjali, which emphasize the practice of one-pointed meditation (samadhi)

Reincarnation: The rebirth of the soul in a new body. A central teaching in both Indian religion and philosophy and Pythagoreanism, Orphism, and Platonism. There is a distinction between Transmigration, in which the soul can be reborn in any type of body, human, animal, or even (in the Vedic and Shramanic version) a god or a being suffering in hell (so that heaven and hell are not afterlife rewards or punishment but simply other types of bodies), and the more recent (19th century onwards) idea of

Reincarnation in the sense of spiritual evolution or ascent (as in Theosophy, Sri Aurobindo, Meher Baba, etc). Buddhists, who deny the existence of a metaphysical soul entity, use the term "rebirth", but otherwise hold to the standard Transmigration model.

Samsara: The cycle of death and rebirth in Indian philosophy and religion, by which sentient beings, driven by craving and the karma of their past thoughts and deeds, are reborn into new bodies. The cycle continues endlessly until the individual achieves the state of liberation or spiritual enlightenment.

Shade: In various mythic beliefs, the soul is identified with the breath and the life of the body, and the afterlife is therefore portrayed as a gloomy or miserable existence. In some cultures such as Egypt and China, this can be countered by Ancestor Worship (offerings to the deceased). The Axial Age revolution introduced the concept of a more positive afterlife (although this is also found in Egypt).

Shadow: In Jungian psychology, the repressed contents of the psyche, which are denied by the Ego. In addition to these individual contents, there is the collective Shadow-archetype. The Shadow tends to be projected onto the world or onto other individuals and groups as the hatred of the Other (by which is meant everyone and everything that is not part of the in-group) and the personification of evil.

Shamanic Flight: The shaman as having the form of a bird and the power of flight. During trance, the shaman can leave his or her body and journey to the Spirit World. Equivalent to astral travel or out-of-body experience, which often features the experience of floating or flying.

Shamanism: While strictly speaking refers to the spiritual practices of the indigenous Tungus people of Siberia, the word tends to be used in the broader context, adopted here, of any of a range of magical and animistic practices involving the use of visualization, dance, drumming, entheogens, or other means to connect with the spirit world and to bring about individual healing or success for the tribe as a whole.

Shramana: Sanskrit "One who performs acts of austerity." Indian movement that developed around the 7th to 6th centuries B.C.E., based on liberation through asceticism and practice of Yoga or meditation techniques. While their teachings and practices parallel and include much in common with those of the Upanishadic sages, they differ in an emphasis on self effort and austerity rather than reliance on God. Includes a number of different atheistic and mystic traditions of which Jainism, Buddhism, and Ajivika are the best known.

Socio-Cultural Evolution: Human evolution and macrohistory, presented in terms of broad culturally-driven transformations of consciousness.

Soteriology: The doctrine of religious salvation, which only began with the Axial Age. There are two very different types. Religious salvation is through belief or faith in an external messiah or savior. Spiritual Liberation is through individual ascetic, yogic, or mystic self-effort.

Spatial Archetypes: Hypothesis developed by feminist architect Mimi Lobell, according to whom cultural evolution can be represented in terms of cycles of spatial archetypes and architectural designs.

Spiral Dynamics: Personal and cultural developmental model describing the stages of development of consciousness and of society in terms of alternating outgoing and introvertive stages. Several interpretations, some of which have been incorporated into Integral Philosophy.

Spiritual Enlightenment: The individual realization of the Absolute, whether through long mystical and contemplative discipline and practice or spontaneous self-awakening. It may involve identity (nonduality, in which the psychophysical ego or self disappears entirely and there is only the Real), union in duality (devotional mysticism or God-realization, in which an aspect of the relative self remains as the lover of God), or even higher states of attainment and transformation (e.g. the Supramental State of Integral Yoga).

Spiritual Hierarchy: A god or archetype, a metaphysical reality or series of realities that stands behind or above the natural world and individual and collective consciousness, an intermediate divine reality, emanation, or personality, between Absolute Reality and creation.

Spirit World: Dimension of existence beyond the physical world and that is inhabited by spirits and other supernatural beings. Equivalent to the Astral Plane of Theosophy and the New Age. In part equivalent with the Imaginal world.

Subtle Body: The energy or life force body that maintains the organic material physical body. Includes a subtle anatomy consisting of chakras, nadis, meridians, and so on.

Subtle Physical: Dimension of existence intermediate between the empirical physical world and the spirit world. Includes afterlife states where one has a body.

Surface Personality: The ordinary waking consciousness, the surface being, the opposite of the transpersonal or inner being.

Tanha: (Sanskrit) Usually translated as craving, but also meaning thirst, desire, longing, greed. In Buddhism it refers to lower tendencies, either physical or mental, that perpetuate samsara and rebirth.

Taoism: Also spelt Daoism. A mystico-philosophical Chinese system that emphasises living in harmony with the Tao, literally: "the Way," or "The Path."

Theism: Faith in and worship of a personal deity. Includes Kathenotheism, Monaltry, Monistic Theism, Monotheism, Polytheism, etc. The opposite of Atheism.

Theogony: Creation story concerning the origin of the gods. Also the name of a poem by Hesiod on this topic, describing the generations of gods. Egyptian theologies are also theogonies, although they don't go into the elaborate detail Hesiod does, and they don't feature generations of gods.

Theology: From Greek, "Doctrine about God." In reference to ancient Egypt, refers to the creation myths of particular gods, deities, and pantheons. In Abrahamic monotheism, especially Christianity and Islam, refers to the intellectual justification for the theistic deity of one's particular religion.

Theosophy: Greek "Divine Wisdom." Refers to esoteric and gnostic intellectual inquiry as to the Nature of Reality, God or the gods, emanation, spiritual psychology, cosmology, the subtle body, the evolution of the soul, and so on. As the word is used there are two definitions. As a common noun, it refers to cosmological gnosis and esoteric cosmology in general (e.g. Porphyry's Neoplatonism, Luria's Kabbalah, or Boehme's mystical theology). As a proper noun, refers to the modern East-West intellectual evolutionary-esoteric movement established by Madame Blavatsky in the late 19th century, and later developments (e.g. New Age teachings based on Blavatskyian or Post-Blavatskyian Theosophy; an exception here is made with Rudolf Steiner's Anthroposophy, a spin-off that adopted a more Western, aesthetic, feeling-orientated, and esoteric Christian orientation).

Theurgy: From Greek "divine-working." A type of mysticism which involves the use of magical rituals to invoke the action or presence of one or more deities, with the goal of achieving henosis (unity, that is, nonduality) and spiritual enlightenment.

Thinking: The logical, analyzing, problem-solving function of consciousness, centered in the head chakra. Tends more to science and philosophy than feeling does. For Jung one of the four ego-functions and the counterpole to Feeling; for Steiner one of three aspects of consciousness (along with feeling and willing).

Three Worlds: In Siberian Shamanism, the Earth, the underworld (a spirit world, not a place of punishment) and heaven or the sky. In Hinduism the three worlds of existence (skt. Triloka,) referred to in the Vedas: Earth (bhu), Air (bhuva), and Heaven (swar). In the Puranas an additional four higher worlds are added.

Thumos: From Greek, spirit. In Plato's tripartite psychology, the fiery emotional, in the sense of spirited debate or righteous anger, part of the soul. Located near the chest region (equivalent to the Anahata chakra). Associated with the warrior principle.

Traditionalism: A 20th and 21st century anti-modernist, anti-evolutionary, esoteric movement, represented by esotericists such as Rene Guenon, Frithjof Schuon, Martin Lings, Seyyed Hossein Nasr, and others, emphasising symbolism, metaphysics, a common transcendent revelation or perennial philosophy behind the various exoteric religions, and the necessity of exoteric religion as a gateway or starting point. Despite their claim to timelessness, Traditionalist and perennialist themes go back no further than the Axial Age. Modern writers with a similar anti-modernist approach to esotericism, but not strictly speaking part of the Traditionalist movement, include R.A. Schwaller de Lubicz, Julius Evola, Mircea Eliade, Henry Corbin, and Huston Smith, among others.

Transcendent "I": The pure center of awareness, the persisting subjectivity, which experiences the Psychophysical Ego's various states and phenomena of consciousness without being tainted by or bound to them. Most clearly referred to in Indian philosophy as the seer, the doer, or the witness. Some technical terms include paramatman (Vedanta), purusha (Samkhya), Original Mind (Mahayana Buddhism), Nous (Hellenistic esotericism), Transcendental Ego (Phenomenology), and so on. Spiritual Liberation means the permanent detachment from the Psychophysical Ego and the return of attention to the Transcendent Ego, at which point consciousness becomes infinite.

Transpersonal: Expanding beyond the surface being and its individual and personal consciousness; the intuitive states of consciousness, gnosis to a greater or lesser degree.

Underworld: In Mesopotamian, early Persian, Greek, and other early Mediterranean cultures, a gloomy region under the Earth, where the shades of the dead are said to go.

Upanishads: Vedic commentaries, early mystical and inspired teachings, composed from the 7th or 8th century B.C.E. onwards. Later formed the basis of Vedanta.

Varna: Sanskrit, "color." The four castes of the Vedic system which according to the Rig Vedic myth of creation emerged from the Primordial Human. These are brahmin (priests), kshatriya (warriors and rulers), the vaishya (merchants and artisans), and the shudra (workers and servants). Plato's *Republic* features a similar but three-fold system of social archetypes, each with a psychological correspondence: philosophers (logos), warriors (thumos), and the common people (epithumia).

Veda: From Sanskrit "knowledge". The oldest scriptures of India, dating to 1500 to 900 B.C.E. and the foundation texts of Hinduism. According to legend they were revealed in profound meditation to the Vedic Rishis (seers). "Vedic" can refer either to the original Vedas themselves and the associated culture, myth, and ritual, or to the Hindu religions which developed later but consider the Vedas sacred, as opposed to the atheistic Shramanas.

Vedanta: Sanskrit, "end (or culmination) of the Vedas." One of the six traditional schools of Vedic, specifically Hindu philosophy, based on the ideas about the Nature of the Self and of ultimate Reality found in the Upanishads.

Venus: Paleolithic, Late Pleistocene, female fertility figurine, often emphasizing the breasts, hips, and belly.

Yin and Yang: In Chinese philosophy, the two inseparable aspects of reality, each contained within the other. They represent the negative or receptive (Yin) and positive or creative (Yang) polarities of reality.

Visible Gods: The Mesopotamian association of the visible planets with gods, which have an effect on circumstances on Earth. This was the foundation of astrology, and was carried through to the Hellenistic period, especially Neoplatonism. With the dominance of monotheism, the planets were no longer considered gods, but the idea of their influence on earthly events remained.

Vital: As described in Integral Yoga, the individual and also cosmic principle intermediate between the physical body and the pure thinking mind (or the physical and the mental); corresponds to Plato's Epithumia and Thumos.

Yoga: From Sanskrit "yoking", "union." In Indian spirituality any set of specific practices that leads to Liberation. Also called marga, path. Swami Vivekananda popularized the idea of four Yogas: Bhakti, Jnana, Karma, and Raja. Sri Aurobindo made Integral Yoga the summation of Bhakti, Jnana, and Karma.

Younger Dryas: Sudden period of global cooling and return of glacial conditions, from around 10,900 to 9,700 years B.C.E. It marked the end of the Pleistocene, and may have driven the Neolithic revolution and the beginning of agriculture in the Near East.

BIBLIOGRAPHY

Alex, Bridget (2018, September 22). Neanderthal Brains: Bigger, Not Necessarily Better. *Discover Magazine*. https://www.discovermagazine.com/planet-earth/neanderthal-brains-bigger-not-necessarily-better

Alfassa, Mirra (The Mother) (1979-1993). *Mother's Agenda*. (Satprem, Ed.). Institute of Evolutionary Research.

Argüelles, José (1984). *Earth Ascending: An Illustrated Treatise on Law Governing Whole Systems*. Shambhala Publications.

Arney, Kat (2020, January 30). Back to the Womb – Fish, Fraud and Dodgy Embryology. *Genetics Unzipped*. https://geneticsunzipped.com/transcripts/2020/1/30/back-to-the-womb

Asprem, Egil (2015). Intermediary Beings. in *The Occult World*, edited by Christopher Partridge, 646-58. Abingdon & New York: Routledge.

Aurobindo, Sri (1995). *Secret of the Veda*. Lotus Light Publications.

Aurobindo, Sri (2005). The Life Divine. *The Complete Works of Sri Aurobindo*, vol. 21-22. Pondicherry: Sri Aurobindo Ashram Trust.

Aurobindo, Sri (2012). Letters on Yoga - I. *The Complete Works of Sri Aurobindo*, vol. 28. Pondicherry: Sri Aurobindo Ashram Press.

Baker, Matthew James (2015). *Psychological Type and Atheism : Why Some People Are More Likely Than Others to Give Up God*. PhD thesis, University of Warwick. http://webcat.warwick.ac.uk/record=b2860410~S1

Baker, Matthew James (2020, April 18). Which Bible Characters are Historical? UsefulCharts. YouTube. https://youtu.be/aLtRR9RgFMg

Baron-Cohen, Simon (2009). Autism: The Empathizing–Systemizing (E-S) Theory. *The Year in Cognitive Neuroscience 2009*: Ann. N.Y. Acad. Sci. 1156: 68–80. doi: 10.1111/j.1749-6632.2009.04467.x

Barron, Bishop Robert (2014, June 13). Bill Maher and Not Understanding Either Faith or the Bible. https://www.wordonfire.org/articles/barron/bill-maher-and-not-understanding-either-faith-or-the-bible/

Barton, Tamsyn (1994). *Ancient Astrology.* London and New York: Routledge.

Basham, A.L. (1951). *History and Doctrines of the Ajivikas* (2nd ed.). Delhi, India: Moltilal Banarsidass.

Bauval, Robert, and Gilbert, Adrian (1994). *The Orion Mystery: Unlocking The Secrets of the Pyramids.* London: Heinemann.

Beck, Don (2006). Spiral Dynamics Integral. Sounds True.

Beck, Roger (2007). *A Brief History of Ancient Astrology.* Blackwell Publishing.

BeDuhn, Jason (2020). The Co-formation of the Manichaean and Zoroastrian Religions in Third-Century Iran. *Entangled Religions* 11.2 (2020) DOI: 10.13154/er.11.2020.8414

Begley, Sharon (2020, September 24). Brainiacs, Not Birdbrains: Crows Possess Higher Intelligence Long Thought a Primarily Human Attribute. STAT News. https://www.statnews.com/2020/09/24/crows-possess-higher-intelligence-long-thought-primarily-human/

Bekoff, Marc (2005). *Animal Passions and Beastly Virtues: Reflections on Redecorating Nature.* Temple University Press.

Bekoff, Marc (2010). *Wild Justice: The Moral Lives of Animals.* University of Chicago Press.

Berlin, Isiah (2013). *The Hedgehog and the Fox. An Essay on Tolstoy's View of History* (2nd ed.). Princeton University Press.

Beschizza, Rob (2016, February 19). Here are all of North Korea's new official slogans. BoingBoing https://boingboing.net/2016/02/19/here-are-all-of-north-koreas.html

Binet, Alfred (1889). *The Psychic Life of Micro-Organisms: A Study in Comparative Psychology.* Translated from the French by Thomas McCormack. (Chicago: The Open Court Publishing Company.

Bleicher, Joseph (1982). *The Hermeneutical Imagination: Outline of a Positive Critique of Scientism and Sociology,* London. Routledge and Kegan Paul.

Bloomberg Technology (2022, June 24). Google Engineer on his Sentient AI Claim. YouTube. https://youtu.be/kgCUn4fQTsc

Bodhisattva (2021, December 27). Ajivika, Buddhism, and Jainism: Why the third Shramana religion "Ajivika" was lost after 2000 years. Youtube. https://youtu.be/jfFBFArv-8Y

Bolen, Jean Shinoda (2004). *Goddesses in Everywoman: Powerful Archetypes in Women's Lives.* HarperCollins.

Bolen, Jean Shinoda (2009). *Gods in Everyman: Archetypes That Shape Men's Lives.* Harper Collins.

Brandon, S. G. F. (1967). *The Judgment of the Dead.* London: Weidenfeld and Nicolson.

Brown, David (2000). *Mesopotamian Planetary Astronomy-Astrology.* Styx.

Budge, E. A. Wallis (1967). *The Egyptian Book of the Dead.* New York: Dover Publications.

Cairns, Douglas (2019, March 26). Thymos. *Oxford Classical Dictionary.* https://doi.org/10.1093/acrefore/9780199381135.013.8180

Campbell, Joseph (1960). *The Masks of God, Volume 1: Primitive Mythology.* London:Secer and Warburg.

Campbell, Joseph (1962). *The Masks of God, Volume 2: Oriental Mythology.* London: Secer and Warburg.

Campbell, Joseph (1964/2017). *The Masks of God, Volume 3: Occidental Mythology.* Joseph Campbell Foundation (Digital edition).

Capra, Fritjof (1975). *The Tao of Physics.* Shambhala Publications.

Capra, Fritjof (1982). *The Turning Point.* Bantam Books.

Carey, Samuel Warren (1976). *The Expanding Earth.* Elsevier.

Carey, Samuel Warren (1988). *Theories of the Earth and Universe: A History of Dogma in the Earth Sciences.* Stanford University Press.

Carl Jung Depth Psychology (2020, November 14). Reflections on the Jung-White Letters. https://carljungdepthpsychologysite.blog/2020/11/14/reflections-on-the-jung-white-letters/

Cathie, Bruce (1990). *Energy Grid: Harmonic 695: The Pulse of the Universe.* American West Publishers.

Cawthorne, Ellie (2020, October 2). Q&A: Why and how did the Aztecs practise human sacrifice? History Extra. https://www.historyextra.com/period/medieval/human-sacrifice-aztecs-why-how-ritual-common/

Chaisson, Eric J. (2001). *Cosmic Evolution: Rise of Complexity in Nature.* Harvard University Press.

Chaisson, E. J. (2006). *Epic of Evolution: Seven Ages of the Cosmos.* Columbia University Press.

Chaisson, Eric J. (2012). Researching and Teaching Cosmic Evolution. In B. Rodrigue, L. Grinin, & A. V. Korotaev (eds.), *From Big Bang to Global Civilization.* Berkeley, CA: University of California Press.

Chalmers, David (1996). *The Conscious Mind: In Search of a Fundamental Theory.* Oxford University Press.

Chaudhuri, Haridas (1977). *The Evolution of Integral Consciousness.* Wheaton, Illinois: Quest Books.

Childress, David Hatcher (2003). *The Anti-Gravity Handbook.* Adventures Unlimited Press.

Christian, David (2018). *Origin Story: A Big History of Everything.* New York: Little, Brown and Co

Clark, Gerald (2013). *The Anunnaki of Nibiru: Mankind's Forgotten Creators, Enslavers, Destroyers, Saviors and Hidden Architects of the New World Order.* Createspace.

CENIEH (2023, January 26). The CENIEH participates in a study that confirms that the Neanderthals possessed symbolic capacity. https://www.cenieh.es/en/press/news/cenieh-participates-study-confirms-neanderthals-possessed-symbolic-capacity

Cole, James (2017). Assessing the Calorific Significance of Episodes of Human Cannibalism in the Palaeolithic. *Scientific Reports* volume 7, 44707. https://doi.org/10.1038/srep44707

Corbin, Henry (1989). *Spiritual Body and Celestial Earth: From Mazdean Iran to Shi'ite Iran.* Princeton University Press.

Corbin, Henry (1995), Mundus Imaginalis, or the Imaginary and the Imaginal. in Leonard Fox transl. *Swedenborg and Esoteric Islam.* Swedenborg Foundation.

Critchlow, Keith (1988). Introduction. in Iamblichus, *The Theology of Arithmetic: On the Mystical, Mathematical and Cosmological Symbolism of the First Ten Numbers.* Grand Rapids: Phanes Press.

Crowley, Aleister (1986). *777 and Other Qabalistic Writings of Aleister Crowley.* Weiser Books.

David-Neel, Alexandra (1977). *Magic and Mystery in Tibet.* Abacus, Sphere.

DeConnick, April D. (2016). *The Gnostic New Age - How a Countercultural Spirituality Revolutionized Religion from Antiquity to Today.* New York: Columbia University Press.

DeKorne, James (2002). The Out-Of-Body Experience as Gnostic Revelation. *New Dawn*, No. 72, May-June 2002. http://jamesdekorne.com/NewDawn/obegnostic.htm

Delaforge, Gaeten (1987). "The Templar Tradition: Yesterday and Today". Gnosis Magazine. No. 6. https://www.masonicworld.com/education/files/artjun02/TEMPTRAD.htm

Derrat, Max (2020). Aion, Youtube playlist, 18 January to 23 June 2020 https://youtube.com/playlist?list=PLDYqIK_NYzw6I41Mk9P2qDW-IocC5DLk4

Descartes, Rene (1968). *Meditations and Other Metaphysical Writings.* Penguin.

Deshpande, R. Y. (2018). *The First Hymn of Rishi Vamadeva: Rig Veda Mandal IV Sukta 1.* CreateSpace.

de Waal, Frans (2016). *Are We Smart Enough to Know How Smart Animals Are?* WW Norton.

Dibble, Flint (2022, November 19). With Netflix's *Ancient Apocalypse*, Graham Hancock has declared war on archaeologists.

The Conversation. https://theconversation.com/with-netflixs-ancient-apocalypse-graham-hancock-has-declared-war-on-archaeologists-194881

S. J. Dick & M. L. Lupisella (2009). Cosmos & Culture; Cultural Evolution in a Cosmic Context. National Aeronautics and Space Administration, Office of External Relations, History Division.

Doley, Kusum (2015). Concept of Soul and Liberation in Jainism. *International Journal of Humanities & Social Science Studies.* vol. 2, issue 2, September 2015, pp. 297-302.

Dundas, Paul (2002). *The Jains.* Routledge (Second ed.).

Earney, Tim (n.d.). What is Gnosis? A critical appraisal of a vague category. Academia edu. https://www.academia.edu/8519480What_is_Gnosis_A_critical_appraisal_of_a_vague_category

Eck, Diana L. (ed.) (1994). Glossary. *The Pluralism Project.* World religions in Boston. Harvard University. https://pluralism.org/glossary

Eliade, Mircea (1964). *Shamanism: Archaic Techniques of Ecstasy.* Princeton University Press.

Emadinia, Arash (2017). *The Soul in the Afterlife: Individual Eschatological Beliefs in Zoroastrianism, Mandaeism and Islam.* Doctoral Thesis, George-August-Universität Göttingen.

Evola, Julius (1995). *Revolt Against the Modern World: Politics, Religion, and Social Order in the Kali Yuga.* Inner Traditions.

Faivre, Antoine (1994). *Access to Western Esotericism.* New York: SUNY Press.

Farthing, Geoffrey (1978). *Exploring the Great Beyond.* Quest Books.

Feldblyum, Vivian (2016). Aristotle on Thumos and Phantasia. *Ithaque* 18, pp.1-23 http://hdl.handle.net/1866/133357

Ferguson, Marilyn (1980). *The Aquarian Conspiracy: Personal and Social Transformation in the 1980s,* Penguin Putman.

Ferrer, Jorge N. (2002). *Revisioning Transpersonal Theory: A Participatory Vision of Human Spirituality.* State University of New York Press.

Ferrone, Giuseppe (2021). *Big History - A Journey From the Big Bang to the Modern World and into the Future.* Thorpe Bowker.

Fix, William R. (1979). *Star Maps: Astonishing New Evidence From Ancient Civilisations and Modern Scientific Research of Man's Origins and Return to the Stars.* Popular Culture Ink.

Forel, Auguste (2016). *Ants and Some Other Insects: An Inquiry into the Psychic Powers of These Animal.* Transl. William Morton Wheeler. Project Gutenberg (originally published 1904, Chicago: The Open Court Publishing Company, and London: Kegan Paul, Trench, Trübner & Co. Ltd.)

Gebser, J. (1986). *The Ever-Present Origin,* (transl. by Noel Barstad with Algis Mickunas) Ohio University Press.

Gidley, Jennifer M. (2007). Evolution of Consciousness as a Planetary Imperative: An Integration of Integral Views. *Integral Review: A Transdisciplinary and Transcultural Journal for New Thought, Research and Praxis,* 5, pp. 4-226.

Gier, N. F. (1994). *Theology Bluebook.* University of Idaho, 3rd ed.

Gill, N. S. (2019, October 29). *Hesiod's Five Ages of Man.* Thought Co. https://www.thoughtco.com/the-five-ages-of-man-111776

Gill, N.S. (2021, April. 12). "The Myth of Er From the Republic of Plato." ThoughtCo. thoughtco.com/the-myth-of-er-120332.

Godwin, Joscelyn (2016). Pythagoras and the Pythagorean Tradition." In Glenn Alexander Magee, ed., *The Cambridge Handbook of Mysticism and Western Esotericism*. Cambridge: Cambridge University Press, 13-25.

Goldfield, Anna (2019, May 9). The Neanderthal Brain—Clues About Cognition. Sapiens org. https://www.sapiens.org/biology/neanderthal-brain/

Gooch, Stan (1972). *Total Man*. Abacus.

Gooch, Stan (1977). *The Neanderthal Question*. Wildwood House.

Gooch, Stan (1980). *Guardians of the Ancient Wisdom*. HarperCollins.

Goodall, Jane (2005). Primate spirituality. In *The Encyclopedia of Religion and Nature*. edited by B. Taylor. New York: Thoemmes Continuum, pp. 1303-1306

Graeber, David and Wengrow, David (2021). *The Dawn of Everything*. Allen Lane.

Graves, Clare W. (2005). *The Never Ending Quest*. Christopher C. Cowan & Natasha Todorovic, Eds. Santa Barbara, CA: ECLET Publishing.

Greer, John Michael (2021). *The King in Orange: The Magical and Occult Roots of Political Power*. Inner Traditions.

Gregory, David (2010, January 28). Gregory's First Law: I see a pattern emerging. BBC. https://www.bbc.co.uk/blogs/davidgregory/2010/01/i_see_a_pattern_emerging.html

Guglielmi, Giorgia (2018, June 07). Honeybees can count to zero. Nature News. doi: https://doi.org/10.1038/d41586-018-05354-z

Guth, Steven Otto (2003). The Double, a new paradigm for understanding the human psyche. Kheper Website. http://malankazlev.com/kheper/topics/double/

Guthrie, Kenneth Sylvan (1987). *The Pythagorean Sourcebook and Library: An Anthology of Ancient Writings which Relate to Pythagoras and Pythagorean Philosophy*. Red Wheel/Weiser.

Hallam, A., Wignall, P. B. (1997). *Mass Extinctions and Their Aftermath*. Oxford University Press.

Harner, Michael (1980). *The Way of the Shaman: A Guide to Power and Healing*. NY: Harper & Row.

Harvey-Wilson, Simon Brian (2000). Shamanism and alien abductions: a comparative study. https://ro.ecu.edu.au/theses/1389

Hayward, Peter, Voros, Joseph, and Morrow, Rowena (2012). "Foresight Education in Australia — Time for a Hybrid Model?" *Futures*. Special Issue: University Learning, 44 (2): 181–88. doi:10.1016/j.futures.2011.09.011.

Healy, Melissa (2018, June 26). The surprising thing the 'marshmallow test' reveals about kids in an instant-gratification world. *LA Times*. https://www.latimes.com/science/

sciencenow/la-sci-sn-marshmallow-test-kids-20180626-story.html

Heidel, Alexander (1963). *The Babylonian Genesis: The Story of the Creation*. University of Chicago Press. (Originally published 1942).

Heyning, Eduard C. (2017). Star Music, T*he Ancient Idea of Cosmic Musicas a Philosophical Paradox*. Phd thesis, Canterbury Christ Church University.

Hill, Donald R. (1987). *Magic: Magic in Indigenous Societies*. Encyclopedia of Religion. NY: Macmillan.

Hodson, Geoffrey (1997). *The Kingdom of the Gods*. Theosophical Publishing House.

Hood, Ralph W. (2006). *The Common Core Thesis in the Study of Mysticism*.

Huxley, Aldous (1970). *The Perennial Philosophy*. Harper Colophon Books.

In P. McNamara (Ed), Where God and Science Meet: How Brain and Evolutionary Studies Alter Our Understanding of Religion, Vol. 3. *The Psychology of Religious Experience*. Westport, CT: Praeger. Online: https://doi.org/10.1093/acrefore/9780199340378.013.241

Horkheimer, Max, and Adorno, Theodor W. (2007). *Dialectic of Enlightenment* (Cultural Memory in the Present). Stanford University Press; 1st edition.

JAINA org (n.d.). *The Philosophy of Karma and the Nine Jain Tattvas*. https://www.jaina.org/page/KarmaTattvas/The-Philosophy-of-Karma-and-the-Nine-Jain-Tattvas.htm

Jainpedia (n.d.). Samgrahani-ratna. https://jainpedia.org/manuscript/samgrahani-ratna-9/

James, William (1971). *The Varieties of Religious Experience*. HarperCollins (First published 1902).

Jaynes, Julian (1976). *The Origin of Consciousness in the Breakdown of the Bicameral Mind*. Houghton Mifflin, Mariner Books.

Johnson, Khari (2022, June 14). LaMDA and the Sentient AI Trap. Wired. https://www.wired.com/story/lamda-sentient-ai-bias-google-blake-lemoine/

Jung, C. G. (1973). *Synchronicity: An Acausal Connecting Principle*. Princeton, NJ: Princeton University Press.

Kaelber, Walter O. (1976). "Tapas", Birth, and Spiritual Rebirth in the Veda. *History of Religions*. 15(4), 343-386.

Kazlev, M Alan (2000). The "Materialisms" Plane - Four Lower Divisions. Kheper website. http://malankazlev.com/kheper/topics/Theon/Materialisms.html

Kazlev, M. A. (2009). Esotericism. Kheper Website. http://malankazlev.com/kheper/topics/esotericism/

Kazlev, M. Alan (2011). Sri Aurobindo, the Mother, and the Integral Movement. Collaboration: *Journal of the Integral Yoga of Sri Aurobindo and the Mother*. Spring 2011, Vol. 35, No. 3.

Kazlev, M. Alan (2020). *Wisdom of the Gods*. Manticore Press.

Kazlev, M. Alan (2021). *Mythopoesis and the Modern World*. Manticore Press.

Kazlev, M. Alan (2022). The Collective Unconscious and the Media Sphere: An Esoteric Analysis of the Disinformation Crisis Facing Western Civilisation. In *Global Media's Preternatural Influence on Global Technological Singularity, Culture, and Government*. (Stephen Schafer and Alex Bennet, eds). IGI Global.

Kloetzli, W. Randolph and Patton, Laurie Louise (1987 / 2005). *Cosmology: Hindu Cosmology*. Encyclopedia of Religion, vol.03. NY, Macmillan. Online, Encyclopedia com https://www.encyclopedia.com/environment/encyclopedias-almanacs-transcripts-and-maps/cosmology-hindu-cosmology

Kolankaya-Bostanci, Neyir (2014). The Evidence of Shamanism Rituals in Early Prehistoric Periods of Europe and Anatolia. In *Colloquium Anatolicum XIII*, 185-204.

Kraut, Richard (2004/2022). Plato. Stanford Encyclopedia of Philosophy. https://plato.stanford.edu/entries/plato

Kruger, Justin, and Dunning, David (1999). Unskilled and Unaware of it: How Difficulties in Recognizing One's Own Incompetence Lead to Inflated Self-Assessments. *Journal of Personality and Social Psychology*, 77(6), 1121–1134. https://doi.org/10.1037/0022-3514.77.6.1121

Kung, Hans (1987). *Christianity and the World Religions*. HarperCollins.

Lachman, Gary (2018). *Dark Star Rising: Magick and Power in the Age of Trump*. TarcherPerigee.

Lamy, Lucy (1981). *Egyptian Mysteries*. Art and Imagination Series, Thames & Hudson.

Larson, Gerald. J. (1979). *Classical Samkhya*. Delhi: Motilal Banarsidass.

Le Page, Michael (2022, September 8). A single gene mutation may have made us smarter than Neanderthals. *New Scientist*. https://www.newscientist.com/article/2337133-a-single-gene-mutation-may-have-made-us-smarter-than-neanderthals/

The Living Philosophy (2022, January 10). Modernism vs Postmodernism. YouTube. https://youtu.be/iMVjI3pcwcU

Lobell, Mimi (1983). Spatial Archetypes ReVision, *A Journal of Consciousness and Change*, vol.6 no.2, Fall 1983.

Lobell, Mimi (2018). *Spatial Archetypes: The Hidden Patterns of Psyche and Civilization*, Createspace.

Lovelock, James (1979). *Gaia: A New Look at Life on Earth*. Oxford University Press.

Lovelock, James (1988). *The Ages of Gaia: A Biography of Our Living Earth*. Bantam.

MacLennan, Bruce (2019). The Psychodynamics of the Numbers. In *Platonic Interpretations: Selected Papers from the Sixteenth Annual Conference of the International Society for Neoplatonic Studies* (edited by John F. Finamore and Eric D. Perl). Lydney: The Prometheus Trust.

Mapacadamy (2022, April 21). Pashupati Seal. https://mapacademy.io/article/

pashupati-seal/

Magee, Glenn Alexander (2016). Jacob Boehme and Christian Theosophy. In Glenn Alexander Magee (ed.), *The Cambridge Handbook of Western Mysticism and Esotericism*. Cambridge University Press.

Marino, Lori (2022). "The Culture of Killer Whales" The Whale Sanctuary Project https://whalesanctuaryproject.org/intelligence-cognition-emotion-cetaceans/ Animal Minds.

Mark, Joshua J. (2019, December 20). Death and the Afterlife in Ancient Persia. World History Encyclopedia. https://www.worldhistory.org/article/1485/death-and-the-afterlife-in-ancient-persia/

Mark, Joshua J. (2020a, January 10). Chinvat Bridge. World History Encyclopedia. https://www.worldhistory.org/Chinvat_Bridge/

Mark, Joshua J. (2020b, September 28). The Dates of the Buddha. World History Encyclopedia. Retrieved from https://www.worldhistory.org/article/493/the-dates-of-the-buddha/

McEvilley, Thomas (2002). *The Shape of Ancient Thought*. New York: Allworth Press.

McLuhan, Marshall (1962). *The Gutenberg Galaxy*. University of Toronto Press.

Meher Baba (1973). *God Speaks*. *Sufism Reoriented*, Inc, 2nd edition. (Avatar Meher Baba Trust eBook, June 2011).

Melton, J. Gordon (ed.) (2001). *Encyclopedia of Occultism & Parapsychology*. Farmington Hills, MI: Gale Group, Inc.

Meyer, Michael (2005). *The Bedford Introduction to Literature*. Bedford: St. Martin's Press.

Middleton, John (1987 and 2005). Magic: Theories of Magic. *Encyclopedia of Religion*. NY: Macmillan.

Milner, Richard (2023, January 27). The bull-leaping women of ancient Minoan Greece. Grunge. https://www.grunge.com/1180844/the-bull-leaping-women-of-ancient-minoan-greece/

Monroe, Robert A. (1977). *Journeys Out Of The Body*. Garden City, NY: Anchor Press/Doubleday

Mooney, James (1991). *The Ghost-Dance Religion and Wounded Knee*. Dover Publications.

Mudgal, S. G. (1975). *Advaita of Sankara, a Reappraisal: Impact of Buddhism and Samkhya on Sankara's thought*. Motilal Banarsidass.

Nai, Alessandro, and Martínez i Coma, Ferran (2019). The personality of populists: provocateurs, charismatic leaders, or drunken dinner guests? *West European Politics*, Volume 42, 2019 - Issue 7, Pages 1337-1367 https://www.tandfonline.com/doi/full/10.1080/01402382.2019.1599570

NateTalksToYou (2023, February 1). Disney Star Calls Out Atheists - Christians of TikTok. YouTube. https://youtu.be/9S5jxqgA-q4

Neumann, Erich (1973). *The Origins and History of Consciousness*. Princeton University Press (originally published 1949).

Neumann, Erich (1983). *The Great Mother: An Analysis of the Archetype*. Transl. Ralph Manheim. Princeton University Press (Originally published: 1955).

Newman, Hugh (2018). *Earth Grids: The Secret Patterns of Gaia's Sacred Sites*. Wooden Books.

Ocean Keltoi (2022, June 21). Arguments for Atheism Don't Work Against Polytheism. YouTube. https://youtu.be/WL__XolIlIY

Oesch, Sean (2022, August 25). Why Google's LaMDA AI Is Not Sentient and Why It Matters. Reasons to Believe. https://reasons.org/explore/blogs/voices/why-googles-lamda-ai-is-not-sentient-and-why-it-matters

Owen, Iris M. and Sparrow, Margaret (1976). *Conjuring Up Philip: An Adventure in Psychokinesis*. New York: Harper & Row.

Oxford Reference (2023). Sensus Communis. Retrieved 11 Jan. 2023, from https://www.oxfordreference.com/view/10.1093/oi/authority.20110810105824261.

Paglia, Camille, (2006). *Erich Neumann: Theorist of the Great Mother*. Arion, 13.3 (Winter 2006).

Pakenham, Thomas (1992). *The Scramble for Africa: White Man's Conquest of the Dark Continent from 1876 to 1912*. HarperCollins.

Parks, Anton (2007). *Chronicles of Girku*, Volume 2. Adam Genesis. New Earth.

Parks, Anton (2014). *Chronicles of Girku*, Volume 0 (Prequel). Dream of Eternal Time. "Book of Nurea."

Pearson, Carol S. (1991). *Awakening the Heroes Within: Twelve Archetypes to Help Us Find Ourselves and Transform Our World*. San Francisco: HarperElixer.

Pezarkar, Leora (2017, August 25). The Jain Tirthankaras. Live History India. https://www.livehistoryindia.com/story/living-culture/the-jain-tirthankaras

Persinger, Michael A. (1976). Transient Geophysical Bases for Ostensible UFO-Related Phenomena and Associated Verbal Behavior? Perceptual and Motor Skills, 43(1), 215–221. https://doi.org/10.2466/pms.1976.43.1.215

Pinchbeck, Daniel (2022, November 28). What's Wrong with "Ancient Apocalypse"? https://danielpinchbeck.substack.com/p/whats-wrong-with-ancient-apocalypse

Poortman, J. J., (1978). Ochema, *Vehicles of Consciousness – the Concept of Hylic Pluralism*. Utrecht: Adyar.

Powell, A. E. (1927). *The Astral Body: and Other Astral Phenomena*. Quest Books.

Quispel, Gilles (2008). *Gnostica, Judaica, Catholica: Collected Essays of Gilles Quispel*. Edited by Johannes van Oort. Leiden & Boston: Brill.

Rackley, Rosanna (2014). *Kingship, Struggle, and Creation: The Story of Chaoskampf.*

Masters Thesis, University of Birmingham.

Radhakrishnan, S. (1953). *The Principle Upanishads*. London: George Allen & Unwin Ltd.

Radovčić D, Sršen AO, Radovčić J, Frayer DW (2015). Evidence for Neandertal Jewelry: Modified White-Tailed Eagle Claws at Krapina. PLoS ONE 10(3): e0119802. https://doi.org/10.1371/journal.pone.0119802

Rendu, William et al (2014). Evidence supporting an intentional Neandertal burial at La Chapelle-aux-Saints. 4100 - https://www.pnas.org/doi/full/10.1073/pnas.1316780110

SO - Proceedings of the National Academy of Sciences 2014-01-07 111(1): 81-86. https://www.pnas.org/doi/abs/10.1073/pnas.1316780110

Roberts, Jennifer (2009/2019). *Greek History: Archaic to Classical Age*. Oxford Bibliographies. DOI: 10.1093/OBO/9780195389661-0021

Rubarth, Scott (2002). Stoic Philosophy of Mind. Internet Encyclopedia of Philosophy. https://iep.utm.edu/stoicmind/

Satprem (1982). *The Mind of the Cells*. Trans; by Francine Mahak and Luc Venet. New York NY: Institute for Evolutionary Research.

Schnell, A.K., Amodio, P., Boeckle, M. and Clayton, N.S. (2021), How Intelligent is a Cephalopod? Lessons from Comparative Cognition. Biol Rev, 96: 162-178. https://doi.org/10.1111/brv.12651

Schonberger, Martin (1992). *I Ching & the Genetic Code: The Hidden Key to Life*. Aurora Press.

School of Life (2015, October 2). Philosophy - Schopenhauer. YouTube. https://youtu.be/q0zmfNx7OM4

Schumacher, E. F. (1977). *A Guide for the Perplexed*. Harper & Row.

Schuon, Frithjof (1975). *The Transcendent Unity of Religions*. Harper & Row.

Schwaller de Lubicz, R. A. (1981). *The Temple in Man: Sacred Architecture and the Perfect Man*. Inner Traditions.

Scott, Aaron (2022, March 30). Want to Study How Aliens Might Think? Look to the Octopus. Oregon Public Broadcasting. https://www.opb.org/article/2022/03/29/want-to-study-how-aliens-might-think-look-to-the-octopus/

Seth, Anil (2017, July 28). If you want to know what aliens will be like, just look at an octopus. Ted https://ideas.ted.com/want-to-know-what-aliens-will-be-like-just-look-at-an-octopus/

Sharma, Pratul (2019, September 06). New DNA Study Debunks Aryan Invasion Theory. The Week. https://www.theweek.in/news/india/2019/09/06/new-study-debunks-aryan-invasion-theory.amp.htm

Shermer, Michael (2017, June 1). No, There Wasn't an Advanced Civilization 12,000 Years Ago. Scientific American. https://www.scientificamerican.com/article/no-there-wasnt-an-advanced-civilization-12-000-years-ago/

Shields, Christopher (2000/2020). Aristotle's Psychology. *Stanford Encyclopedia of Philosophy*. https://plato.stanford.edu/entries/aristotle-psychology/

Sinclair Thomson, Brent & Challis, Sam. (2017). The 'Bullets to Water' Belief Complex: A Pan-Southern African Cognate Epistemology for Protective Medicines and the Control of Projectiles. Journal of Conflict Archaeology. Vol. 12, no. 3.

Singh, Jaideva (1980). *Pratyabhijnahrdayam*. Delhi: Motilal Banarsidass.

Sinnett, A. P. (1883). *Esoteric Buddhism*. Trübner & Co.

Skrbina, David (2007). "Panpsychism" The Internet Encyclopedia of Philosophy. https://iep.utm.edu/panpsych/

Sledge, Justin (2023, March 4). Who is Yahweh - How a Warrior-Storm God became the God of the Israelistes and of World Monotheism. Esoterica. YouTube. https://youtu.be/mdKst8zeh-U

Smith, Huston (1977). *Forgotten Truth: The Primordial Tradition*. New York: Harper & Row.

Soubrier, J., Gower, G., Chen, K. et al. (2016). Early Cave Art and Ancient DNA Record the Origin of European Bison. *Nature Communications* 7, 13158. https://doi.org/10.1038/ncomms13158

Sledge, Justin (2021, October 30). The Dead Sea Scrolls - The War Scroll - Apocalyptic War against Belial and the Sons of Darkness. Esoterica, You Tube https://youtu.be/mWave1tX-ko

Spier, Fred (2015). *Big History and the Future of Humanity*. 2nd edn. Chichester, UK: Wiley-Blackwell.

Stace, W. T. (1961). *Mysticism and Philosophy*. London: Macmillan.

Stavish, Marc (2018). *Egregores: The Occult Entities That Watch Over Human Destiny*. Simon and Schuster.

Sterkenberg, Zack (2019, March 28). Are Plants Intelligent? Science is Beginning to Think So. Ambius. https://www.ambius.com/blog/are-plants-intelligent/

Stoa, The (2022, March 24). Swarms, Egregores, and Autocults, w/ John Robb, BJ Campbell, Patrick Ryan, and Jordan Hall. YouTube. https://youtu.be/sTxuLoI80Vg

Story, Ronald (1976). *The Space-Gods Revealed: A Close Look at the Theories of Erich Von Däniken*. New York: Harper & Row.

Teja, Charan (2019, April 17). At the Heart of Andhra's Booming Capital Lies a Quaint Ashram for Rationalists. The News Minute. https://www.thenewsminute.com/article/heart-andhra-s-booming-capital-lies-quaint-ashram-rationalists-100193

TheraminTrees (2015, May 8). Respecting Beliefs: Why We Should Do No Such Thing. YouTube https://youtu.be/r_5yUXjXizQ

Teilhard de Chardin, Pierre (1965). *The Phenomenon of Man*. Fontana Collins.

TREY the Explainer (2018, November 25). What's the Deal with the Nephilim? YouTube. https://youtu.be/4Kpkp2vxX3I

Trompf, Garry W. (2006). "Macrohistory", in Wouter J. Hanegraaff, ed. *Dictionary of Gnosis & Western Esotericism*. Leiden & Boston: Brill. pp.701-716.

Uzdavinys, Algis (2010). *Philosophy and Theurgy in Late Antiquity*. Angelico Press/Sophia Perennis.

Van Den Doel, Marieke J.E. and Hanegraaff, Wouter J. (2006). "Imagination". In: *Dictionary of Gnosis and Western Esotericism* (Wouter J. Hanegraaff, ed.). Leiden & Boston: Brill.

van Inwagen, Peter and Sullivan, Meghan (2021). "Metaphysics", *The Stanford Encyclopedia of Philosophy* (Winter 2021 Edition), Edward N. Zalta (ed.) https://plato.stanford.edu/archives/win2021/entries/metaphysics/

van Prooijen, J.-W., Douglas, K. M., and De Inocencio, C. (2018). Connecting the Dots: Illusory Pattern Perception Predicts Belief in Conspiracies and the Supernatural. Eur. J. Soc. Psychol., 48: 320– 335. https://doi.org/10.1002/ejsp.2331.

Versluis, Arthur (2007). *Magic and Mysticism: An Introduction to Western Esoteric Traditions*. Rowman & Littlefield Publishers.

Viegas, Jennifer (2010, October 9). Animals Said to Have Spiritual Experiences. NBC News. https://www.nbcnews.com/id/wbna39574733

von Franz, Marie-Louise (1975). Number and Time: Reflections Leading Toward a Unification of Depth Psychology and Physics. Rider.

von Stuckrad, Kocku (2005). *Western Esotericism: A Brief History of Secret Knowledge*. London: Equinox Publishing.

Voros, Joseph (2022a, June 6). The Sum Total of All Human Knowledge', Part I. The Voroscope. https://thevoroscope.com/2022/06/06/sum-total-human-knowledge-1/

Voros, Joseph (2022b, June 13). The Sum Total of All Human Knowledge', Part II. The Voroscope. https://thevoroscope.com/2022/06/06/sum-total-human-knowledge-2/

Wehr, Gerhard (2003). *Jung and Steiner: The Birth of a New Psychology*. SteinerBooks.

White, David Gordon (2014). *The Yoga Sutra of Patanjali A Biography*. Princeton University Press.

Wigner, Eugene P. (1960). "The Unreasonable Effectiveness of Mathematics in the Natural Sciences. Richard Courant lecture in mathematical sciences delivered at New York University, May 11, 1959". *Communications on Pure and Applied Mathematics*. 13: 1–14. doi:10.1002/cpa.3160130102.

Wilber, Ken (1986). *Up From Eden*. New Science Library.

Wilber, Ken (2002). "Participatory Samsara: The Green-Meme Approach to the Mystery of the Divine." http://wilber.shambhala.com/html/books/boomeritis/sidebar_f/index.cfm/

Williams, Matt (2020, July 23). Beyond "Fermi's Paradox" III: What is the Great Filter? Universe Today. https://www.universetoday.com/145512/beyond-the-fermi-paradox-iii-what-is-the-great-filter/

Wilson, Colin (1995). Humankind's Origins. Colin Wilson talks About the Achievements of Author Stan Gooch. Aulis Publishers. https://www.aulis.com/twothirds_colin_wilson.htm

Winell, Marlene (2011). *Religious Trauma Syndrome* (Series of 3 articles), Vol. 39, Issue 2, May 2011, Vol. 39, Issue 3, September 2011, Vol. 39, Issue 4.

Winkelman, Michael (2008). "Shamanism". *International Encyclopedia of the Social Sciences* (2nd edition), MacMillan.

Woodford, Stephen (2021, November 25). Every Argument for God DEBUNKED! Rationality Rules. YouTube https://youtu.be/o9Ctc9LlfiA

Wu, Kuang-Ming (1990). *The Butterfly as Companion: Meditations on the First Three Chapters of the Chuang-Tzu*. State University of New York Press.

Wurges, Jennifer; and Frey, Rebecca (2005). "Shamanism" *Gale Encyclopedia of Alternative Medicine*. Thomson Gale.

Yamauchi, Edwin M. (1978). "The Descent of Ishtar, the Fall of Sophia, and the Jewish Roots of Gnosticism." *Tyndale Bulletin* 29 (1): 143–75. https://doi.org/10.53751/001c.30626.

Yes Vedanta (n.d.). Sanskrit Glossary – Yoga and Vedas Terms. https://www.yesvedanta.com/sanskrit-glossary-1/

Zabel, Gary (n.d.). Therianthropes, Shamans, and Sorcerers. *Philosophy* 281: Philosophy of Magic, Witchcraft, and The Occult.

https://www.faculty.umb.edu/gary_zabel/Courses/Phil%20281/Philosophy%20of%20Magic/My%20Documents/Therianthropes.htm

Zukav, Gary (1984). *The Dancing Wu Li Masters: An Overview of the New Physics*. Bantam.

INDEX

A

Achaemenid Empire 119

Achilles 110, 213

Adonis 131-133

Advaita 167, 169, 180, 204, 213, 249, 254

Afterlife 62, 85, 111, 121, 124, 131, 135-140, 154-155, 159, 164, 181-182, 200-201, 208, 215, 226, 230, 241-242, 245, 248, 250, 257-258, 260

Ahimsa 131, 166, 170-174, 215

Ahura Mazda 149-153

Ajivika 170, 181-183, 223, 242, 259

Akenaten 140

Akh 124, 137-138, 242, 250

Akhenaten 123, 140-141

Akkadians 98, 101

Alienation from Nature 48, 83, 94, 147, 253

Aliens 52, 97-101, 122

Amesha Spenta 151-152

Amun-Ra 129

Anatolia 75-77, 93, 211, 229, 244

Ancestors 68, 76, 94, 106, 111, 114

Ancestor Worship 111, 154, 241, 258

Ancient Apocalypse 57-58

Ancient Astronaut 58, 98-101, 122

Angra Mainyu 151-153

Anima 64, 82, 235, 237

Animal Consciousness 50

Animal Soul 50

Animism 61, 64, 66, 117, 140, 195, 242, 252

Anubis 90, 132, 138

Apis 128-129, 131, 133

Apsu 101, 103

Archon 87, 201

Aristotle 218, 220, 223, 228-229, 233-237

Arithmosophy 218, 234, 242-243

Asgard 110

Asha 151

Astral Plane 62, 66, 107, 110-111, 242, 251, 255, 260

Astral Projection 63, 254

Astrology 26, 30-31, 66, 116-119, 128, 159, 233, 239, 242, 254, 263

Atlantis 55-57, 79, 97, 122, 208

Atman 163, 167-169, 183, 193, 212, 226-227, 238

Atomism 182, 220-221, 234, 243

Atum 5, 124-129

Aubrey, John 78

Aurignacian 70-72

Aurobindo, Sri 25, 32, 37, 44, 46, 49-50, 89, 106, 109, 127, 137, 151, 162, 169, 204-205, 210, 228, 235-237, 247, 250, 258, 264-265

Auroch 68

Avebury 78

Avesta 150-152

Axial Age 29, 141, 143, 145, 147, 149, 207, 209, 243, 247, 253, 255-256, 258-259, 262

B

Ba 76, 136-138, 196, 242-243, 250

Baal 23, 196-197

Babylonians 98, 101, 109, 130, 135, 200

Behe, Michael 44

Bekoff, Marc 50

Bergson, Henry 45

Berry 46

Bhakti 22-24, 205, 243, 248, 252, 264

Big Bang Theory 46

Blavatsky, Helena Petrova 16, 20, 32, 35, 54-57, 97, 122, 236, 261

Boehme, Jakob 45, 261

Bonaventure 19

Book of Coming Forth by Day 136

Book of Enoch 107

Brahmacharya 166

Brahman 163, 166, 168-169, 191, 212, 241

Brennan, Barbara Ann 37

Breuil, Henri 68-70

Bronze Age 77, 82-83, 97, 99, 122, 157, 197-198, 207-209, 243-244

Bruno, Giordano 31, 221

Buddha, the 23-24, 146, 171-172, 175, 178-181, 189, 213, 248

Buddhi 50, 167-168, 227

Buddhism 16, 19, 23, 25, 30, 137, 145-146, 152, 163-165, 170-171, 173-175, 177-183, 189-192, 225, 237, 242, 250-251, 254, 259-260, 262

C

Campbell, Joseph 32, 63, 68, 70-71, 83, 125, 132-134, 150, 171-172, 180, 208

Canaan 198

Carey, Samuel Warren 56

Cartesian Dualism 243, 245

Catal Hoyuk 76-77

Cathie, Bruce 80-81

Catholic 66, 68, 111, 155, 201, 221, 229

Chalmers, David 49

Chaos 49, 61, 81, 83, 94, 101-103, 115, 126-128, 130, 134-135, 147, 166, 197, 204, 225, 244, 246

Chaoskampf 102, 127, 134, 151, 244

Charvaka 181-182

Chaudhuri, Haridas 44

Chimpanzees 53

Christian, David 42

Christianity 18, 30, 38, 46, 56, 101, 132,

153, 155, 201-203, 205, 215, 230, 241, 246, 261

Chuang-Tzu 189, 191-192, 202

Civilization 28, 32, 43, 48, 57-58, 64, 73, 76, 93-97, 99, 109, 114, 117, 121-122, 130, 133, 135, 137, 146-147, 157, 159-160, 162, 172, 185-186, 190-191, 198, 207-209, 226, 253, 256

Collective Unconscious 36, 45, 73, 86, 98, 103, 105-106, 153, 164, 166, 242, 244, 249, 253

Confucius 145, 189-190

Contextualism 35

Continental Drift 55-56

Copernican Principle 52

Corbin. Henry 16, 45, 62, 87, 262

Cosmic Man 90-91, 162, 228

Cosmological Gnosis 20, 41, 233, 245, 249-250, 261

Cosmology 16, 20, 25-26, 31, 42-43, 56, 99, 101, 110, 117, 119, 127, 139, 155, 164-167, 177, 186, 188-189, 205, 210, 220, 225, 229-230, 234, 243, 245, 250, 255, 261

Crowley, Aleister 32, 38, 65, 88, 126, 140

Cyrus, the Great 150, 201

D

Dawn 24, 26, 32, 61, 85, 88-89, 125

Demiurge 104, 231-232

Democritus 220-221

Denisovians 54

Descartes, Rene 192, 221

Deuteronomistic Theology 200

Devas 64, 80, 85, 104

de Waal, Frans 50

Divination 28, 63, 79, 81, 117, 159, 186, 188

Donnelly, Ignatius 56-57, 97, 122

Downward Causation 108

Dreamtime 62

Druids 78

Druj 151

Duality 17, 21, 127, 134, 151-154, 189, 204, 217-218, 226-227, 252, 259

Dubois, Eugene 53

Dunning-Kruger Effect 17

E

Earth Mysteries 79

Egregore 106-109, 111, 246, 248

Egypt 16, 57, 66, 76, 82, 93, 97, 99-100, 104, 121-126, 129, 132, 134, 140, 152, 157, 160, 162-164, 166, 195, 214, 242-243, 250, 258, 261

Eleatic School 213, 221

Eliade, Mircea 21, 62, 262

Empedocles 8, 219-220

Empiricism 18, 33, 37, 42, 45, 182, 224, 234, 252, 257

Enki 101, 103, 115

Enkidu 112-113

Enlil 101, 115, 118, 198

Ennead 124, 126, 128

Enuma Anu Enlil 118

Enuma Elish 101-103, 106, 199

Epicurus 221

Epithumia 50, 107-108, 227-228, 237, 246, 263-264

Esotericism 16-21, 23-34, 36-39, 41, 43, 45, 47, 49-50, 52, 59, 69, 73, 104, 109, 111, 124, 130-131, 137, 143, 146, 168, 189, 202, 212, 214-215, 217-218, 220, 233, 239, 242-243, 247, 249-250, 254-256, 262

Evolution 16, 27, 32, 42-54, 57, 74, 140-141, 162, 183, 195, 222, 236, 245, 247, 250, 256, 258-259, 261

Exoteric 17, 22, 25, 73-74, 104, 202, 235, 241, 248, 256, 262

Expanding Earth 56

F

Faith 17-20, 23, 38, 75, 149, 155, 168, 175, 199, 203, 207, 248-249, 252, 259-260

Faivre, Antoine 16

Federov, Nikolai 46

Feng Shui 80-81, 186

Ferrer, Jorge 35

Fertile Crescent 93

Field of Reeds 138-139, 248

Fourth Way 138, 175

Fox and the Hedgehog 34

Frazer, James George 64-65, 131-132

G

Gaia 47-48, 126-127, 222

Gandhi, Mahatma 173-174

Gathas 150-151

Gebser, Jean 32, 44, 48, 57-58, 162

Genesis 42, 94, 101-103, 114-116, 127, 198-199, 202, 209

Gilgamesh 95, 112-115, 210

Giza 57, 97

Gnosis 17-20, 23, 27-29, 32-34, 38-39, 41, 43, 50, 52, 57, 59, 107, 114, 131, 143, 163, 176, 204, 207, 228, 231, 233, 242-243, 245, 247-250, 252-253, 261-262

God 20-24, 27, 29-30, 37-38, 43-46, 69, 85-88, 90, 94-97, 101-104, 106, 108, 110-112, 115, 118, 123, 125-126, 128-135, 138, 140, 149, 154, 158, 161, 163-164, 175, 179, 182, 195-204, 208, 212, 231, 236, 238, 242-246, 248, 251-252, 255, 257, 259, 261

God-King 28, 83, 93, 95, 97, 121-122, 135, 147

Gods 16, 28, 38, 43, 57, 68, 85-88, 94-95, 97-101, 103-106, 108-109, 111-113, 115-119, 121-124, 126-132, 134, 137-139, 141, 150, 154-155, 161, 163-164, 166, 196-200, 202, 204, 209-210, 212, 221, 224, 231, 238, 242-244, 246, 249, 252, 256, 260-261, 263-264

Golden Bough, the 65, 131

Golden Dawn 24, 26, 32, 88

Golden Verses 216

Gooch, Stan 54, 134, 180, 187

Gorgias 223-224

Graves, Clare W. 44, 102

Gravettian 71

Great Flood 114-115

Great Round 49, 83, 86

Guatama 164

Gudea 117

Guenon, Rene 16, 32, 204, 255, 262

Gunkel, Hermann 102-103

Gurdjieff, George Ivanovich 38, 113, 138

Guth, Steven Otto 50, 80

H

Hades 109-110

Hancock, Graham 57-58, 76

Hanegraaff, Wouter 17-19, 231

Harmony of the Spheres 230

Hatha Yoga 23, 80, 168, 238

Hermetic Kabbalah (Qabalah) 24, 88, 106

Heimarmene 238-239

Heliopolis Theology 125

Hepatoscopy 117

Heraclitus 146, 213

Hermopolis 127,

Hero's Journey 62

Hesiod 94, 210, 214, 260-261

Homer 95, 109-110, 146, 209-210

Hominids 53, 98-99

Homo erectus 53, 98

Homo heidelbergensis 53

Horoscope 117, 119

Horus 88, 132, 134, 152

Hun 50, 138

Huxley, Aldous 35, 163, 255

I

Iamblichus 88, 105, 214, 218, 233

I Ching 128, 185-188, 213, 216

Id 50, 257

Iliad 109, 209

Imaginal World 47, 58, 62, 93, 242, 244, 249-250, 252, 260

Indo-Aryans 159

Indus Valley 82, 93, 133, 157-160

Integral Philosophy 22, 43-46, 48-49, 64, 74, 249, 259

Integral Yoga 25, 37, 46, 50, 154, 177, 205, 228, 236, 247, 250-251, 259, 264

Intelligent Design 44, 100, 245

Intuition 20-21, 29, 38, 51-52, 82, 87, 114, 228, 249-250

Irrational 33, 50, 135, 182, 227-228, 237, 246, 250-251

Ishtar 113, 133

Isis 82, 126, 129, 132-133

Ismailism 105

J

Jainism 18, 164-165, 170-175, 177-183, 193, 259

James, William 21, 64, 88, 126, 131

Jaspers, Karl 29, 49, 145, 209, 243

Jnana 18, 22-24, 171, 176, 205, 233, 250, 252, 254, 264

Jones, William 159

Jung, Carl Gustav 18, 26, 32, 36-37, 45, 57, 73-74, 79, 83, 105, 107, 109, 113, 118,

130, 147, 153-155, 177, 190, 217, 228-229, 244, 248, 250, 253, 257, 261

K

Ka 111, 136-138, 242-243, 248, 250

Kabbalah 21, 24, 50, 88, 105-106, 153, 162, 174, 189, 202, 217, 219, 225, 227, 256, 261

Kama 50, 108, 179

Kama-rupa 50

Kant, Immanuel 34, 182-183, 192

Kapila 170-171, 179

Karma 22, 131, 164-165, 174-176, 178-179, 181-182, 231, 258, 264

Kathenotheism 104, 123, 195, 204, 251, 260

Khepri 89, 125

Kleshas 175, 227

Krishna 66, 91, 106

Kundalini 24, 251

L

Lagash 117

Lao-Tzu 189-191, 202, 213

Lascaux 68, 70

Law of Sympathy 65

Lemuria 55-56

Levi 32, 107

Liberation 24, 29-30, 41, 50, 147, 162, 164, 166, 168-169, 173-179, 181, 204, 215, 237, 243, 245, 251, 253, 258-259, 262, 264

Life 36, 42-52, 55, 67-68, 73-74, 82, 86, 91, 99-100, 105, 107, 109, 113, 125, 128, 132, 136, 140, 149, 155, 159, 161, 164-166, 168-170, 172, 174-178, 180-181, 183, 191-192, 208, 210, 213-214, 216, 221, 230, 238, 245-247, 258, 260

Lobell, Mimi 49, 83, 93, 122, 259

Logos 25, 50, 151, 213, 226-228, 235, 238, 251, 263

Loka 161

Loosh 103-104, 106

Lovelock, James 47, 126

Lowenmensch 72

Lucretius 221

Lunar Mystery 133

Luria, Isaac 45, 261

Lurianic Kabbalah 153, 162, 174, 219

M

Macrohistory 41, 259

Magical flight 62

Mahavakya 163

Mahavira 164, 171, 177-179, 181, 213

Malinowski, Bronislaw 64

Mana 61

Manas 50, 167-169, 227

Manichaeism 135, 153, 155, 162, 174, 229, 246

Marduk 101-103, 106, 199, 256

Maslow, Abraham 20-21, 44

Maspero, Gaston 123-124

Massignon, Louis 201

Matter 3, 20, 24, 33, 41, 45-47, 49, 52,

55, 62, 66, 97, 104, 107, 113, 125-128, 154, 169, 171-172, 174-176, 201, 208, 211, 221, 236, 238, 245, 247, 255

McLuhan, Marshall 32, 48

Megalithic culture 4, 77, 83

Memphis 6, 124, 128-129, 140

Mental body 110, 236

Mesopotamia 57, 82, 90, 93, 95-97, 112, 133, 157, 159-160, 195, 256

Metamodernism 33, 46

Metaphysical Gnosis 20, 114, 228

Metaphysics 19-20, 26, 29-30, 34, 36, 43, 127, 131, 136, 140, 146, 153, 162, 164, 166-167, 170, 175, 177, 182, 204, 213, 224, 227, 231-232, 234, 236, 253, 255, 262

Michell, John 79

Mind 19, 21, 45-47, 49-50, 66, 152, 162, 167-171, 175-176, 183, 200, 211-212, 227-228, 235, 245, 247, 255, 262, 264

Minoan 207-208

Mirra 25, 37, 44, 89, 109

Miyazaki, Hayao 65

Modernity 15, 18, 26, 29, 31-33, 37-38, 42, 44-45, 63-64, 98-99, 117, 130, 154, 162, 165, 178, 182, 203, 215, 219-220, 228, 234, 236, 247, 251-252, 256

Monaltry 195, 200, 252, 260

Monism 7, 30, 167, 204, 252

Monotheism 66-67, 86, 98, 123, 140-141, 149-151, 195, 198, 200-204, 252, 260-261, 263

Monroe, Robert 48, 87, 100, 103, 106-108, 139, 254

Moses 96, 140, 200, 202

Mul.Apin 119

Muller, Max 123, 251

Murray, Margaret 69

Mysticism 17, 19-26, 38, 41, 131, 162, 164-166, 176-177, 202, 218, 220, 222, 225-228, 234, 242-243, 247, 250, 252-254, 259, 261

Myth 28, 32, 64, 73-74, 81, 86-87, 90-91, 95, 100-102, 104, 112, 114-115, 127, 129, 131-132, 164, 179, 195, 197, 202, 208, 229, 245, 249, 252-254, 263

Myth of Progress 32, 64, 74

Mythohistory 57-58, 177

Mythology 65, 85-86, 88, 90, 99, 111, 125-126, 130, 133-134, 140, 153, 160, 172, 180, 186, 196, 198, 208, 210, 218, 248

N

Nammu 101

Neanderthal man 54

Neopagan 78

Neoplatonism 19, 21, 26, 29, 31, 88, 126, 163, 177, 191, 204, 215, 218, 225, 256, 261, 263

Neo-Sumerian 112, 210

Nephilim 109

Neumann 57, 65, 72, 81-83, 103, 208

Nevalı Cori 76

New Age 16, 20, 32-33, 37-38, 57, 62-64, 79, 93, 97, 100, 107, 111, 118, 122, 165, 169, 174, 190, 222, 233, 236, 242, 246, 249-251, 260-261

New Paradigm 222

Nineveh 112, 118

Nisaba 117

Noosphere 48-49, 87

Nun 126-127, 129

Nut 126

O

Occultism 16, 20, 25-26, 37, 107, 109, 111, 126, 130-131, 137, 159, 218, 247, 254

Odysseus 110

Ogdoad 127-129, 244

Old Testament 95, 123, 196-197

Olympic Games 209

Omega Point 46, 49

Orexis 237

Orphism/Ophics 210, 254, 257

Otherworld 5, 89-90

Overmind 106

P

Paleolithic 28, 54, 63-65, 67-72, 76, 82, 254, 263

Panpsychism 49, 66, 222, 238, 242, 255

Parker, Matt 79

Parks, Anton 99-100

Parmenides 146, 212-213, 254

Pashupati Seal 157-159, 172

Pattern-recognition 79

Perennialism 27, 35-37, 255

Phanerozoic Eon 47

Phenomenology 37, 45, 49, 94, 175, 192, 220, 262

Pherecydes 210, 214

Philolaus 215

Plastic Shamans 62

Plato 27, 50, 56, 79, 97, 107, 114, 121-122, 146, 208, 212-213, 215, 218, 223-237, 246, 251, 257, 262-264

Pleistocene 53-54, 58, 67-69, 72, 75-76, 99, 249, 256, 263-264

Positivism 32-33, 63, 66, 109, 140, 221, 234, 256

Postmodern Philosophy 34-35

Post-Truth World 33

Prana 80, 168-169, 238, 246

Prayer to the Gods of the Night 117

Presocratics 211-212

Princess Mononoke 65

Process Philosophy 213

Proclus 88, 105

Protagoras 223-224

Proterozoic Eon 47

Proto-Indo-European 85-86, 88, 90, 126, 154, 187

Ptah 128-129, 131, 133

Ptolemy 118-119

Purgatory 111

Purusha 91, 124, 126, 161, 167-168, 171, 193, 228, 257, 262

Pyramid of the Sun 97

Pyrrho 182

Pythagoras 121, 146, 210, 212-216, 218, 226, 233, 254, 257

Pythagorean 16, 128, 162, 187-188, 215-216, 218, 231, 233-234, 236, 242-243

Q

Qabalah 88

Quispel, Gilles 18

R

Ra 125-127, 129, 134, 245

Ramana Maharshi 23, 50

Rational Soul 235, 251

Reason 3, 17-20, 37-38, 44, 50, 62, 80, 130, 137, 151, 153, 183, 200, 207, 224, 226-228, 235-236, 238, 248-249, 251-252, 257

Reincarnation 6, 16, 164-165, 181, 215, 236, 257-258

Religion 5, 17-19, 22-32, 34, 36-38, 41, 43, 54-55, 62, 64-65, 74, 85-86, 91, 94-95, 101-102, 104, 106, 108, 111, 117, 121-123, 127, 129-133, 140-141, 146, 149-150, 152, 155, 159-160, 163, 166, 169, 171, 179, 181, 186, 189, 195-198, 200-201, 203-204, 208-209, 218, 223, 231, 241-242, 246-248, 252, 256-258, 261-262

Rig Veda 89-91, 150, 161, 228, 244, 257

Russian Cosmism 46

S

Sacred Geometry 79, 122

Sagan, Carl 43

Saints 111

Sakkara 124

Samkhya 30, 126-127, 167-168, 170, 175, 179, 181-182, 193, 227-228, 257, 262

Sapience 50, 52

Schopenhauer, Arthur 7, 183

Schuon, Frithjof 16, 18, 204, 262

Schwaller de Lubicz, René Adolphe 122, 129

Science 15, 17-20, 28, 31-32, 34, 37, 41-44, 46, 55, 64-66, 75, 80, 94, 97, 99-101, 107, 114, 130-131, 134, 146, 175, 186, 210, 215, 218, 220-222, 224, 234, 236, 243, 245, 247, 249, 252, 254-256, 261

Scientism 63, 67, 80

Sensitive Chaos 49, 61, 81, 83, 246

Sentience 47, 50, 52, 235, 247

Set 27, 78, 99, 105, 126, 132, 134, 137, 152-153, 255, 264

Shadow 50, 109, 118, 121, 135-136, 153-155, 229, 257-258

Shakti 82, 217, 251

Shamanism 2, 4, 61-65, 67, 70, 116-117, 124, 161, 180, 242, 245, 252, 258, 261

Shen 50, 138

Shiva 133, 157-159, 217

Shramana 167, 169-170, 173, 181, 183, 220, 259

Sitchin, Zecharia 98-99

Sky Deity 126

Smith, Huston 21, 25, 27, 45, 262

Solar Symbolism 150

Song-Lines 80

Sophia 82, 104, 223

Sophists 8, 223-224

Sorcerer, the 68-69

Soul 16, 21-22, 24, 29-30, 48, 50, 52, 62-64, 66-67, 76, 95, 104, 109-111, 113-114, 124, 132, 136-138, 153-155, 164-165, 171, 173-176, 179, 181-182, 193, 200, 204,

214-215, 226-232, 235-238, 242-243, 245-247, 250-251, 257-258, 261-262

Spatial Archetypes 49, 83, 86, 259

Spengler, Oswald 49, 83

Spenta Mainyu 151-152

Spiral Dynamics 44, 88, 259

Spirit 19-22, 37, 61-64, 67, 69, 76, 95, 104, 107-108, 110-111, 124, 137-139, 147, 151, 153-154, 189, 195, 230-231, 238, 245, 254, 258, 260-262

Spiritual Hierarchies 16, 30, 38, 45, 98, 105-106, 113, 154, 196, 233

Spirit World 61, 63, 67, 95, 110, 124, 138, 153, 258, 260-261

Srimrad Bhagavatam 106

Stace 21, 163

Steiner, Rudolf 16, 32, 37-38, 45, 50, 54, 56-58, 87, 99, 105, 107, 113, 130, 233, 235-236, 248, 256, 261

Stoicism 66, 204, 237-238

Stonehenge 76-78

Storm God 86, 102, 196-198

Storytelling 74-75

Stukeley, William 78

Subtle Physical 81, 108, 138-139, 220, 242, 249, 260

Sumeria 95, 100, 104

Summerlands 90, 139, 248

Superintelligence 87, 103

Supermind 25, 106, 169

Supramental 44, 46, 49, 89, 137, 151, 210, 259

Swastika 7, 160, 180

Swimme, Brian 46

Symbolic Thinking 54

Synchronicity 26, 36, 73, 79, 81, 105, 118, 187

T

Tammuz 131-133

Tanha 178, 237, 260

Tantra 24-25, 82, 159, 166-168, 189, 200, 217, 251

Teilhard de Chardin, Pierre 46, 53, 247

Tepe 75-76

Tetraktys 187, 216, 232

Theban Theology 129

Theogony 94, 127, 210, 254, 260

Theology 6, 19-22, 25, 46, 105, 124-125, 127-129, 151, 164, 167-168, 200, 203-205, 232, 244, 254, 261

Theon, Max 38

Theosophy 16-17, 20-21, 26, 33, 41, 45, 48, 50, 56, 107, 165, 174, 177, 225, 235, 245, 247, 249-251, 255, 258, 260-261

Theurgy 24-26, 30, 252, 261

Thoth 130, 132, 138

Thought Forms 38, 107, 110, 219

Tiamat 101-103

Tolkien, John Ronald Reuel 32, 75, 94, 210

Toynbee, Arnold 49

Traditionalism 16, 262

Transcendental Ego 164, 192-193, 262

Transcendent One 98, 106

Trump Egregore 108

Tungus People 62, 258

Tylor, Edward 64, 195

U

UFO 38, 48, 62, 80

Underworld 89, 101, 109-110, 128, 133, 138, 154, 208, 230, 254, 261-262

Upanishads 66, 106, 125, 145, 160, 162-164, 166-168, 170, 172, 179-180, 183, 212, 227, 238, 242, 244, 253, 263

Uruk 95, 112-114

Urvan 154

Utnapishtim 113, 115

V

Varna 161, 263

Vedas 6, 123, 160-163, 168, 261, 263

Venus (figure) 70-72, 82, 215, 263

Vernadsky, Vladimir 46

Versluis, Arthur 20

Vishnu 106, 248

Vital, the 29, 50, 80, 168-169, 228, 235, 237, 242, 250, 264

Vivekananda, Swami 22, 35, 255, 257, 264

Vohu Manah 149, 151

von Daniken, Erich 122

W

Wakan Tanka 195

Warring States Period 185, 191

Watkins, Alfred 78

Weak Perennialism 35-36

Wellhausen, Julius 198

Whitehead, Alfred North 46, 213

Wicca 26, 173

Wilber, Ken 19, 35, 44, 46, 50, 64, 74, 249

X

Xenophanes 212, 214, 253

Y

Yahweh 101, 103, 109, 123, 129, 155, 196-198, 200

Yajnavalkya 163

Yama 91, 154

Yima 154

Yoga 21-25, 30, 37, 44, 46, 50, 80, 151, 154, 157, 159, 168-171, 175, 177, 193, 205, 227-228, 233, 236, 238, 243, 247, 249-251, 254, 256-257, 259

Yogi 70

Younger Dryas 75, 249, 264

Z

Zarathustra 146, 149-150, 154, 213

Ziggurat 97, 112

Zodiac 119, 128

Zoroastrianism 123, 135, 139, 147, 149-155, 160-161, 165, 189, 201, 226, 229-230, 246-247, 250

www.ingramcontent.com/pod-product-compliance
Lightning Source LLC
Chambersburg PA
CBHW020943230426
43666CB00005B/146